Taste of Home

THE
Market Fresh
COOKBOOK

Reader's Digest

The Reader's Digest Association, Inc.
Pleasantville, New York/Montreal

Taste of Home

A TASTE OF HOME/READER'S DIGEST BOOK

Editor: Jennifer Olski
Associate Editor: Janet Briggs
Art Director: Lori Arndt
Layout Designer: Kathy Crawford
Proofreader: Linne Bruskewitz
Editorial Assistant: Barb Czysz
Recipe Testing and Editing: Taste of Home Test Kitchen
Food Photography: Reiman Photo Studio

Additional photography shot on location at
The Elegant Farmer in Mukwonago, Wisconsin, by Jim Wieland

Senior Editor, Retail Books: Jennifer Olski
Executive Editor, Books: Heidi Reuter Lloyd
Creative Director: Ardyth Cope
Senior Vice President/Editor in Chief: Catherine Cassidy
President: Barbara Newton
Founder: Roy Reiman

International Standard Book Number (10): 0-89821-696-6
International Standard Book Number (13): 978-0-89821-696-7
Library of Congress Control Number: 2007943499

For other Taste of Home books and products,
visit www.tasteofhome.com.
For more Reader's Digest products and information, visit
www.rd.com (in the United States)
www.rd.ca (in Canada).

Printed in China
1 3 5 7 9 10 8 6 4 2

Table of Contents

A Bounty of Flavors
Ripe for the Picking...

Walk into any grocery store or farmers market and you'll find an abundance of fresh, flavorful and nutritious fruits and vegetables. With so many colorful options, it can be difficult to choose.

Whether you fill your basket with produce because there's an irresistible sale, it's your family's favorite or you're simply curious about a fruit or veggie you haven't tried, you'll find hundreds of delicious ways to use produce inside *The Market Fresh Cookbook*.

These 302 scrumptious recipes provide a bountiful array of options for main dishes, side dishes, appetizers, breads and desserts using nature's freshest ingredients. They've been individually selected to give you a wide range of tastes so you can please even the pickiest eater at your table.

Chapters have been arranged by produce variety so you can quickly scan for recipes that use the items you have on hand. A special bonus chapter, Cornucopia, showcases fruits and vegetables not included in other sections. Inside every chapter, you'll generally find recipes ordered from appetizers and snacks to soups, salads and sides, followed by main dishes, then breads and desserts.

Best of all, these recipes come from the private collections of outstanding home cooks. Browse the pages of *The Market Fresh Cookbook* to read their personal stories and discover what these great cooks across the country create with their bounty of the best produce.

What's more, each recipe has been tasted and tested by the professional home economists in the Taste of Home Test Kitchen, the team also responsible for producing America's #1 cooking magazine, *Taste of Home*. And that means you're guaranteed a mouth-watering winner every time you dish up one of these recipes.

On the following pages, you'll find handy information for many vegetables and fruits, including availability, buying tips, storage pointers and general yield amounts. This information is simply a guideline. For example, if you purchase vegetables or fruits that are overripe, their storage life will be shorter than the times suggested here.

The inside front and back covers of this book feature useful cooking charts for common vegetables. These charts recommend cooking methods and times. Keep in mind that cooking times vary depending on the size, freshness and ripeness of the vegetable you are preparing.

Produce Handling Guidelines

Buying

Handle all produce gently since fruits and vegetables bruise easily. A bruised spot will lead to decay and make the fruit or vegetable unsuitable for use in your recipes.

When selecting fresh-cut produce, such as sliced watermelon, cored pineapple or bagged mixed greens, purchase only those items that are refrigerated or surrounded by ice.

At the checkout, pack produce separately from meat, poultry and seafood products when bagging them to take home from the market.

Storing

After purchasing produce, promptly refrigerate vegetables and fruits that need to stay chilled. All produce that is purchased precut or peeled should be refrigerated to maintain freshness and avoid safety concerns. For best results, keep your refrigerator set at 40°F or below.

Many types of underripe fruits such as apricots, nectarines, plums and pears can be placed in a closed paper bag and left at room temperature to ripen. Other fruits such as bananas, mangoes, melons and papayas can be placed in a bowl out of direct sunlight to ripen at room temperature.

Don't leave cooked or raw vegetables that require refrigeration at room temperature for more than 2 hours.

Proper storage of fresh produce can affect both quality and safety. For detailed instructions on how best to store produce, follow the guidelines beginning on the next page.

Preparing

When you're ready to prepare your produce, start with clean hands. Wash your hands thoroughly (about 20 seconds) with warm water and soap.

Next, cut away damaged or bruised areas on produce and discard them. Rinse fruits and vegetables, including pre-packaged items from a market or homegrown produce, under cool, running water. Do not wash with detergent or bleach.

Some firm vegetables, like potatoes and carrots, should be gently scrubbed with a vegetable brush if you are going to eat the peel. Always peel vegetables with a wax coating.

Dry produce with a clean cloth towel or paper towel to further reduce the presence of bacteria.

Safety

Make sure your countertops, cutting boards and utensils have been washed in hot, soapy water. For safest food handling, don't place raw or cooked produce on the same surfaces that came in contact with raw meat, and do not use the same utensils to handle both.

If you use plastic or other non-porous cutting boards, run them through the dishwasher after use to prevent cross-contamination.

For added protection, periodically use a kitchen sanitizer on cutting boards and countertops. Try a solution of one teaspoon chlorine bleach to one quart water.

How to Buy Fresh Produce

Buy in Season
* Supply is greater, quality is better and prices are generally lower.
* Buy only what you need.
* Fresh vegetables and fruits are perishable.

Shop Carefully
* Don't buy damaged produce even if the price is low.
* Handle produce carefully to avoid causing damage.

Buy Quality
* Some packages carry a USDA grade. Use the grade as your guide to quality.
* Buy mature produce that looks fresh, has good color and is free from bruises, skin punctures and decay.
* At the produce counter, you are your own best judge of quality.

Produce Reference

Vegetables

Artichokes

Season: Year-round; peaks March–May.

Buying: Select artichokes that are heavy for their size with tightly closed leaves. Slight brown discoloration does not affect the quality. Avoid ones with spreading leaves and a lot of brown areas.

Storage: Refrigerate unwashed for up to 4 days.

Yield: 1 medium artichoke (8 to 10 ounces) = 1 serving

Asparagus

Varieties: Green, white

Season: February through late June; peaks April–May.

Buying: Select small, straight stalks with tightly closed, compact tips. Spears should be smooth and round. Green asparagus should have bright green stalks and tips with a slight lavender tint. White asparagus should have straight, firm stalks.

Storage: Refrigerate unwashed green asparagus in a sealed plastic bag for up to 4 days (2 days for white asparagus).

Yield: 1 pound asparagus = 3-1/2 cups cut

Beans

Varieties: Green, wax

Season: Year-round; peaks July–October.

Buying: Select brightly colored, straight, smooth pods that are unblemished. Should be crisp and have a firm, velvety feel. Seeds inside should be small.

Storage: Store unwashed in a sealed plastic bag or covered container in the refrigerator crisper drawer for up to 3 days.

Yield: 1 pound green or wax beans = about 4 cups cut

Beets

Season: June through October; peaks June–August.

Buying: Select firm, deep red, round beets with unwilted green tops and smooth, unblemished and unbroken skin. Small and medium-sized beets are usually the most tender.

Storage: Remove greens 2 inches from beets. Refrigerate greens separately in a sealed plastic bag for up to 3 days. Refrigerate uncooked beets in an open plastic bag for about 2 weeks.

Yield: 1 pound beets = 2-1/2 cups cooked, sliced or cubed

Broccoli

Season: Year-round.

Buying: Select firm but tender stalks of broccoli with compact, dark green or slightly purplish florets.

Storage: Refrigerate unwashed in an open plastic bag for up to 4 days.

Yield: 1 pound broccoli = 3-1/2 cups florets

Brussels Sprouts

Season: September through May; peaks October–February.

Buying: Select small, firm, tightly closed heads that have a bright green color.

Storage: Refrigerate unwashed in an open plastic bag for up to 3 days.

Yield: 1 pound brussels sprouts = 22 to 28 medium sprouts or 4 cups trimmed

Cabbage

Varieties: Green, red

Season: Year-round.

Buying: Cabbage heads will vary in size; for green cabbage, select round, compact, solid heads. Red cabbage heads are not as compact.

Storage: Refrigerate unwashed for up to 2 weeks.

Yield: 1 medium head cabbage (2-1/2 pounds) = 8 cups

Carrots

Season: Year-round.

Buying: Select crisp, firm, smooth, well-shaped carrots with deep orange color. Smaller carrots are tender and sweet. Carrots sold in bunches with fern-like green tops are fresher than those sold in plastic bags.

Storage: Trim tops and roots when present. Refrigerate unwashed, unpeeled carrots in a sealed plastic bag for 1 to 2 weeks.

Yield: 1 pound carrots (6 to 7 medium) = 3 to 3-1/2 cups sliced (uncooked); 2 medium carrots = 1 cup sliced or shredded

Cauliflower

Season: Year-round; peaks October–March.

Buying: Select firm, solid white or creamy-colored heads that are heavy for their size. Florets should be clean and tightly packed; surrounding jacket leaves should be fresh and green.

Storage: Refrigerate unwashed and keep in an open plastic bag for up to 5 days.

Yield: 1-1/2 pounds of cauliflower (about 1 head) trimmed = 4 cups florets

Corn

Season: May through August; peaks July–August.

Buying: Select corn that has fresh green, tightly closed husks with dark brown, dry (but not brittle) silk. The stem should be moist but not chalky, yellow or discolored. Ears should have plump, tender, small kernels in tight rows up to the tip. Kernels should be firm enough to resist slight pressure. A fresh kernel will spurt "milk" if punctured.

Storage: Refrigerate unshucked ears in an open plastic bag; use within 2 days.

Yield: 1 ear of corn = 1/3 to 1/2 cup kernels

Cucumbers

Varieties: Kirby, English (also called burpless or hothouse)

Season: Year-round; peak summer.

Buying: Select firm cucumbers with round ends. Avoid those with soft spots, bulging middles or withered ends.

Storage: Refrigerate unwashed for up to 1 week.

Yield: 1 medium = 1-1/4 to 1-1/2 cups peeled and sliced or chopped

Eggplant

Season: Year-round; peaks July–September.

Buying: Select firm and heavy eggplant that has a uniformly smooth color and glossy taut skin. The eggplant should be free from blemishes and rust spots with intact green caps and mold-free stems.

Storage: Refrigerate unwashed in an open plastic bag for up to 3 days.

Yield: 1 medium eggplant (1 pound) = 5 cups cubes

Greens

Varieties: Collards, dandelion greens, kale, mustard greens, Swiss chard, turnip greens

Season: Varies.

Buying: Select fresh crisp greens with a bright color; avoid withered, yellow or blemished leaves or stems.

Storage: Remove any ties before storing greens; discard yellow or bruised leaves. Refrigerate in a plastic bag for up to 3 days.

Yield: 1 pound = about 3 cups cooked

Kohlrabi

Season: Year-round; peaks June–July.

Buying: Select small (no larger than 3 in.), firm, pale green bulbs with tender skins. Leaves should appear fresh and crisp.

Storage: Refrigerate unwashed kohlrabi in an open plastic bag for up to 5 days. Refrigerate greens separately in a sealed plastic bag for up to 3 days.

Yield: 1 pound kohlrabi (without leaves) = 3 to 4 medium bulbs

Mushrooms

Varieties: Button or white, chantrelle, cremini or brown, enoki, oyster, portobello, shiitake

Season: Year-round.

Buying: Select mushrooms with fresh, firm, smooth caps and closed gills; avoid cracks, brown spots or blemishes or ones that are shriveled or moist.

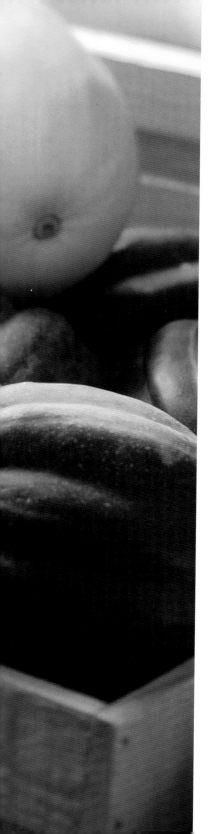

Mushrooms (continued)

Storage: Refrigerate unwashed, loose mushrooms in a brown paper bag for up to 5-10 days depending on the variety. Keep packaged mushrooms wrapped in their package. Store away from other vegetables with strong aromas.

Yield: 1 package (8 ounces) = 3 cups whole or sliced (varies by size and shape)

Okra

Season: Year-round; peaks June–November.

Buying: Select young, tender, unblemished, bright green pods less than 4 in. long. Pods can be smooth or ridged, should snap easily and should not have any hard seeds. The tips should bend under slight pressure.

Storage: Refrigerate in a sealed plastic bag for up to 2 days.

Yield: 1 pound okra = 3 to 4 cups sliced

Onions

Varieties: Green, white, yellow, red

Season: Year-round.

Buying: Select firm onions that have dry, papery skins; avoid those with soft spots, blemishes or green sprouts.

Storage: Keep in a dark, cool, dry, well-ventilated area for up to 3 weeks.

Yield: 1 small onion = 1/3 cup chopped; 1 medium onion = 1/2 to 3/4 cup chopped; 1 large onion = 1 to 1-1/4 cups chopped

Onions, Green (Scallions)

Season: Year-round.

Buying: Select green onions with bright green tops, white bulbs and short roots; avoid those with dry, withered or slimy greens.

Storage: Refrigerate unwashed in a plastic bag for up to 1-2 weeks.

Yield: 1 green onion = 2 tablespoons, sliced

Peas, Green

Season: Year-round; peaks May–June.

Buying: For maximum freshness, select peas in their pods; choose ones that are crisp and firm and have a bright green color. Avoid large pods or those with thick skin, which indicates they are past mature.

Storage: Refrigerate unwashed, unshelled in an open plastic bag for up to 2 days.

Yield: 1 pound unshelled green peas = 1-1/2 cups shelled

Peas, Snow and Sugar Snap

Season: Snow peas available year-round; sugar snap peas available in spring and fall.

Buying: Select snow peas that are flat, are about 3 in. long and have a light green color with a shiny appearance. Select sugar snap peas that have crisp plump looking dark green pods. Avoid dry or moldy pods.

Storage: Refrigerate unwashed snow or sugar snap peas in an open plastic bag for up to 2 days.

Yield: 1 pound snow peas or sugar snap peas = about 4 cups

Peppers, Chili

Varieties: Anaheim, banana, Cubanelle, ancho, pasilla, jalapeno, serrano, habanero

Season: Year-round.

Buying: Select peppers with firm, smooth, glossy skin. Avoid those that are shriveled or have soft spots.

Storage: Refrigerate unwashed fresh

chili peppers wrapped in paper towels for up to 2 weeks.

Yield: (varies by size and shape)

Peppers, Sweet

Varieties: Green, yellow, red, orange, purple

Season: Year-round; peaks March–October.

Buying: Select firm peppers with smooth, shiny skin and bright colors. Avoid those that are shriveled or have soft spots.

Storage: Refrigerate unwashed for up to 5 days.

Yield: 1 medium sweet pepper = 3/4 cup chopped

Potatoes

Varieties: New, round, round whites, russets, yellow-fleshed

Season: Year-round.

Buying: Select well-shaped, firm potatoes that are free from cuts, decay, blemishes or green discoloration under the skin. Avoid sprouted or shriveled potatoes.

Storage: Keep potatoes in a dark, cool, dry, well-ventilated area for up to 2 months. Do not store with onions or in the refrigerator.

Yield: 1 pound russet potatoes = 3 medium; 1 pound small new potatoes = 8 to 10; 1 pound potatoes = 2-1/4 cups diced or sliced

Pumpkin

Season: Fall.

Buying: Select pumpkins that have firm, blemish-free rinds and are bright orange in color.

Storage: Keep in a cool, dry place for up to 1 month. A cut pumpkin may be refrigerated in an open plastic bag for up to 1 week.

Yield: 1 pie pumpkin (3 pounds) = about 2 cups cooked pureed

Spinach

Season: Year-round; peaks late spring through early summer.

Buying: Select crisp, dark green, tender leaves; avoid yellowed or wilted spinach.

Storage: Refrigerate unwashed in a sealed plastic bag for up to 5 days.

Yield: 1 to 1-1/2 pounds fresh spinach = 1 cup cooked

Squash, Summer

Varieties: baby squash, zucchini, summer squash, pattypan, sunburst

Season: Year-round; peaks late summer through early fall.

Buying: Select firm, plump squash with bright, smooth skin.

Storage: Refrigerate unwashed for up to 4 days.

Yield: 1 pound = 4 cups grated or 3-1/2 cups sliced

Squash, Winter

Varieties: Acorn, buttercup, butternut, delicata, hubbard, spaghetti, sweet dumpling, turban

Season: Year-round; peaks October–December.

Buying: Select squash that is heavy for its size; shells should be hard with a deep color and no cracks or soft spots.

Storage: Keep unwashed winter squash in a cool, dry, well-ventilated area for up to 4 weeks.

Yield: 1-3/4 pounds winter squash = 1-3/4 cups cooked mashed

Sweet Potatoes

Season: Year-round; peaks in November.

Buying: Select potatoes that have a thin, smooth skin and tapered ends that feel heavy for their size. Avoid those with shriveled skin, soft spots or bruises.

Storage: Keep in a dark, cool, dry, well-ventilated area for up to 1 week.

Yield: 1 pound = 2 cups cooked, mashed

Tomatoes

Varieties: beefsteak, cherry, grape, plum, roma, sun-dried

Season: Year-round; peaks summer through early fall.

Buying: Select tomatoes that are smooth and free from blemishes. Fully ripe tomatoes have a slight softness. Avoid overripe or bruised tomatoes and ones with green or yellow areas near the stem, as well as ones with growth cracks, water-soaked spots or depressed areas.

Storage: Keep unwashed at room temperature until ripe; store out of direct sunlight; can be refrigerated for up to 3 days.

Yield: 1 pound of tomatoes (about 2-3 medium) = 1-1/2 to 1-3/4 cups chopped; 1 pound plum tomatoes (5 medium) = about 2-1/2 cups chopped; 1 pint cherry or grape tomatoes = 2 cups halved

Turnips

Season: Year-round; peaks fall through winter.

Buying: Select firm turnips that are unblemished and heavy for their

Turnips *(continued)*

size. Any attached greens should be bright and fresh looking. Greens can be removed and cooked separately.

Storage: Refrigerate unwashed for up to 1 week.

Yield: 1 pound trimmed = 3 cups cubed

Fruit

Apples

Varieties: Braeburn, Cortland, Empire, Fuji, Gala, Golden Delicious, Granny Smith, Jonathan, McIntosh, Pink Lady, Red Delicious, Rome Beauty

Season: Year-round.

Buying: Select apples that are firm and have a smooth, unblemished skin free of any bruises. Handle gently to prevent bruising.

Storage: Refrigerate unwashed for up to 6 weeks.

Yield: 1 pound (3 medium) = 2-3/4 cups sliced

Apricots

Season: May–August.

Buying: Select apricots that are plump and fairly firm, not hard, and are orange-yellow to orange in color.

Storage: Keep firm apricots at room temperature. Once the fruit yields to gentle pressure, refrigerate for up to 3 days.

Yield: 1 pound (8 to 12 medium) = 2-1/2 cups sliced

Bananas

Varieties: Cavendish, finger, red, plantain

Season: Year-round.

Buying: Select plump bananas that are free from bruises. The banana skin goes from green to yellow to yellow with speckles to black, depending upon its ripeness.

Storage: Keep at room temperature until ripe, then refrigerate or freeze.

Yield: 1 pound (3 medium) = 1-1/3 cups mashed or 1-1/2 to 2 cups sliced

Blackberries

Season: May–September.

Buying: Select berries that are plump; avoid those that are bruised, mushy or moldy. Avoid packages with juice-stained bottoms.

Storage: Sort and discard any crushed, mushy or moldy fruit. Refrigerate a single layer on a paper towel-lined baking sheet covered with a paper towel for 2 days.

Yield: 1 pint = 1-1/2 to 2 cups

Blueberries

Season: May–October.

Buying: Select berries that are plump; avoid those that are bruised, mushy or moldy. Avoid packages with juice-stained bottoms.

Storage: Sort and discard any crushed, mushy or moldy fruit. Refrigerate blueberries in their container or tightly covered for up to 1 week.

Yield: 1 pint = 1-1/2 to 2 cups

Cherries

Varieties: Bing, Royal Ann, Montmorency

Season: May–July.

Buying: Select cherries that are plump and firm with a shiny skin.

Storage: Before refrigerating, sort through and discard any crushed, mushy or moldy fruit. Refrigerate unwashed cherries in a closed plastic bag for 1-2 days.

Yield: 1 pound = 3 cups whole or 3-1/2 cups halved

Cranberries

Season: October–December.

Buying: Select berries that are plump; avoid those that are bruised, mushy or moldy. Avoid packages with juice-stained bottoms.

Storage: Sort and discard any crushed, mushy or moldy fruit. Refrigerate in original bag for up to 2 months.

Yield: 12 ounces = 3 cups whole; 2-1/2 cups finely chopped.

Melons

Varieties: Muskmelons (cantaloupes), crenshaw, honeydew, Persian

Season: Year-round.

Buying: Select melons that feel heavy for their size and have no cracks or dents in the skin. A ripe melon should have a fruity, pleasant aroma.

Storage: Keep underripe melons at room temperature for 2-3 days. Refrigerate ripe melons for up to 1 week.

Yield: Varies by type/size

Nectarines and Peaches

Season: May–November.

Buying: Select plump fruit. Avoid fruit with bruises, soft spots or cuts. Avoid peaches with a green background as these will not ripen or be sweet. Ripe nectarines and peaches will give slightly when gently pressed and have a sweet aroma.

Storage: Refrigerate ripe fruit for 3-5 days. Store firm fruit at room temperature until ripened.

Yield: 1 pound nectarines (3 medium) = 3 cups sliced; 1 pound peaches (4 medium) = 2-3/4 cups sliced

Pears

Varieties: Anjou, Bartlett, Bosc, Comice, Seckel

Season: Year-round; peaks July–January.

Buying: Select pears that are plump. For some varieties, the color of the skin will change as the pear ripens. Select firm pears for baking. For eating, select pears that give slightly when gently pressed.

Storage: Refrigerate unwashed ripe pears for 3-5 days. To ripen firm pears, place in a paper bag at room temperature for 2-3 days.

Yield: 1 pound (3 medium) = 3 cups sliced

Plums

Varieties: Greengage, Kelsey, mirabelle, Santa Rosa

Season: June–November.

Buying: Select plump fruit. Ripe plums will give slightly when gently pressed and have a fruity aroma.

Storage: Refrigerate unwashed ripe plums for 3-5 days. To ripen, place in a paper bag at room temperature for 1-3 days.

Yield: 1 pound (4-5 medium) = 2 to 2-1/2 cups halved or 2-1/2 cups sliced

Raspberries

Season: Peaks June–July and September–October.

Buying: Select berries that are plump; avoid those that are bruised, mushy or moldy. Avoid packages with juice-stained bottoms.

Storage: Sort and discard any crushed, mushy or moldy fruit. Refrigerate a single layer on a paper towel-lined baking sheet covered with a paper towel for 3 days.

Yield: 1 pint = 1-1/2 to 2 cups

Rhubarb

Season: April–June.

Buying: Select rhubarb that is firm and crisp. Avoid limp stalks.

Storage: Refrigerate unwashed for up to 1 week.

Yield: 1 pound = 3 cups chopped raw or 2 cups cooked

Strawberries

Season: Year-round; peaks April–June.

Buying: Select berries that are plump; avoid those that are bruised, mushy or moldy. Avoid packages with juice-stained bottoms.

Storage: Sort and discard any crushed, mushy or moldy fruit. Refrigerate in a paper towel-lined, moisture-proof container for 2 to 3 days.

Yield: 1 pint = 1-1/2 to 2 cups

Watermelon

Season: Year-round; peaks May–September.

Buying: Select watermelons with a hard, green rind that has a dull appearance. The part that rested on the ground will be creamy yellow or white color. To test for ripeness, slap the side with the palm of your hand. A deep thump means it is ripe.

Storage: Refrigerate for up to 1 week.

Yield: 1 pound = about 1 cup cubes

Apples

Apple Dumpling Dessert, p. 24

Apple Luncheon Salad

Served with fresh bread, this makes a nice light meal. While it's a delicious way to use up leftover beef, I sometimes serve it with cold ham and cheese instead.

Audrey Marsh
Arva, Ontario

3 cups diced red apples
1 cup julienned cooked roast beef
1 cup thinly sliced celery
4 green onions, thinly sliced
1/4 cup minced fresh parsley

1/3 cup vegetable oil
2 tablespoons cider vinegar
1 garlic clove, minced
1/2 teaspoon salt
1/4 teaspoon pepper
Lettuce leaves

In a bowl, combine the first five ingredients. In a small bowl, combine oil, vinegar, garlic, salt and pepper; mix well. Pour over apple mixture; toss to coat. Cover and refrigerate for at least 1 hour. Serve on lettuce. **Yield:** 4-6 servings.

When you take a bite of this salad, you may think you're eating a tasty candied apple. It's yummy!

Cathy LaReau
Sumava Resorts, Indiana

Taffy Apple Salad

1 can (20 ounces) crushed pineapple
4 cups miniature marshmallows
1 egg, lightly beaten
1/2 cup sugar
1/4 cup packed brown sugar
1 tablespoon all-purpose flour

4-1/2 teaspoons cider vinegar
1 carton (8 ounces) frozen whipped topping, thawed
3 cups diced unpeeled apples
1-1/2 cups lightly salted peanuts, coarsely chopped

1. Drain pineapple, reserving juice. In a large bowl, combine pineapple and marshmallows; cover and refrigerate for several hours.

2. In a saucepan, combine the egg, sugars, flour, vinegar and reserved pineapple juice; cook and stir until mixture thickens and reaches 160°. Remove from the heat; cool. Cover and refrigerate.

3. Fold whipped topping into the chilled dressing. Add the apples and peanuts to the pineapple and marshmallows. Fold dressing into fruit mixture. Refrigerate leftovers. **Yield:** 10-12 servings.

Apple Salsa with Cinnamon Chips

Salsa:
- 2 medium tart apples, chopped
- 1 cup chopped strawberries
- 2 medium kiwifruit, peeled and chopped
- 1 small orange
- 2 tablespoons brown sugar
- 2 tablespoons apple jelly, melted

Chips:
- 8 flour tortillas (8-inches)
- 1 tablespoon water
- 1/4 cup sugar
- 2 teaspoons ground cinnamon

1. In a bowl, combine apples, strawberries and kiwi. Grate orange peel to measure 1-1/2 teaspoons; squeeze juice from orange. Add peel and juice to apple mixture. Stir in brown sugar and jelly.

2. For chips, brush tortillas lightly with water. Combine sugar and cinnamon; sprinkle over tortillas. Cut each tortilla into eight wedges. Place in a single layer on ungreased baking sheets. Bake at 400° for 6-8 minutes or until lightly browned. Cool. Serve with salsa. **Yield:** 4 cups salsa.

Both my husband and I were raised on farms, and we prefer home cooking. That works out fine since I love trying new recipes! I've served this treat as an appetizer. Since it's easy to transport, it's a great take-along snack, too.

Carolyn Brinkmeyer
Aurora, Colorado

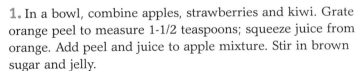

Avoid Discoloration

To keep peeled apple slices from turning brown, sprinkle on a bit of lime juice or lemon-lime soda.

Apple-Ham Grilled Cheese

1 cup chopped tart apples
1/3 cup mayonnaise
1/4 cup finely chopped
    walnuts
8 slices process American
    cheese
8 slices sourdough bread
4 slices fully cooked ham
1/4 cup butter, softened

This is a recipe I found years ago. I altered it to fit our tastes by adding fresh apples. We look forward to fall, when we gather apples for this delicious treat.

Shirley Brazel
Rocklin, California

1. In a bowl, combine apples, mayonnaise and walnuts. Place a slice of cheese on four slices of bread. Layer each with 1/3 cup of the apple mixture, a slice of ham and another slice of cheese; cover with remaining bread.

2. Butter the outsides of the sandwiches. In a large skillet over medium heat, cook sandwiches until each side is golden brown and cheese is melted. **Yield:** 4 servings.

Apple Yeast Bread

2 tablespoons butter, melted
1/2 cup sugar
1 teaspoon ground cinnamon
1 large tart apple, peeled
and thinly sliced
1/4 cup raisins
1 package (1/4 ounce)
active dry yeast

3/4 cup warm water (110°
to 115°)
1/4 cup sugar
1 teaspoon salt
2-1/4 cups all-purpose flour,
divided
1 egg, lightly beaten
1/4 cup shortening

1. Pour butter into a 9-in. square baking pan. Mix sugar and cinnamon; sprinkle over butter. Arrange apple slices in pan. Sprinkle with raisins.

2. In a mixing bowl, combine yeast, water, sugar, salt and 1 cup flour; beat for 1-2 minutes. Add egg, shortening and remaining flour. Beat for 1 minute. Drop dough by spoonfuls over apples. Cover and let rise in a warm place until almost doubled, about 1 hour.

3. Bake at 350° for 30-35 minutes or until golden brown. Invert pan on a serving platter. **Yield:** 9 servings.

This is one of the recipes I included in a cookbook I put together after my grown children kept calling home to ask how to make some of their favorite dishes.

Marilyn Strickland
Williamson, New York

Autumn Casserole

3 cups sliced unpeeled tart
apples
3 cups sliced carrots,
cooked
1/2 cup packed brown sugar
2 tablespoons all-purpose
flour

1 teaspoon ground
cinnamon
1/2 teaspoon salt
1 tablespoon cold butter
3/4 cup orange juice

1. Place half the apples in a greased 2-qt. baking dish. Cover with half the carrots.

2. In a bowl, combine brown sugar, flour, cinnamon and salt. Cut in butter until crumbly; sprinkle half over apples and carrots. Repeat layers. Pour orange juice over all. Bake, uncovered, at 350° for 30-35 minutes. **Yield:** 6 servings.

Since our state is second in the country in apple production, I make many recipes using them. My family often requests this dish for Sunday dinners and Thanksgiving.

Shirley Brownell
Amsterdam, New York

German Apple Pancake

Pancake:
- 3 eggs
- 1 cup milk
- 3/4 cup all-purpose flour
- 1/2 teaspoon salt
- 1/8 teaspoon ground nutmeg
- 3 tablespoons butter

Topping:
- 2 tart apples, peeled and sliced
- 3 to 4 tablespoons butter
- 2 tablespoons sugar
- Confectioners' sugar
- Lemon wedges

1. Preheat oven and 10-in. cast-iron skillet to 425°.

2. Meanwhile, place eggs, milk, flour, salt and nutmeg in a blender container; process until smooth.

3. Add butter to skillet; return to oven until butter bubbles. Pour batter into skillet.

4. Bake, uncovered, for 20 minutes or until pancake puffs and edges are browned and crisp.

5. For topping, place apples, butter and sugar in a skillet; cook and stir over medium heat until apples are tender. Spoon into baked pancake. Sprinkle with confectioners' sugar. Cut and serve immediately with lemon wedges. **Yield:** 6-8 servings.

Everyone I've served this brunch dish to has enjoyed it...except for one time when my husband tried to make it following my recipe, which I'd written down incorrectly! If you don't leave out the flour like I did, it'll turn out terrific!

Judi Van Beek
Lynden, Washington

Coring an Apple

Use an apple corer to core a whole apple. Push apple corer down into center of a washed apple. Twist and remove the center seeds and membranes.

Core an apple quarter by cutting out the core with a sharp knife.

Pork Roast With Apple Topping

1 boneless rolled pork loin roast (3 to 3-1/2 pounds), trimmed
1/2 teaspoon poultry seasoning
1 jar (10 ounces) apple jelly
1 cup apple juice
1/2 teaspoon ground cardamom
1 cup chopped peeled tart fresh *or* dried apples
3 tablespoons chopped fresh *or* dried cranberries
5 teaspoons cornstarch
2 tablespoons water

1. Place roast on a rack in a shallow roasting pan and rub with poultry seasoning. Bake, uncovered, at 350° for 1-1/4 to 1-1/2 hours or until a meat thermometer reads 160°.

2. For topping, combine the apple jelly, juice and cardamom in a saucepan. Cook and stir over low heat until smooth. Add apples and cranberries; cook until tender, about 5-10 minutes. Combine cornstarch and water; stir into apple mixture. Bring to a boil. Cook and stir over medium heat until thickened, about 1-2 minutes.

3. Remove roast from oven and let stand for 10 minutes before slicing. Serve with apple topping. **Yield:** 8-10 servings (about 2 cups topping).

This recipe's one my mother-in-law and I developed together. The topping also goes great with pork chops, lean sausage balls or patties and ham.

Paula Neal
Dolores, Colorado

Apple Ladder Loaf

2 packages (1/4 ounce
each) active dry yeast
1/4 cup warm water (110°
to 115°)
1/2 cup warm milk (110°
to 115°)
1/2 cup butter, softened
1/3 cup sugar
1 teaspoon salt
4 eggs
4-1/2 to 4-3/4 cups all-purpose
flour

Filling:
1/3 cup packed brown sugar
2 tablespoons all-purpose
flour
1-1/4 teaspoons ground
cinnamon
1/2 teaspoon ground nutmeg
1/8 teaspoon ground allspice
4 cups thinly sliced peeled
tart apples
1/4 cup butter, softened

Icing:
1 cup confectioners' sugar
1 to 2 tablespoons orange
juice
1/4 teaspoon vanilla extract

I first served my family this rich bread with its spicy apple filling years ago. From the first bite, it was a hit with everyone.

Norma Foster
Compton, Illinois

1. In a large mixing bowl, dissolve yeast in water. Add the milk, butter, sugar, salt, eggs and 2 cups flour. Beat on low speed for 3 minutes. Stir in enough remaining flour to form a soft dough.

2. Turn onto a lightly floured surface; knead until smooth and elastic, about 6-8 minutes. Place in a greased bowl, turning once to grease top. Cover and refrigerate for 1-2 hours; punch dough down. Cover and refrigerate overnight.

3. Punch dough down. Turn onto a lightly floured surface; divide in half. Roll each half into a 12-in. x 9-in. rectangle. Place each on a greased baking sheet. Spread with butter. For filling, combine the brown sugar, flour, cinnamon, nutmeg and allspice in a large bowl; add apples and toss to coat. Spread filling down center third of each rectangle.

4. On each long side, cut 1-in.-wide strips about 3 in. into center. Starting at one end, fold alternating strips at an angle across filling; seal ends. Cover and let rise until nearly doubled, about 45-60 minutes.

5. Bake at 350° for 30-40 minutes or until golden brown. Combine icing ingredients until smooth; drizzle over warm loaves. Serve warm or at room temperature. **Yield:** 2 loaves (10 slices each).

Apple Walnut Cake

1 cup butter, softened
2 cups sugar
3 eggs
2 teaspoons vanilla extract
3 cups all-purpose flour
1-1/2 teaspoons baking powder
1 teaspoon ground cinnamon
1/2 teaspoon salt
1/4 teaspoon ground mace
3 cups chopped peeled tart apples
2 cups chopped walnuts

1. In a mixing bowl, cream butter and sugar. Add eggs, one at a time, beating well after each addition. Add vanilla. Combine flour, baking powder, cinnamon, salt and mace; gradually add to creamed mixture. Stir in apples and nuts (batter will be very stiff).

2. Spoon into a greased and floured 10-in. tube pan bake at 325° for 1 hour and 25 minutes or until a toothpick inserted near the center of cake comes out clean. Cool 10 minutes in pan before removing to a wire rack to cool completely. **Yield:** 16 servings.

The aroma and flavor of this old-fashioned tube cake will remind you of cakes your grandma made! The apple-walnut combination makes it perfect for fall...and it can be served for breakfast, brunch or dessert.

Lynne Campbell
Lansing, Michigan

Apple Snack Squares

2 cups sugar
2 eggs
3/4 cup vegetable oil
2-1/2 cups self-rising flour
1 teaspoon ground cinnamon
3 cups diced peeled tart apples
1 cup chopped walnuts
3/4 cup butterscotch chips

In a bowl, combine sugar, eggs and oil; mix well. Stir in flour and cinnamon (batter will be thick). Stir in apples and nuts. Spread into greased 13-in. x 9-in. x 2-in. baking pan. Sprinkle with chips. Bake at 350° for 35-40 minutes or until golden brown and a toothpick inserted near the center comes out clean. Cool before cutting. **Yield:** 2 dozen squares.

Editor's Note: As a substitute for each cup of self-rising flour, place 1-1/2 teaspoons baking powder and 1/2 teaspoon salt in a measuring cup. Add all-purpose flour to measure 1 cup.

As soon as I was old enough to stand on a chair, I started cooking. So when I got this recipe from my sister-in-law, I knew it would be delicious. It's a favorite at our large family gatherings.

Julia Quintrell
Sumerco, West Virginia

Old-Fashioned Apple Crisp

My whole family loves this recipe—fortunately for me, it's a breeze to prepare!

Linda Troyer
Bellville, Ohio

6 large tart apples, peeled and sliced
2 tablespoons plus 1 cup sugar, *divided*
1-1/4 teaspoons ground cinnamon, *divided*
3/4 cup all-purpose flour
1/2 cup cold butter
1/2 cup water

1. Place apples in a greased 8-in. square baking pan. Sprinkle with 2 tablespoons sugar and 1/4 teaspoon cinnamon. In a medium bowl, combine flour and remaining sugar and cinnamon; cut in butter until crumbs form. Drizzle water over apples; sprinkle with crumb topping.

2. Bake at 350° for 60 minutes or until apples are tender. **Yield:** 6-8 servings.

Saucy Spiced Apple Pie

Mom's sweet and saucy apple pie earns a lip-smacking salute from everyone who tastes it. Since it's hard to wait for it to cool, I like to serve slices warm with a scoop of French vanilla ice cream on top.

Lisa Jedrzejczak
Capac, Michigan

Pastry for double-crust pie (9 inches)
1/4 cup butter, softened
2 cups sugar
1 egg
1 egg, *separated*
1/3 cup unsweetened pineapple juice
1-1/2 teaspoons vanilla extract
1/3 cup all-purpose flour
1/2 teaspoon ground cinnamon
1/4 teaspoon ground ginger
1/4 teaspoon ground nutmeg
6 cups sliced peeled tart apples
Additional sugar

1. Line a 9-in. pie plate with bottom pastry; trim even with edge. In a mixing bowl, cream butter and sugar. Add the egg, egg yolk, pineapple juice and vanilla; mix well (mixture will appear curdled). Combine the flour, cinnamon, ginger and nutmeg; add to creamed mixture. Fill crust with apple slices. Top with the creamed mixture.

2. Roll out remaining pastry to fit top of pie; place over filling. Trim, seal and flute edges; cut slits in top. Beat egg white; brush over pastry. Sprinkle with additional sugar.

3. Bake at 350° for 55-60 minutes or until crust is golden brown and filling is bubbly. Cool on a wire rack. Refrigerate leftovers. **Yield:** 6-8 servings.

Apple-of-Your-Eye Cheesecake

1 cup graham cracker crumbs
3 tablespoons sugar
1/2 teaspoon ground cinnamon
1/4 cup butter, melted
2 tablespoons finely
    chopped pecans

Filling:
3 packages (8 ounces *each*)
    cream cheese, softened
3/4 cup sugar
3 eggs
3/4 teaspoon vanilla extract

Topping:
2-1/2 cups chopped peeled
    apples
1 tablespoon lemon juice
1/4 cup sugar
1/2 teaspoon ground cinnamon
6 tablespoons caramel ice
    cream topping, *divided*
Sweetened whipped cream
2 tablespoons chopped
    pecans

1. Combine first five ingredients; press into bottom of a lightly greased 9-in. springform pan. Place pan on a baking sheet. Bake at 350° for 10 minutes; cool.

2. In a mixing bowl, beat cream cheese and sugar until smooth. Add eggs; beat on low just until combined. Stir in vanilla. Pour over crust. Toss apples with lemon juice, sugar and cinnamon; spoon over filling. Place pan on a baking sheet. Bake at 350° for 55-60 minutes or until center is almost set. Cool on a wire rack for 10 minutes.

3. Carefully run a knife around edge of pan to loosen. Drizzle with 4 tablespoons caramel topping. Cool for 1 hour. Chill overnight. Remove sides of pan. Just before serving, garnish with whipped cream. Drizzle with remaining caramel; sprinkle with pecans. Store in refrigerator. **Yield:** 12 servings.

My most-often-requested dessert, this exquisite cheesecake with apples, caramel and pecans wins me more compliments than anything else I make. My husband's co-workers say it's too pretty to cut...but agree it's well worth it to do so.

Debbie Wilson
Sellersburg, Indiana

Apple Dumpling Dessert

Pastry:
- 4 cups all-purpose flour
- 2 teaspoons salt
- 1-1/3 cups shortening
- 8 to 9 tablespoons cold water

Filling:
- 8 cups chopped peeled tart apples
- 1/4 cup sugar
- 3/4 teaspoon ground cinnamon

Syrup:
- 2 cups water
- 1 cup packed brown sugar
- Whipped topping *or* vanilla ice cream, optional
- Mint leaves, optional

My husband loves apple dumplings, but they take so long. So our daughter Kathy created a quick-to-fix variation with a nice bonus: no bites of dry crust without filling since it's all mixed throughout!

Janet Weaver
Wooster, Ohio

1. In a bowl, combine flour and salt; cut in shortening until the mixture resembles coarse crumbs. Sprinkle with water, 1 tablespoon at a time, and toss with a fork until dough can be formed into a ball. Divide dough into four parts.

2. On a lightly floured surface, roll one part to fit the bottom of an ungreased 13-in. x 9-in. x 2-in. baking dish. Place in dish; top with a third of the apples. Combine sugar and cinnamon; sprinkle a third over apples. Repeat layers of pastry, apples and cinnamon-sugar twice.

3. Roll out remaining dough to fit top of dish and place on top. Using a sharp knife, cut 2-in. slits through all layers at once.

4. For syrup, bring water and sugar to a boil in a saucepan. Cook and stir until sugar is dissolved. Pour over top crust. Bake at 400° for 35-40 minutes or until browned and bubbly. Serve warm with whipped topping or ice cream if desired. Garnish with mint if desired. **Yield:** 12 servings.

Caramel Apples

1 cup butter
2 cups packed brown sugar
1 cup light corn syrup
1 can (14 ounces)
   sweetened condensed milk
1 teaspoon vanilla extract
8 to 10 wooden sticks
8 to 10 medium tart apples

Who doesn't love a good, gooey caramel apple? Make a double batch because these treats always go fast!

Karen Ann Bland
Gove, Kansas

1. In a heavy large saucepan, combine butter, brown sugar, corn syrup and milk; bring to a boil over medium-high heat. Cook and stir until mixture reaches 248° (firm-ball stage) on a candy thermometer, about 30-40 minutes.

2. Remove from the heat; stir in vanilla. Insert wooden sticks into apples. Dip each apple into hot caramel mixture; turn to coat. Set on waxed paper to cool. **Yield:** 8-10 apples.

Honey Baked Apples

2-1/4 cups water
3/4 cup packed brown sugar
3 tablespoons honey
6 large tart apples
1 cup golden raisins
Vanilla ice cream, optional
Mint leaves, optional

1. In a saucepan, bring water, brown sugar and honey to a boil. Remove from the heat.

2. Core apples and peel the top third of each. Place in an ungreased 9-in. baking dish. Fill apples with raisins; sprinkle any remaining raisins into pan. Pour sugar syrup over apples.

3. Bake, uncovered, at 350° for 1 hour or until tender, basting occasionally. Serve with ice cream if desired. Garnish with mint if desired. **Yield:** 6 servings.

These tender apples smell so good while they're in the oven—and taste even better. We enjoy the golden raisins inside and the soothing taste of honey.

Chere Bell
Colorado Springs, Colorado

Asparagus

Asparagus Appetizer
Roll-Ups, p. 30

Oriental Asparagus Salad

A delightful change of pace from hot vegetable side dishes, this lovely asparagus salad gets an Oriental twist with a simple marinade and sesame seeds. Once you try it, you'll serve it time and again.

Linda Hutton
Hayden, Idaho

1 pound asparagus, cut into 2-inch pieces
2 tablespoons soy sauce
1 tablespoon vegetable oil
1 tablespoon white vinegar
1-1/2 teaspoons sugar
1 teaspoon sesame seeds, toasted
1/4 to 1/2 teaspoon ground ginger
1/4 teaspoon ground cumin

1. Place 1/2 in. of water in a large saucepan; add asparagus. Bring to a boil. Reduce heat; cover and simmer for 3-4 minutes or until crisp-tender. Drain well and place in a large bowl.

2. Combine the soy sauce, oil, vinegar, sugar, sesame seeds, ginger and cumin; pour over asparagus and toss to coat. Cover and refrigerate for 1 hour. Drain before serving. **Yield:** 4 servings.

Cheesy Asparagus Bites

When I managed a cafeteria, I would cook up different snacks for the staff. These tiny squares with a big asparagus flavor never lasted long and prompted lots of recipe requests.

Lois McAtee
Oceanside, California

1/2 cup diced onion
1 garlic clove, minced
2 tablespoons vegetable oil
2 cups (8 ounces) shredded sharp cheddar cheese
1/4 cup dry bread crumbs
2 tablespoons minced fresh parsley
1/4 teaspoon salt
1/4 teaspoon pepper
1/8 to 1/4 teaspoon dried oregano
1/8 teaspoon hot pepper sauce
4 eggs, beaten
1 pound fresh asparagus, trimmed and cut into 1/2-inch pieces

1. In a skillet, saute onion and garlic in oil until tender. Combine the cheese, bread crumbs, parsley, salt, pepper, oregano and hot pepper sauce. Stir in the onion mixture and eggs.

2. Place 1/2 in. of water in a large saucepan; add asparagus. Bring to a boil. Reduce heat; cover and simmer for 3-4 minutes or until crisp-tender. Drain well. Stir into cheese mixture. Pour into a greased 9-in. square baking pan.

3. Bake at 350° for 30 minutes or until a knife inserted near the center comes out clean. Let stand for 15 minutes. Cut into small squares; serve warm. **Yield:** 5 dozen.

Asparagus Ham Swirls

- 16 fresh asparagus spears, trimmed
- 3 tablespoons Dijon mustard
- 16 thin slices deli ham
- 16 slices process Swiss cheese
- 2 eggs, beaten
- 1 cup dry bread crumbs

Vegetable oil

1. In a large skillet, bring 1/2 in. of water and asparagus to a boil. Reduce heat; cover and simmer for 3-5 minutes or until crisp-tender. Drain well.

2. Spread about 1 teaspoon of mustard on each ham slice. Top with a slice of cheese. Place an asparagus spear at one end (trim to fit if needed). Roll up each ham slice tightly; secure with three toothpicks. Dip ham rolls in egg, then roll in bread crumbs.

3. In an electric skillet, heat 1 in. of oil to 350°. Fry rolls, a few at a time, for 3-4 minutes or until golden brown. Drain on paper towels; keep warm. Cut each roll between the toothpicks into three pieces. **Yield:** 4 dozen.

I came across the recipe for this hot appetizer years ago and have made it many times to share with friends and co-workers. Asparagus, ham and cheese combine into a fun finger food.

Nancy Ingersol
Midlothian, Illinois

Preparing Asparagus

Rinse asparagus spears well in cold water to clean. Snap off the spear ends as far down as they will easily break when gently bent, or cut off the tough white portion. If spears are large, use a vegetable peeler to gently peel the tough area of the spear from the end to just below the tip. If tips are large, scrape off scales with a knife.

Asparagus Appetizer Roll-Ups

12 slices white bread, crusts removed

1 carton (8 ounces) spreadable cream cheese

2 tablespoons chopped green onions

8 bacon strips, cooked and crumbled

24 fresh asparagus spears, trimmed

1/4 cup butter, melted

3 tablespoons grated Parmesan cheese

When spring is in the air and asparagus is plentiful, consider this pretty appetizer. Serve them right from the oven.

Mrs. Howard Lansinger
Pineola, North Carolina

1. Flatten bread with a rolling pin and set aside. In a small bowl, combine the cream cheese, onions and bacon. Spread mixture over bread slices.

2. Cut asparagus to fit bread; place two spears on each bread slice and roll up jelly-roll style. Place seam side down on a greased baking sheet. Brush with butter, then sprinkle with Parmesan cheese.

3. Bake at 400° for 10-12 minutes or until lightly browned. Serve immediately. **Yield:** 1 dozen.

Asparagus and Wild Rice Casserole

2 tablespoons chopped
onion
1 tablespoon butter
1 tablespoon all-purpose
flour
1/8 teaspoon salt
1 cup milk
1/2 cup sour cream

2 cups cooked wild rice
2 pounds fresh asparagus,
cut into 2-inch pieces
and cooked
3/4 cup shredded cheddar
cheese
6 bacon strips, diced and
cooked

I learned the fun of cooking as a child. I love to create as I cook—this recipe is a combination of several different asparagus dishes. It's also tasty with pieces of cooked duck added to the wild rice.

Theresa Charlson
Forest City, Iowa

1. In a small saucepan, saute onion in butter until tender. Stir in flour and salt until blended. Gradually stir in milk. Bring to a boil over medium heat; cook and stir for 2 minutes or until thickened. Remove from the heat; cool for 1 minute. Stir in sour cream until smooth.

2. In a greased 11-in. x 7-in. x 2-in. baking dish, layer the wild rice, asparagus, sour cream mixture, cheese and bacon. Bake, uncovered, at 350° for 30 minutes or until heated through. **Yield:** 6 servings.

Asparagus Tomato Salad

2 tablespoons lemon juice
1 tablespoon olive oil
1 teaspoon red wine
vinegar
1/2 garlic clove, minced
1/2 teaspoon Dijon mustard
1/4 teaspoon dried basil
1/4 teaspoon salt

1/8 teaspoon pepper

Salad:
12 fresh asparagus spears,
cut into 1-1/2-inch pieces
3 small tomatoes, seeded
and diced
1 small red onion, sliced

This is a delicious way to start off any meal—and a nice change of pace from the usual tossed salad.

Anne Frederick
New Hartford, New York

1. In a medium bowl, whisk together the first eight ingredients; set aside.

2. Place 1/2 in. of water in a large saucepan; add asparagus. Bring to a boil. Reduce heat; cover and simmer for 3-4 minutes or until crisp-tender. Drain well and cool.

3. In a bowl, combine the asparagus, tomatoes and onion. Pour dressing over salad; toss to coat. Serve immediately or refrigerate. **Yield:** 4 servings.

Asparagus with Dill Butter

1/2 cup butter, softened
1/4 cup snipped fresh dill
1-1/2 teaspoons lemon juice
Cooked fresh asparagus spears

1. In a small bowl, combine the butter, dill and lemon juice until well blended. Form into a log. (If necessary, refrigerate until mixture is firm enough to shape easily.) Wrap log in plastic wrap; freeze until firm.

2. When ready to serve, slice butter 1/4 in. thick and place on hot asparagus. **Yield:** Recipe will season about 4 pounds of asparagus.

Cream of Asparagus Soup

1/2 cup chopped onion
1 tablespoon vegetable oil
2 cans (14-1/2 ounces *each*) **chicken broth**
2-1/2 pounds fresh asparagus, trimmed and cut into 1-inch pieces
1/4 teaspoon dried tarragon
1/4 cup butter
1/4 cup all-purpose flour
1/2 teaspoon salt
1/4 teaspoon white pepper
3 cups half-and-half cream
1-1/2 teaspoons lemon juice
Shredded Swiss cheese, optional

1. In a large saucepan, saute onion in oil until tender. Add the broth, asparagus and tarragon. Bring to a boil. Reduce heat; simmer, uncovered, for 5-8 minutes or until asparagus is tender. Cool for 10 minutes. In a blender or food processor, puree the asparagus mixture, a third at a time; set aside.

2. In a Dutch oven, melt butter. Stir in the flour, salt and pepper until smooth. Cook and stir for 2 minutes or until golden. Gradually add cream. Bring to a boil; cook and stir for 2 minutes or until thickened. Reduce heat; stir in the pureed asparagus and lemon juice and heat through. Garnish with cheese if desired. **Yield:** 8 servings (about 2 quarts).

Asparagus Pasta Salad

- 1 pound fresh asparagus, cut into 1-1/2-inch pieces
- 1 package (16 ounces) multicolored corkscrew pasta, cooked and drained
- 1 cup diced cooked chicken
- 1 cup diced fully cooked ham
- 2 medium tomatoes, seeded and diced
- 1/2 cup sliced ripe olives
- 1-1/2 cups bottled zesty Italian dressing
- 1-1/2 teaspoons dill weed

1. Place 1/2 in. of water in a large saucepan; add asparagus. Bring to a boil. Reduce heat; cover and simmer for 3-4 minutes or until crisp-tender. Drain well and cool.

2. In a large bowl, combine asparagus and the remaining ingredients; toss to coat. Cover and refrigerate 3-4 hours or overnight. **Yield:** 12 servings.

I got this recipe from my sister-in-law while visiting her in Texas. I usually prepare this salad in the summer as a light evening meal for my family or as an extra-special lunch for friends.

Jan Nelson
Tallulah, Louisiana

Freezing Asparagus

When fresh asparagus is plentiful and inexpensive, stock up. Blanch, cool and store it covered with water in containers in the freezer. When thawed, it tastes just like fresh-picked.

Sunny Asparagus Tart

1-1/2 cups all-purpose flour
1/2 teaspoon caraway seeds
1/8 teaspoon salt
5 tablespoons cold butter
2 tablespoons shortening
3 to 5 tablespoons ice water

Filling:
1-1/2 pounds fresh asparagus
1 package (3 ounces) cream cheese, softened

1 egg yolk
1 cup heavy whipping cream
3 eggs
3/4 teaspoon salt
1/4 teaspoon white pepper
1/4 pound thinly sliced fully cooked ham, julienned
1/3 cup grated Parmesan cheese

This tart looks as good as it tastes. The distinctive caraway crust and rich, custard-like filling dotted with tender slices of asparagus make it a dish you'll be proud to serve time after time.

Susan Kuklinski
Delafield, Wisconsin

1. In a bowl, combine the flour, caraway and salt; cut in butter and shortening until mixture resembles coarse crumbs. Sprinkle with water, 1 tablespoon at a time; stir with a fork until dough forms a ball. On a floured surface, roll out dough to fit a 10-in. tart pan. Transfer dough to pan. Freeze for 10 minutes.

2. Cut asparagus into 2-1/2-in. pieces. Set tips aside; cut remaining pieces in half. Place 1/2 in. of water in a large saucepan; add asparagus pieces. Bring to a boil. Reduce heat; cover and simmer for 3-4 minutes or until crisp-tender. Drain well and pat dry.

3. In a small mixing bowl, combine the cream cheese and egg yolk; gradually add cream (mixture will be slightly lumpy). Beat in eggs, one at a time. Add salt and pepper.

4. Place ham and asparagus pieces (not tips) over crust; pour half of the cream cheese mixture over the top. Bake, uncovered, at 425° for 15 minutes. Reduce heat to 375°.

5. Pour remaining cream cheese mixture over top. Arrange asparagus tips over tart; sprinkle with Parmesan cheese. Bake for 40 minutes or until a knife inserted near the center comes out clean. Let stand for 15 minutes before cutting. **Yield:** 6-8 servings.

Asparagus Salmon Pie

1 pound fresh asparagus,
  trimmed
1/2 cup chopped onion
2 tablespoons butter
3 eggs, lightly beaten
1/2 cup milk
2 tablespoons minced fresh
  parsley

1/2 teaspoon dried basil
1/2 teaspoon salt
1 can (14-3/4 ounces)
  pink salmon, drained,
  boned and flaked
1 unbaked pastry shell
  (9 inches)

1. In a skillet, bring 1/2 in. of water and asparagus to a boil. Reduce heat; cover and simmer for 3-4 minutes or until crisp-tender. Drain. Reserve six spears; cut remaining spears into bite-size pieces. In a small saucepan, saute onion in butter until tender.

2. In small bowl, beat eggs, milk, parsley, basil and salt. Stir in salmon and onion. Place cut asparagus in pastry shell; top with salmon mixture. Arrange reserved asparagus spears on top.

3. Cover edges of crust with foil. Bake at 425° for 30-35 minutes or until filling is set. **Yield:** 6 servings.

I received this recipe from a dear neighbor years ago when we lived in the mountains near Yosemite National Park. Now I make it for my husband, for guests and for my children and grandchildren when they come to visit.

Shirley Martin
Fresno, California

Asparagus Chicken Fajitas

1 pound boneless skinless
  chicken breasts, cut into
  strips
3/4 cup Italian salad dressing
1 tablespoon canola oil
1 pound fresh asparagus,
  trimmed and cut into
  2-inch pieces
1 medium sweet red
  pepper, julienned

1 medium sweet yellow
  pepper, julienned
1/2 cup fresh *or* frozen corn
1/4 cup diced onion
2 tablespoons lemon juice
1/2 teaspoon garlic salt
1/8 teaspoon pepper
12 flour tortillas (6 inches),
  warmed

1. Place chicken in a large resealable plastic bag; add salad dressing. Seal bag; refrigerate for 4 hours, turning twice.

2. Drain and discard marinade. In a nonstick skillet, saute chicken in oil for 3 minutes. Add the vegetables. Stir-fry until the chicken juices run clear and vegetables are crisp-tender.

3. Stir in the lemon juice, garlic salt and pepper. Spoon 1/2 cup on each tortilla; fold in sides. **Yield:** 6 servings.

When my children visited their aunt, she served these colorful fajitas. They were so impressed, they brought the recipe home to me. It's a great way for them to eat vegetables.

Marlene Mohr
Cincinnati, Ohio

Asparagus Cress Soup

3/4 cup chopped green onions
1/4 cup butter
3 tablespoons all-purpose flour
2-1/2 cups chicken broth
1-1/2 pounds fresh asparagus, cut into 1-inch pieces

1/2 bunch watercress, stems removed (about 1 cup, lightly packed)
1-1/2 cups half-and-half cream
3/4 teaspoon salt
1/4 teaspoon white pepper
1/8 teaspoon cayenne pepper
Sour cream

1. In a saucepan, saute onion in butter until tender. Stir in flour until blended; gradually add broth. Bring to a boil. Add asparagus and watercress. Reduce heat; cover and simmer 5-7 minutes or until vegetables are tender. Cool.

2. Puree soup, in batches, in a blender or food processor until smooth. Return to saucepan; stir in cream. Heat over low heat (do not boil). Add seasonings. Dollop servings with sour cream. **Yield:** 6 servings.

Gingered Pork and Asparagus

6 tablespoons apple juice
6 tablespoons soy sauce
4 garlic cloves, minced
1 tablespoon ground ginger
1 pound pork tenderloin, thinly sliced

1-1/2 teaspoons cornstarch
2 tablespoons vegetable oil, *divided*
1 pound fresh asparagus, cut into 1-inch pieces
Hot cooked rice, optional

1. Combine the first four ingredients; set aside 1/3 cup. Pour remaining marinade into a large resealable plastic bag; add pork. Seal bag and turn to coat; refrigerate for 1 hour.

2. Combine cornstarch and reserved marinade until smooth; set aside. In a skillet, stir-fry half of the pork in 1 tablespoon oil for 2-3 minutes or until no longer pink. Remove pork with a slotted spoon. Repeat with remaining pork and oil.

3. In the same skillet, stir-fry the asparagus for 2-3 minutes or until crisp-tender. Stir cornstarch mixture and stir into skillet. Bring to a boil; cook and stir for 2 minutes or until thickened. Return pork to skillet and heat through. Serve over rice if desired. **Yield:** 4 servings.

Asparagus Crab Quiche

3/4 **pound fresh asparagus, cut into 2-inch pieces**
1 **unbaked pastry shell (9 inches)**
1 **can (6 ounces) crabmeat, drained, flaked and cartilage removed**
1 **cup (4 ounces) shredded Swiss cheese**
1 **tablespoon all-purpose flour**
3 **eggs, beaten**
1-1/2 **cups half-and-half cream**
1/2 **teaspoon salt**
3 **drops hot pepper sauce**
2 **tablespoons grated Parmesan cheese**
8 **fresh asparagus spears for garnish**

1. Place 1/2 in. of water in a large saucepan; add asparagus. Bring to a boil. Reduce heat; cover and simmer for 3-4 minutes or until crisp-tender. Drain well and pat dry. Arrange cooked asparagus over bottom of pastry. Top with crab. Toss Swiss cheese and flour; sprinkle over crab.

2. In a small bowl, combine the eggs, cream, salt and hot pepper sauce. Pour into pastry. Sprinkle with Parmesan cheese. Arrange asparagus spears, spoke fashion, on top of quiche.

3. Bake, uncovered, at 350° for 35-40 minutes or until a knife inserted near the center comes out clean. Let stand for 5 minutes before cutting. **Yield:** 6 servings.

I almost always serve this easy-to-make quiche when I have company for lunch because it makes such a pretty presentation. It gets rave reviews from family and friends—almost everyone who tastes it asks for a copy of the recipe.

Karen Templeton
Montrose, Pennsylvania

Simple Side

For a quick and easy side dish, drizzle olive oil over trimmed fresh asparagus spears, sprinkle with salt and bake at 450° for 10-20 minutes, depending on the thickness of the asparagus spears.

Asparagus Puff Ring

3/4 cup water
6 tablespoons butter
3/4 cup all-purpose flour
1/2 teaspoon salt
3 eggs
1/4 cup grated Parmesan cheese, *divided*

Filling:
1 pound fresh asparagus, cut into 1-inch pieces
1/4 cup diced onion

2 tablespoons butter
2 tablespoons all-purpose flour
1/2 teaspoon salt
1/4 teaspoon pepper
1-1/2 cups milk
1/2 cup shredded Swiss cheese
2 tablespoons grated Parmesan cheese
2 cups diced fully cooked ham

Every spring when I make this family-favorite entree, I'm struck by how impressive it looks. Ham and asparagus in a creamy sauce are piled high in a cheesy cream puff shell. It's delicious and deceivingly simple to prepare!

Shirley De Lange
Byron Center, Michigan

1. In a saucepan over medium heat, bring water and butter to a boil. Add flour and salt all at once; stir until a smooth ball forms. Remove from heat; let stand for 5 minutes. Add eggs, one at a time, beating well after each addition. Continue beating until mixture is smooth and shiny. Stir in 3 tablespoons Parmesan cheese.

2. Drop dough by 1/4 cupfuls around the sides of a greased 10-in. quiche pan or pie plate (mounds should touch), forming a ring. Top with the remaining cheese.

3. Bake at 400° for 35 minutes or until golden brown. Meanwhile, place 1/2 in. of water in a large saucepan; add asparagus. Bring to a boil. Reduce heat; cover and simmer for 3-4 minutes or until crisp-tender. Drain well.

4. In a saucepan, saute onion in butter until tender. Stir in flour, salt and pepper until blended. Gradually add milk. Bring to a boil over medium heat; cook and stir for 2 minutes or until thickened. Reduce heat; add cheeses and stir until melted. Stir in ham and asparagus; spoon into ring. Serve immediately. **Yield:** 6 servings.

Chicken-Asparagus Pasta Supper

4 tablespoons vegetable oil, *divided*

1-1/2 pounds fresh asparagus, cut into 2-inch pieces

8 ounces sliced fresh mushrooms

1-1/2 cups broccoli florets

2 carrots, julienned

2 medium zucchini, sliced

3 green onions, sliced into 1/2-inch pieces

1/2 teaspoon salt

4 boneless skinless chicken breasts, cut into 1-inch pieces

1/2 cup frozen peas

Sauce:

2 tablespoons butter

2 tablespoons all-purpose flour

1/4 teaspoon pepper

2 cups milk

1 chicken bouillon cube

1 pound thin spaghetti, cooked and drained

I've used this recipe for years as a side dish for family gatherings and potluck suppers. At home, though, we make an entire meal of it...my family can't seem to get enough!

Ginny Truwe
Mankato, Minnesota

1. In a large skillet, heat 2 tablespoons oil. Add the asparagus, mushrooms, broccoli, carrots, zucchini, onions and salt. Cook and stir for 5 minutes. Remove vegetables from the skillet; set aside.

2. Add remaining oil to the skillet. Cook chicken for 5-6 minutes or until it is no longer pink, stirring constantly. Return vegetables to the skillet; add peas and cook for 3-5 minutes. Set aside.

3. For sauce, melt butter in a saucepan. Stir in flour and pepper until smooth. Gradually add milk and bouillon cube. Bring to a boil; cook and stir for 2 minutes or until thickened. Pour over chicken mixture; toss to coat. Serve over spaghetti. **Yield:** 8 servings.

Beans

String Bean Chicken Skillet, p. 50

Beans 'n' Greens

1 cup olive oil
1/4 cup cider vinegar
1-1/2 teaspoons salt
1-1/2 teaspoons sugar
1/2 teaspoon celery seed
1/2 teaspoon paprika

4 cups fresh green beans, cut into 2-inch pieces
8 cups torn lettuce
4 cups torn fresh spinach
2 cups (8 ounces) shredded Swiss cheese

1. In a jar with tight-fitting lid, combine the first six ingredients; shake well. Pour over green beans; let stand for 15 minutes. Just before serving, drain beans, reserving the marinade.

2. In a salad bowl, combine the beans, lettuce, spinach and Swiss cheese. Drizzle with the reserved marinade and toss to coat. **Yield:** 14-18 servings.

German-Style Green Beans

1 pound fresh green beans, cut into 2-inch pieces
3 bacon strips, diced
1 medium onion, quartered and sliced
2 teaspoons cornstarch

1/4 teaspoon salt
1/4 teaspoon ground mustard
1/2 cup water
1 tablespoon brown sugar
1 tablespoon cider vinegar
Apple slices, optional

1. Place beans in a saucepan and cover with water; bring to a boil. Cook, uncovered, for 8-10 minutes or until crisp-tender; drain and set aside.

2. In a skillet, cook bacon over medium heat until crisp. Remove to paper towels. Drain, reserving 1 tablespoon drippings. In the same skillet, saute onion in reserved drippings until tender.

3. In a small bowl, combine the cornstarch, salt, mustard and water until smooth. Stir into onion. Bring to a boil; cook and stir for 1-2 minutes or until thickened. Stir in brown sugar and vinegar. Add the beans; heat through. Sprinkle with bacon. Garnish with apples if desired. **Yield:** 3-4 servings.

Dilly Bean Potato Salad

1 pound fresh green beans

4 pounds red potatoes

1 medium red onion, thinly sliced and separated into rings

1 medium Vidalia *or* sweet onion, thinly sliced and separated into rings

1 cup chopped celery

8 dill pickles, sliced

2 tablespoons minced fresh dill *or* 2 teaspoons dill weed

2 tablespoons minced fresh parsley

4 garlic cloves, minced

Vinaigrette:

3/4 cup olive oil

1/3 to 1/2 cup tarragon vinegar

1 envelope Italian salad dressing mix

2 tablespoons sugar

1 teaspoon salt

1 teaspoon pepper

Celery salt and seasoned salt to taste

1. Place 1 in. of water and beans in a skillet; bring to a boil. Reduce heat. Cover and simmer for 8-10 minutes or until crisp-tender; drain and set aside.

2. Place potatoes in a large saucepan or Dutch oven and cover with water. Bring to a boil. Reduce heat. Cover and cook for 15-20 minutes or until tender; drain and cool. Cut into 1/4-in. slices; place in a large bowl. Add the onions, celery, pickles, dill, parsley and garlic.

3. In a jar with a tight-fitting lid, combine the vinaigrette ingredients; shake well. Drizzle over potato mixture. Add beans; gently toss. **Yield:** 14-16 servings.

Green beans and dill pickles perk up this pretty potato salad, and the Italian-style dressing adds a refreshing tang. My Irish grandmother made it for family gatherings; even though I've changed it a bit, Nanny always comes to mind when I dish it up.

Marguerite Novicke
Vineland, New Jersey

Italian Green Beans

1 small onion, chopped
2 tablespoons olive oil
2 to 3 garlic cloves, minced
1 can (14-1/2 ounces) stewed tomatoes, coarsely mashed
1/2 cup water
3 tablespoons minced fresh oregano *or* 1 tablespoon dried oregano
4-1/2 teaspoons minced fresh basil *or* 1-1/2 teaspoons dried basil
1 teaspoon sugar
1 teaspoon salt
1/4 to 1/2 teaspoon coarsely ground pepper
2 pounds fresh green beans, cut into 1-inch pieces
2 tablespoons grated Romano *or* Parmesan cheese

When I was first married, I wasn't a great cook. Over 20 years later, I have many dishes I'm proud of, including this family favorite. Basil, oregano and Romano cheese give these beans their Italian accent. I serve them with broiled steak, pork roast, lamb chops or pork chops.

Andrea Ibzag
Gordon, Wisconsin

1. In a small saucepan, saute onion in oil until tender. Add garlic; saute 1 minute longer. Add the tomatoes, water, oregano, basil, sugar, salt and pepper. Bring to a boil. Reduce heat; simmer, uncovered, for 40 minutes.

2. Meanwhile, place beans in a large saucepan and cover with water; bring to a boil. Cook, uncovered, for 8-10 minutes or until crisp-tender; drain. Add tomato mixture and cheese; cook for 5 minutes or until heated through. **Yield:** 10 servings.

Roasted Green Bean Salad

2 pounds fresh green beans
3 tablespoons olive oil, *divided*
3/4 teaspoon salt, *divided*
2 tablespoons white wine vinegar
1-1/2 teaspoons Dijon mustard
2 tablespoons snipped fresh dill *or* 2 teaspoons dill weed
1-1/2 teaspoons sugar
1/4 teaspoon pepper

1. In a bowl, toss beans with 1 tablespoon oil and 1/2 teaspoon salt. Spread in a single layer in an ungreased 15-in. x 10-in. x 1-in. baking pan. Bake, uncovered, at 400° for 30-40 minutes or until beans are tender and lightly browned, stirring twice.

2. Meanwhile, in a small bowl, whisk the vinegar, mustard, dill, sugar, pepper and remaining salt. Slowly whisk in remaining oil. Transfer beans to a large serving bowl. Add vinaigrette and toss to coat. **Yield:** 4-6 servings.

This easy-to-fix recipe turns homegrown green beans into something special. A tangy dill and Dijon vinaigrette coats the crisp-tender beans without overpowering them so the fresh-from-the-garden flavor comes through.

Kathy Shell
San Diego, California

Picnic Beans with Dip

1 pound fresh green *and/or* wax beans
1/2 cup mayonnaise
1/2 cup half-and-half cream
6 tablespoons vegetable oil
2 tablespoons white vinegar
1 tablespoon Dijon mustard
1 small onion, quartered
1 teaspoon salt
1/4 teaspoon ground coriander
1/4 teaspoon dried savory
1/4 teaspoon pepper
1/8 teaspoon dried thyme

1. Place beans in a saucepan and cover with water; bring to a boil. Cook, uncovered, for 8-10 minutes or until crisp-tender. Drain and rinse with cold water. Refrigerate until serving.

2. In a blender or food processor, combine the remaining ingredients; cover and process until smooth. Refrigerate for at least 1 hour. Serve with beans for dipping. **Yield:** 1-2/3 cups dip.

Here's a fun way to enjoy fresh-picked beans...with a creamy well-seasoned dip. I first enjoyed it at a friend's house and have made it for several years. Try the dip with other vegetables, too, such as broccoli, celery and carrots.

Martha Bergman
Cleveland Heights, Ohio

Chicken Green Bean Casserole

6 tablespoons butter
6 tablespoons all-purpose flour
1-1/2 cups chicken broth
1/2 cup milk
1 to 2 teaspoons soy sauce
1/2 teaspoon salt
Dash pepper

2/3 cup shredded Parmesan cheese, *divided*
8 cups cut fresh green *or* wax beans, cooked and drained
2 cups cubed cooked chicken

1. In a saucepan, melt butter. Stir in flour until smooth. Gradually add broth, milk, soy sauce, salt and pepper. Bring to a boil; cook and stir for 2 minutes or until thickened. Remove from heat.

2. Stir in 1/3 cup Parmesan cheese until melted. Add beans and chicken; toss to coat. Transfer to a greased 2-qt. baking dish; sprinkle with the remaining cheese. Bake, uncovered, at 375° for 15-18 minutes or until golden brown. **Yield:** 6-8 servings.

Nutty Onion Green Beans

1/2 pound fresh green beans, cut in half
1 small red onion, sliced and separated into rings
1/3 cup chopped pecans

3 tablespoons butter
2 tablespoons brown sugar
2 tablespoons orange juice
1 tablespoon Dijon mustard
1/2 teaspoon salt

1. Place beans in a saucepan and cover with water; bring to a boil. Cook, uncovered, for 8-10 minutes or until crisp-tender; drain and set aside.

2. In a skillet, cook onion and pecans in butter until onion is tender. In a small bowl, combine the brown sugar, orange juice, mustard and salt; stir into the onion mixture. Cook 2-3 minutes longer or until sauce begins to thicken. Stir in beans; heat through. **Yield:** 3-4 servings.

Green Bean Potato Bake

- 6 cups cubed peeled cooked potatoes
- 2 cups fresh green beans
- 2 cups cubed fully cooked ham
- 2-1/2 cups (10 ounces) shredded Colby-Monterey Jack cheese, *divided*
- 2 tablespoons dried minced onion
- 1 can (10-3/4 ounces) condensed cream of mushroom soup, undiluted
- 1/2 cup milk
- 1/3 cup mayonnaise
- 1/3 cup sour cream

1. In a greased 13-in. x 9-in. x 2-in. baking dish, layer the potatoes, beans, ham, 2 cups cheese and onion. In a bowl, combine the soup, milk, mayonnaise and sour cream; pour over the top and gently stir to coat.

2. Cover and bake at 350° for 45 minutes. Uncover and sprinkle with remaining cheese. Bake 5-8 minutes longer or until cheese is melted. **Yield:** 8 servings.

Editor's Note: Reduced-fat or fat-free mayonnaise is not recommended for this recipe.

As a pastor's wife, I often cook up contributions to church dinners using on-hand ingredients. This creamy bake was such a hit, I now take it to family get-togethers as well. I make it up ahead, refrigerate it and bake it shortly before serving.

Charlene Wells
Colorado Springs, Colorado

Flavorful Green Beans

Instead of cooking green beans in plain water, add some beef bouillon granules and sugar to give them subtle flavor.

Green Bean Mushroom Pie

Fresh green bean flavor stands out in this pretty, lattice-topped pie. A flaky golden crust holds the savory bean, mushroom and cream cheese filling. It tastes wonderfully different every time I make it depending on the variety of mushroom I use.

Tara Walworth
Maple Park, Illinois

3 cups sliced fresh mushrooms
4 tablespoons butter, *divided*
2-1/2 cups chopped onions
6 cups fresh green beans, cut into 1-inch pieces
2 teaspoons minced fresh thyme *or* 3/4 teaspoon dried thyme
1/2 teaspoon salt
1/4 teaspoon pepper
1 package (8 ounces) cream cheese, cubed
1/2 cup milk

Crust:
2-1/2 cups all-purpose flour
2 teaspoons baking powder
1 teaspoon dill weed
1/4 teaspoon salt
1 cup cold butter
1 cup (8 ounces) sour cream
1 egg
1 tablespoon heavy whipping cream

1. In a skillet, saute mushrooms in 1 tablespoon butter until tender; drain and set aside. In the same skillet, saute onions and beans in remaining butter for 18-20 minutes or until beans are crisp-tender. Add the thyme, salt, pepper, cream cheese, milk and mushrooms. Cook and stir until the cheese is melted. Remove from the heat; set aside.

2. In a bowl, combine the flour, baking powder, dill and salt. Cut in butter until mixture resembles coarse crumbs. Stir in sour cream to form a soft dough. Divide dough in half. On a well-floured surface, roll out one portion to fit a deep-dish 9-in. pie plate; trim pastry even with edge.

3. Pour green bean mixture into crust. Roll out remaining pastry; make a lattice crust. Trim, seal and flute edge. In a small bowl, beat the egg and cream; brush over lattice top. Bake at 400° for 25-35 minutes or until golden brown. **Yield:** 8-10 servings.

Mixed Beans with Lime Butter

This is a simple yet delicious way to showcase beans. It is best with beans fresh from your garden or the farmers market.

Lois Fetting
Nelson, Wisconsin

1/2 pound *each* fresh green and wax beans, trimmed
2 tablespoons butter
2 teaspoons snipped fresh dill
2 teaspoons lime juice
1 teaspoon grated lime peel
1/2 teaspoon salt
1/4 teaspoon pepper

1. Place beans in a saucepan and cover with water; bring to a boil. Cook, uncovered, for 8-10 minutes or until crisp-tender; drain and set aside.

2. In a skillet, melt butter; add the dill, lime juice and peel, salt, pepper and beans. Stir to coat and cook until heated through. **Yield:** 4 servings.

Creole Green Beans

4 cups cut fresh green beans
5 bacon strips, diced
1 medium onion, chopped
1/2 cup chopped green pepper
2 tablespoons all-purpose flour
2 tablespoons brown sugar
1 tablespoon Worcestershire sauce
1 teaspoon salt
1/2 teaspoon pepper
1/2 teaspoon ground mustard
1 can (14-1/2 ounces) diced tomatoes, undrained

1. Place beans in a large saucepan and cover with water. Bring to a boil. Cook, uncovered, for 8-10 minutes or until crisp-tender. Meanwhile, in a skillet, cook bacon, onion and green pepper over medium heat until bacon is crisp and vegetables are tender. Remove with a slotted spoon.

2. Stir the flour, brown sugar, Worcestershire sauce, salt, pepper and mustard into the reserved drippings until blended. Stir in tomatoes. Bring to a boil; cook and stir for 2 minutes or until thickened. Drain beans and add to skillet. Stir in bacon mixture. **Yield:** 6 servings.

Even though our children are grown, my husband and I remain busy. So we rely on speedy recipes that call for everyday ingredients. This peppery treatment really wakes up green beans.

Sue Kuhn
Dublin, Ohio

Green Bean Bundles of Joy

I like to serve baked green beans in little bundles, secured with strips of bacon, as a special side dish. A few minutes under the broiler makes the bacon crispy. The dish gets its tang from Italian dressing, which the beans are baked in.

Ame Andrews
Little Rock, Arkansas

6 cups water
1/2 pound fresh green beans, trimmed

4 to 6 bacon strips
3/4 cup Italian salad dressing

1. In a saucepan, bring water to a boil. Add beans; cover and cook for 3 minutes. Drain and set aside. Cut bacon in half lengthwise; place on a microwave-safe plate. Microwave on high for 2-1/2 to 3 minutes or until edges curl. Place four or five beans on each bacon strip; wrap bacon around beans and tie in a knot.

2. Place bundles in an 8-in. square baking dish. Drizzle with salad dressing. Bake, uncovered, at 350° for 10-15 minutes or until beans are crisp-tender. Broil 4 in. from the heat for 2-3 minutes or until bacon is crisp. **Yield:** 4-6 servings.

String Bean Chicken Skillet

1/2 pound fresh green beans, cut into 2-inch pieces
1/2 pound fresh wax beans, cut into 2-inch pieces
3 boneless skinless chicken breast halves
2 tablespoons vegetable oil
2 tablespoons plus 1-1/2 teaspoons cornstarch

3 tablespoons soy sauce
1 can (8 ounces) pineapple chunks
1 medium sweet red pepper, julienned
1 small onion, thinly sliced
1/4 teaspoon salt
1/4 teaspoon ground ginger
Hot cooked rice

1. Place beans in a saucepan and cover with water; bring to a boil. Cook, uncovered, for 3 minutes; drain and set aside. Flatten chicken to 1/4-in. thickness; cut into 1/2-in. strips. In a large skillet, stir-fry chicken in oil for 3-4 minutes or until no longer pink. Remove with a slotted spoon.

2. In a small bowl, combine cornstarch and soy sauce until smooth. Drain the pineapple, reserving juice; set pineapple aside. Stir the juice into the soy sauce mixture; set aside.

3. In the skillet, stir-fry red pepper and onion for 5 minutes. Add the chicken, beans, pineapple, salt and ginger. Gradually stir in the soy sauce mixture. Bring to a boil; cook and stir for 2 minutes or until thickened. Serve with rice. **Yield:** 6 servings.

I started to prepare a chicken stir-fry one day and discovered I was out of frozen snow peas. So I tossed in green beans instead with a few leftover wax beans for color. I've been making the recipe this way ever since.

Priscilla Gilbert
Indian Harbour Beach, Florida

Three-Bean Tomato Cups

3/4 **pound fresh green beans,
cut into 2-inch pieces**

1/2 **pound fresh wax beans,
cut into 2-inch pieces**

1 **can (15 ounces) black
beans, rinsed and
drained**

1 **medium sweet red
pepper, cut into
1-1/2-inch strips**

3 **green onions, sliced**

1/4 **cup minced fresh cilantro**

1/4 **cup olive oil**

3 **tablespoons red wine
vinegar**

1 **teaspoon ground cumin**

1 **garlic clove, minced**

1/2 **teaspoon salt**

1/4 **teaspoon pepper**

6 **large firm tomatoes**

1. Place the beans in a saucepan and cover with water; bring to a boil. Cook, uncovered, for 8-10 minutes or until crisp-tender. Drain and place in a large bowl. Add the black beans, red pepper, onions and cilantro.

2. In a jar with a tight-fitting lid, combine the oil, vinegar, cumin, garlic, salt and pepper; shake well. Pour over bean mixture and toss to coat. Cover and refrigerate for 30 minutes.

3. Cut a 1/4-in. slice off the top of each tomato; scoop out and discard pulp. Using a slotted spoon, fill tomato cups with bean mixture. **Yield:** 6 servings.

Cilantro and cumin give this delightful salad a Mexican flair. Served in hollowed-out tomatoes, the tasty bean blend makes a pretty addition to a ladies' luncheon or special-occasion meal. Garlic lovers might want to add a second clove.

Audrey Green Ballon
Kentwood, Louisiana

Shepherd's Bean Pie

1-1/4 pounds fresh green beans, cut into 2-inch pieces

1-1/4 pounds fresh wax beans, cut into 2-inch pieces

3 medium carrots, cut into 2-inch julienned strips

1/2 small onion, chopped

1 teaspoon butter

1 can (10-3/4 ounces) condensed cream of chicken soup, undiluted

1/2 cup heavy whipping cream

1/2 cup chicken broth

3-1/4 teaspoons dill weed, *divided*

6 ounces cubed fully cooked ham

1-1/2 cups (6 ounces) shredded Swiss cheese, *divided*

1/4 cup slivered almonds

7 cups hot mashed potatoes (with added milk and butter)

This comforting casserole is a variation on the traditional English pie. It is chock-full of fresh green and wax beans, carrots, cubed ham and a handful of crunchy almonds in a creamy Swiss cheese sauce. Topped with mashed potatoes, it makes a hearty side dish.

Karen Cleveland
Spring Valley, Minnesota

1. Place beans and carrots in a saucepan and cover with water; bring to a boil. Cook, uncovered, for 8-10 minutes or until crisp-tender; drain and set aside. In a small skillet, saute onion in butter for 3-4 minutes or until tender.

2. In a large bowl, whisk the soup, cream, broth and 3 teaspoons dill. Add the beans, carrots and onion; gently stir to coat. Transfer to a greased shallow 3-qt. baking dish. Top with the ham, 1 cup cheese and almonds. Spread mashed potatoes over the top.

3. Cover and bake at 350° for 30 minutes. Uncover and sprinkle with remaining cheese and dill. Bake 5-10 minutes longer or until heated through and the cheese is melted. **Yield:** 12-15 servings.

Tortellini Vegetable Soup

1 large onion, chopped
2 celery ribs, chopped
2 tablespoons vegetable oil
2 cans (14-1/2 ounces each) beef broth
1 cup *each* fresh *or* frozen corn, sliced carrots and cut green beans
1 cup diced uncooked potatoes
1 teaspoon dried basil
1 teaspoon dried thyme
1/2 teaspoon minced chives
2 cans (14-1/2 ounces each) diced tomatoes
2 cups frozen beef *or* cheese tortellini

1. In a Dutch oven or soup kettle, saute the onion and celery in oil. Add the broth, corn, carrots, beans, potatoes, basil, thyme and chives; bring to a boil. Reduce heat; cover and simmer for 10-15 minutes or until potatoes are tender.

2. Add the tomatoes and tortellini. Simmer, uncovered, for 4-5 minutes or until heated through. **Yield:** 10 servings (2-1/2 quarts).

Tomatoes, carrots, green beans, potatoes, corn and celery are the perfect complements to convenient frozen tortellini in this heartwarming soup. Add a crusty loaf of bread and a green salad, and dinner is ready in no time.

Deborah Hutchinson
Enfield, Connecticut

Green Bean Quiche

1-1/2 cups fresh cut green beans
1/2 cup chopped onion
2 tablespoons butter
1/2 cup sliced fresh mushrooms
1/4 cup diced green pepper
1/2 cup mayonnaise
1/4 cup sour cream
1/4 teaspoon salt
1/4 cup crushed saltines (about 8 crackers)
6 eggs, beaten
1 medium tomato, seeded and chopped
3/4 cup shredded sharp cheddar cheese

1. Place beans in a small saucepan and cover with water. Bring to a boil. Cook, uncovered, for 8-10 minutes or until crisp-tender; drain and set aside.

2. In a small skillet, saute onion in butter until tender. Add mushrooms and green pepper; saute until tender.

3. In a large bowl, combine the mayonnaise, sour cream and salt; stir in the beans, mushroom mixture and cracker crumbs. Gradually stir in eggs. Pour into a greased deep-dish 9-in. pie plate. Sprinkle with tomato and cheese.

4. Bake at 350° for 25-30 minutes or until a knife inserted near the center comes out clean. Let stand for 5-10 minutes before cutting. **Yield:** 6 servings.

This colorful quiche is perfect for brunch or lunch. I even like to serve it for our Sunday night supper. Each hearty slice is filled with green beans and mushrooms and topped with tomato and cheddar cheese. It's delicious!

Lee Campbell
Bartow, Florida

Blue Cheese Green Beans

Bacon, blue cheese and chopped nuts make this my mom's favorite way to enjoy green beans. I always prepare this side dish when she's coming for dinner.

Kate Hilts
Grand Rapids, Michigan

6 bacon strips, diced
1 pound fresh green beans, cut into 2-inch pieces
1/2 cup crumbled blue cheese
1/3 cup chopped pecans
Pepper to taste

1. In a large skillet, cook bacon over medium heat until crisp. Using a slotted spoon, remove to paper towels. Drain, reserving 2 tablespoons drippings.

2. In the drippings, cook and stir the beans for 8-10 minutes or until crisp-tender. Add the blue cheese, pecans, pepper and bacon. Cook for 2 minutes or until heated through. **Yield:** 6 servings.

Two-Bean Tomato Bake

1-1/2 pounds fresh green beans, cut into 2-inch pieces
1-1/2 pounds fresh wax beans, cut into 2-inch pieces
5 medium tomatoes, peeled and cubed
1/2 pounds fresh mushrooms, sliced
1 medium sweet onion, chopped
10 tablespoons butter, divided
1-1/2 teaspoons minced garlic, divided
1-1/2 teaspoons dried basil, divided
1-1/2 teaspoons dried oregano, divided
1 teaspoon salt
1-1/2 cups soft bread crumbs
1/3 cup grated Parmesan cheese

Parmesan cheese, basil and garlic spice up this mouth-watering medley of beans, mushrooms, onion and tomatoes. A crumb topping adds crunch to this veggie bake that's even more flavorful when you use your garden harvest.

Dorothy Rieke
Julian, Nebraska

1. Place beans in a large saucepan and cover with water; bring to a boil. Cook, uncovered, for 8-10 minutes or until crisp-tender. Drain; add the tomatoes and set aside.

2. In a skillet, saute mushrooms and onion in 4 tablespoons butter. Add 1 teaspoon garlic, basil, 1 teaspoon oregano and salt. Add to the bean mixture; toss to coat. Spoon into a greased 3-qt. baking dish.

3. Melt the remaining butter; toss with bread crumbs, Parmesan cheese and remaining garlic, basil and oregano. Sprinkle over bean mixture. Cover and bake at 400° for 20 minutes. Uncover and bake 15 minutes longer or until golden brown. **Yield:** 14-16 servings.

Stir-Fried Beef 'n' Beans

1/4 cup cornstarch
1/2 cup soy sauce
2 tablespoons water
4 teaspoons minced fresh gingerroot
4 garlic cloves, minced
4 tablespoons vegetable oil, *divided*
1 pound boneless beef sirloin steak, cut into 1/4-inch strips
1/2 pound fresh green beans, cut in half lengthwise
1 teaspoon sugar
1/2 teaspoon salt
Hot cooked rice

1. In a bowl, combine the cornstarch, soy sauce, water, ginger, garlic and 2 tablespoons oil until smooth. Set aside 1/2 cup. Pour the remaining marinade into a large resealable plastic bag; add the beef. Seal bag and turn to coat; refrigerate for 25-30 minutes.

2. Drain and discard marinade from beef. In a wok or skillet, stir-fry beef in remaining oil for 4-6 minutes or until no longer pink. Remove and keep warm. In the same skillet, stir-fry the beans, sugar and salt for 15 minutes or until crisp-tender. Stir in the reserved marinade and beef. Bring to a boil; cook and stir for 1-2 minutes or until thickened. Serve over rice.
Yield: 4 servings.

Garlic, ginger and soy sauce lend a robust flavor to this meaty marinated dish. My mother-in-law took cooking lessons while living in Japan and brought back this recipe. It has become a favorite of family and friends...even those who don't usually eat green beans.

Kristine Lowry
Bowling Green, Kentucky

Berries

Fresh Strawberry Pie, p. 72

Berry Good Ice Cream Sauce

1-3/4 cups sliced fresh *or* frozen rhubarb

2/3 cup pureed fresh *or* frozen strawberries

1/4 cup sugar

1/4 cup orange juice

2 cups sliced fresh *or* frozen strawberries

Vanilla ice cream

In a saucepan, combine the first four ingredients. Cook for 5 minutes over medium heat until rhubarb is tender. Stir in the sliced strawberries. Store in the refrigerator. Serve over ice cream. **Yield:** 3-1/2 cups.

Four-Berry Spread

1 cup fresh *or* frozen blackberries

1 cup fresh *or* frozen blueberries

1-1/2 cups fresh *or* frozen strawberries

1-1/2 cups fresh *or* frozen raspberries

1 package (1-3/4 ounces) powdered fruit pectin

7 cups sugar

1. Crush berries in a large kettle. Stir in pectin; bring to a full rolling boil over high heat, stirring constantly. Stir in sugar; return to a full rolling boil. Boil for 1 minute, stirring constantly.

2. Remove from the heat; skim off any foam. Pour hot into hot sterilized jars, leaving 1/4-in. headspace. Adjust caps. Process for 10 minutes in a boiling-water bath. **Yield:** about 7 half-pints.

Strawberry Tossed Salad

1/2 cup vegetable oil
1/3 cup sugar
1/4 cup cider vinegar
  1 garlic clove, minced
1/4 teaspoon salt
1/4 teaspoon paprika
Pinch white pepper
  8 cups torn romaine
  4 cups torn Bibb *or* Boston lettuce
2-1/2 cups sliced fresh strawberries
  1 cup (4 ounces) shredded Monterey Jack cheese
1/2 cup chopped walnuts, toasted

Combine the first seven ingredients in a jar with tight-fitting lid; shake well. Just before serving, toss the salad greens, strawberries, cheese and walnuts in a large salad bowl. Drizzle with dressing and toss. **Yield:** 6-8 servings.

One reason I particularly like this recipe is that it's so versatile. I've served the salad with poultry, ham and pork all throughout the year and even used it to add color to the table at Christmas.

Patricia McNamara
Kansas City, Missouri

Raspberry Cider

2 cups fresh *or* frozen raspberries

4 cups apple cider
Mint sprigs, optional

In a bowl, crush berries. Add cider and mix well. Strain through a fine sieve or cheesecloth. Chill. Garnish with mint sprigs if desired. **Yield:** about 5 cups.

Here's a refreshing cooler for a late-summer afternoon. The cider is so pretty in a clear sparkling glass!

Pat McIlrath
Grinnell, Iowa

Raspberry-Cranberry Soup

2 cups fresh *or* frozen cranberries

2 cups apple juice

1 cup fresh *or* frozen unsweetened raspberries, thawed

1/2 to 1 cup sugar

1 tablespoon lemon juice

1/4 teaspoon ground cinnamon

2 cups half-and-half cream, *divided*

1 tablespoon cornstarch

Whipped cream, additional raspberries and mint, optional

Served hot, this beautiful tangy soup helps beat the winter "blahs". On a sunny summer day, it's refreshingly cold. I have fun serving it because people are so intrigued with the idea of a fruit soup. Even doubters scrape their bowls clean.

Susan Stull
Chillicothe, Missouri

1. In a large saucepan, bring cranberries and apple juice to a boil. Reduce heat; simmer, uncovered, for 10 minutes. Press through a sieve; return to the pan. Also press the raspberries through the sieve; discard skins and seeds. Add to cranberry mixture; bring to a boil. Add the sugar, lemon juice and cinnamon; remove from the heat.

2. Cool for 4 minutes. Stir 1 cup into 1-1/2 cups cream. Return all to pan; bring to a gentle boil. Combine cornstarch and remaining cream until smooth; stir into soup. Cook and stir for 2 minutes or until thickened. Serve hot or chilled. Garnish with whipped cream, raspberries and mint if desired. **Yield:** 4 servings.

Avoid Moldy Berries

When at the farmers market, select berries that are in dry unstained containers. Stained containers may indicate oversoft berries that are not freshly picked. Since mold on berries spreads quickly, never leave a moldy berry next to a good one.

Cranberry Salsa

2 cups fresh *or* frozen
  cranberries
2 cups water
1/2 cup sugar
1/4 to 1/2 cup minced fresh
  cilantro
2 to 4 tablespoons chopped
  jalapeno peppers

1/4 cup finely chopped onion
2 tablespoons grated
  orange peel
1/2 teaspoon salt
1/4 teaspoon pepper

In a saucepan, bring cranberries and water to a boil; cook
for 2 minutes. Drain. Stir in sugar until dissolved. Add the
cilantro, peppers, onion, orange peel, salt and pepper. Mix
well. Cool and refrigerate. **Yield:** 2 cups.

Editor's Note: When cutting or seeding hot peppers, use rubber
or plastic gloves to protect your hands. Avoid touching your face.

*Wisconsin grows an
abundance of cranberries
and celebrates the harvest
with many cranberry
festivals. I don't remember
where I obtained this recipe,
but it's easy, different...and
good! Try it with pork or
leftover turkey.*

Arline Roggenbuck
Shawano, Wisconsin

Spinach Berry Salad

4 cups packed torn fresh
  spinach
1 cup sliced fresh
  strawberries
1 cup fresh *or* frozen
  blueberries
1 small sweet onion, sliced
1/4 cup chopped pecans,
  toasted

Curry Salad Dressing:
  2 tablespoons white wine
    vinegar
  2 tablespoons balsamic
    vinegar
  2 tablespoons honey
  2 teaspoons Dijon mustard
  1 teaspoon curry powder
  1/4 teaspoon salt
  1/8 teaspoon pepper

1. In a large salad bowl, toss together the spinach, strawberries,
blueberries, onion and pecans.

2. In a jar with a tight-fitting lid, combine the dressing
ingredients; shake well. Pour over salad and toss to coat. Serve
immediately. **Yield:** 4 servings.

*My mother shared this
recipe with me because of
my passion for light dishes.
Delicious and colorful, it's as
pleasing to the eye as it is to
the palate. It wins me raves
whenever I serve it.*

Lisa Lorenzo
Willoughby, Ohio

Strawberry Salsa

This different salsa is versatile, fresh-tasting and colorful. People are surprised to see a salsa made with strawberries, but it's excellent over grilled chicken and pork and as a dip with corn chips.

Jean Giroux
Belchertown, Massachusetts

1 pint fresh strawberries, diced
4 plum tomatoes, seeded and diced
1 small red onion, diced
1 to 2 medium jalapeno peppers, minced
Juice of 1 lime
2 garlic cloves, minced
1 tablespoon olive oil

In a bowl, combine the strawberries, tomatoes, onion and peppers. Stir in the lime juice, garlic and oil. Cover and refrigerate for 2 hours. **Yield:** 4 cups.

Editor's Note: When cutting or seeding hot peppers, use rubber or plastic gloves to protect your hands. Avoid touching your face.

Blueberry Muffins

3/4 cup milk
1/4 cup lemon juice
2 cups all-purpose flour
3/4 cup sugar
1 tablespoon baking powder
1/2 teaspoon ground cinnamon
1/2 teaspoon salt
1 egg, lightly beaten
1/4 cup vegetable oil
1 cup fresh *or* frozen blueberries

1. In a small bowl, mix milk and lemon juice; set aside. In a large bowl, combine flour, sugar, baking powder, cinnamon and salt. Set aside. Add egg and oil to milk mixture; mix well. Gently stir into flour mixture just until moistened.

2. Fold in blueberries. Fill greased or paper-lined muffin cups two-thirds full. Bake at 400° for 22-24 minutes or until a toothpick inserted near the center comes out clean. Cool for 5 minutes before removing from the pan to a wire rack. **Yield:** 1 dozen.

I prepare these muffins with the blueberries that grow wild along the rocky coast of Maine. I have worked on this recipe for several years and finally feel that I have it perfected.

Carolyn Gilman
Westbrook, Maine

Lamb with Raspberry Sauce

- 2 cups fresh *or* frozen unsweetened raspberries
- 3/4 cup finely chopped seeded peeled cucumber
- 1/2 cup finely chopped peeled tart apple
- 2 tablespoons white grape juice
- 1 to 2 tablespoons sugar
- 4 garlic cloves, minced
- 3 tablespoons olive oil
- 8 lamb loin chops (6 to 7 ounces *each* and 1 to 1-1/2 inches thick)

1. Place raspberries in a blender or food processor; cover and process until pureed. Strain and discard seeds; transfer puree to a small saucepan. Stir in the cucumber, apple, grape juice and sugar. Bring to a boil. Reduce heat; simmer, uncovered, for 5-7 minutes or until cucumber and apple are tender.

2. Meanwhile, in a large skillet, saute garlic in oil until tender. Add lamb chops. Cook, uncovered, for 7-10 minutes on each side or until meat reaches desired doneness (for medium-rare, a meat thermometer should read 145°; medium, 160°; well-done, 170°). Serve with raspberry sauce. **Yield:** 4 servings.

Lamb chops are dressed up with a wonderful fruity sauce in this recipe. I enjoy cooking and surprising my wife, Chrissy, with creative dishes like this one.

Scott Beatrice
Lakeland, Florida

Washing Berries

To wash berries, place berries a few at a time in a colander in the sink. Gently spray with sink sprayer. Then spread out on paper towels to pat dry.

Blueberry French Toast

12 slices day-old white bread, crusts removed	**Sauce:**
	1 cup sugar
2 packages (8 ounces *each*) cream cheese	2 tablespoons cornstarch
	1 cup water

1 cup fresh *or* frozen
  blueberries
	1 cup fresh *or* frozen
	  blueberries

12 eggs	1 tablespoon butter
2 cups milk	
1/3 cup maple syrup *or* honey	

This is the best breakfast dish I've ever tasted. With luscious blueberries inside and in a sauce, it's almost more a dessert. The recipe was shared with me by a local blueberry grower.

Patricia Walls
Aurora, Minnesota

1. Cut bread into 1-in. cubes; place half in a greased 13-in. x 9-in. x 2-in. baking dish. Cut cream cheese into 1-in. cubes; place over bread. Top with blueberries and remaining bread cubes.

2. In a large bowl, beat eggs. Add milk and syrup; mix well. Pour over bread mixture. Cover and refrigerate for 8 hours or overnight.

3. Remove from the refrigerator 30 minutes before baking. Cover and bake at 350° for 30 minutes. Uncover; bake 25-30 minutes longer or until golden brown and center is set.

4. For sauce, in a small saucepan, combine the sugar, cornstarch and water until smooth. Bring to a boil; cook and stir for 2 minutes or until thickened. Stir in blueberries; reduce heat. Simmer; uncovered, for 8-10 minutes or until berries burst. Stir in butter until melted. Serve with French toast. **Yield:** 6-8 servings (1-3/4 cups sauce).

Editor's Note: If using frozen blueberries, do not thaw.

Blueberry-Sausage Breakfast Cake

1/2 cup butter, softened
3/4 cup sugar
1/4 cup packed brown sugar
2 eggs
2 cups all-purpose flour
1 teaspoon baking powder
1/2 teaspoon baking soda
1 cup (8 ounces) sour cream
1 pound bulk pork sausage, cooked and drained
1 cup fresh *or* frozen blueberries
1/2 cup chopped pecans

Blueberry Sauce:
1/2 cup sugar
2 tablespoons cornstarch
1/2 cup water
2 cups fresh *or* frozen blueberries

1. In a mixing bowl, cream butter and sugars. Add eggs, one at a time, beating well after each addition. Combine the flour, baking powder and baking soda; add to creamed mixture alternately with sour cream, beating well after each addition. Fold in sausage and blueberries.

2. Pour into a greased 13-in. x 9-in. x 2-in. baking pan. Sprinkle with pecans. Bake at 350° for 35-40 minutes or until a toothpick inserted near the center comes out clean.

3. For sauce, combine sugar and cornstarch in a saucepan. Add water and blueberries. Bring to a boil; cook and stir for 2 minutes or until thickened. Spoon over individual servings.
Yield: 9-12 servings.

I fix this recipe for my co-workers often. It's very simple and can be prepared the night before.

Peggy Frazier
Indianapolis, Indiana

Instead of the usual ham and cheese, try dressing up eggs with strawberries and cream cheese. I first tasted this dish while vacationing at the beach and now make it as a change of pace for dinner.

Selina Smith
Frostburg, Maryland

Strawberry Bliss Omelet

6 eggs
2 tablespoons water
1/2 teaspoon salt
Dash pepper
2 tablespoons butter

2 ounces cream cheese, cut into 1/2-inch cubes
3 tablespoons brown sugar
1-1/2 cups sliced fresh strawberries, *divided*
Confectioners' sugar

1. In a bowl, beat the eggs, water, salt and pepper. Heat butter in a 10-in. nonstick skillet over medium heat; add egg mixture. As the eggs set, lift edges, letting uncooked portion flow underneath.

2. When the eggs are almost set, sprinkle cream cheese, brown sugar and 1 cup strawberries over one side. Fold omelet in half. Cover and cook for 1-2 minutes or until brown sugar begins to melt. Slide omelet onto a plate; top with remaining strawberries and dust with confectioners' sugar. **Yield:** 2-3 servings.

Blackberry Dumplings

3 pints fresh *or* frozen blackberries
1 cup sugar
3/4 cup water
1 tablespoon butter

Dumplings:
1 cup all-purpose flour

5 teaspoons baking powder
5 teaspoons sugar
1/2 teaspoon salt
1 egg
1/3 cup milk
Cream *or* whipped cream, optional

1. In a large Dutch oven, combine the blackberries, sugar, water and butter; bring to a boil.

2. For dumplings, combine the flour, baking powder, sugar and salt. In a bowl, beat egg and milk; stir in dry ingredients until a soft dough forms. Drop by tablespoonfuls onto boiling berry mixture. Reduce heat; cover and simmer for 15-20 minutes or until a toothpick inserted in the dumplings comes out clean (do not lift the cover while simmering). Serve warm with cream if desired. **Yield:** 8 servings.

I received this recipe from a Native American woman. We've exchanged many tips and recipes over the years, and this dessert has become a favorite.

Maria Stuhlemmer
London, Ontario

Super Strawberry Shortcake

1 quart fresh strawberries, sliced

1 to 2 tablespoons sugar

Shortcake:

1-3/4 cups all-purpose flour

2 tablespoons sugar

1 teaspoon baking powder

1/2 teaspoon baking soda

1/2 teaspoon salt

1/4 cup cold butter

1 egg

3/4 cup sour cream

Topping:

1 cup heavy whipping cream

1 to 2 tablespoons sugar

1 teaspoon vanilla extract

1. In a large bowl, combine the strawberries and sugar; set aside.

2. For shortcake, in another large bowl, combine the flour, sugar, baking powder, baking soda and salt; cut in butter until mixture resembles coarse crumbs. In a small bowl, beat egg; add sour cream. Stir into the crumb mixture just until moistened.

3. Knead dough on a floured surface 25 times or until smooth. Roll out into a 7-1/2-in. circle on a lightly greased baking sheet. Cut a 2-in. hole in center to form a ring. Bake at 425° for 12-14 minutes or until golden brown. Remove to a wire rack to cool completely.

4. For topping, in a small chilled mixing bowl, beat cream until it begins to thicken. Add sugar and vanilla; beat until stiff peaks form.

5. Just before serving, split cake into two horizontally layers. Spoon juice from berries over bottom layer. Spoon half of berries over juice. Spread with half of topping. Cover with top cake layer, then spread with remaining topping and spoon remaining berries over top. Cut into wedges. **Yield:** 8 servings.

Berry Shortcake: Use 1 pint each fresh blueberries and fresh strawberries, sliced for the quart of fresh strawberries.

"Wow!" is what people will say when you set this dessert on the table. It's fun to serve since it's not overly sweet and is bursting with flavor.

Renee Bisch
Wellesley, Ontario

Vanilla Cream Fruit Tart

3/4 cup butter, softened
1/2 cup confectioners' sugar
1-1/2 cups all-purpose flour
1 package (10 to 12 ounces) vanilla *or* white chips, melted and cooled
1/4 cup heavy whipping cream
1 package (8 ounces) cream cheese, softened
1 pint fresh strawberries, sliced
1 cup fresh blueberries
1 cup fresh raspberries
1/2 cup pineapple juice
1/4 cup sugar
1 tablespoon cornstarch
1/2 teaspoon lemon juice

It's well worth the effort to prepare this spectacular tart, which is best made and served the same day. A friend gave me the recipe, and it always receives rave reviews at gatherings.

Susan Terzakis
Andover, Massachusetts

1. In a mixing bowl, cream butter and confectioners' sugar. Beat in flour (mixture will be crumbly). Pat into the bottom of a greased 12-in. pizza pan. Bake at 300° for 25-28 minutes or until lightly browned. Cool.

2. In another mixing bowl, beat melted chips and cream. Add cream cheese; beat until smooth. Spread over crust. Chill for 30 minutes. Arrange berries over filling.

3. In a saucepan, combine pineapple juice, sugar, cornstarch and lemon juice; bring to a boil over medium heat. Boil for 2 minutes or until thickened, stirring constantly. Cool; brush over fruit. Chill 1 hour before serving. Store in refrigerator. **Yield:** 12-16 servings.

Strawberry Shortcut

To quickly cut fresh strawberries into perfectly even slices, use an egg slicer. To mash strawberries, use a pastry blender instead of a fork.

Lemon Whirligigs with Raspberries

2/3 cup sugar
2 tablespoons cornstarch
1/4 teaspoon ground cinnamon
1/8 teaspoon ground nutmeg
1/8 teaspoon salt
1 cup water
3 cups fresh raspberries

Whirligigs:
1 cup all-purpose flour
2 teaspoons baking powder
1/2 teaspoon salt
3 tablespoons shortening
1 egg, lightly beaten
2 tablespoons half-and-half cream
1/4 cup sugar
2 tablespoons butter, melted
1 teaspoon grated lemon peel
Whipping cream and additional raspberries, optional

Golden whirligigs with a tart lemon flavor float on a ruby raspberry sauce in this delectable dessert. I love serving it for guests. My children also like it made with blackberries.

Vicki Ayres
Wappingers Falls, New York

1. In a small saucepan, combine the sugar, cornstarch, cinnamon, nutmeg and salt. Gradually add water; bring to a boil. Reduce heat to medium; cook and stir until sauce thickens, about 5 minutes. Place berries in an ungreased 1-1/2-qt. shallow baking dish; pour hot sauce over top. Bake at 400° for 10 minutes. Remove from the oven; set aside.

2. For whirligigs, combine the dry ingredients in a bowl; cut in shortening until crumbly. Combine egg and cream; stir into dry ingredients to form a stiff dough. Shape into a ball; place on a lightly floured surface. Roll into a 12-in. x 6-in. rectangle. Combine the sugar, butter and peel; spread over dough. Roll up jelly-roll style, starting at a long side. Cut into 10 slices; pat each slice slightly to flatten. Place over hot berry mixture.

3. Bake at 400° for 15 minutes or until whirligigs are golden brown. Garnish with cream and raspberries if desired. **Yield:** 10 servings.

Fresh Raspberry Pie

1/4 cup sugar
1 tablespoon cornstarch
1 cup water
1 package (3 ounces) raspberry gelatin

4 cups fresh raspberries
1 graham cracker crust (9 inches)
Whipped cream, optional

1. In a saucepan, combine sugar and cornstarch. Stir in water until smooth. Bring to a boil; cook and stir for 2 minutes or until thickened. Remove from the heat; stir in gelatin until dissolved. Cool for 15 minutes.

2. Place raspberries in the crust; slowly pour gelatin mixture over berries. Chill until set, about 3 hours. Garnish with whipped cream if desired. **Yield:** 6-8 servings.

Cranberry-Orange Bars

3 cups fresh *or* frozen cranberries
2 large unpeeled oranges, cut into quarters and seeded
2-1/2 cups sugar
3 tablespoons cornstarch
1 teaspoon ground ginger
1/2 cup chopped nuts, optional

Crust:
3-1/4 cups all-purpose flour
3/4 cup sugar
1 tablespoon grated lemon peel
1 cup cold butter
3 egg yolks
3/4 teaspoon vanilla extract
1 to 2 tablespoons water

1. Grind cranberries and oranges (including peel). Set aside. In a saucepan, combine sugar, cornstarch and ginger. Add ground fruit; bring to a boil. Reduce heat; cook and stir for 15 minutes or until thick. Remove from the heat; stir in nuts if desired. Set aside to cool.

2. Meanwhile, for crust, combine flour, sugar and lemon peel in a large bowl. Cut in butter until coarse crumbs form. Add egg yolks, vanilla and just enough water so dough holds its shape. Pat two-thirds of dough into a greased 13-in. x 9-in. x 2-in. baking pan. Cover with cranberry-orange mixture. Crumble remaining dough on top.

3. Bake at 425° for 20-25 minutes or until topping is golden brown. Cool; cut into bars. **Yield:** about 2-1/2 dozen.

Tunnel of Berries Cake

6 eggs, *separated*
3/4 cup water
1/2 cup vegetable oil
1-1/2 teaspoons vanilla extract, *divided*
2-1/4 cups cake flour
2 cups sugar, *divided*
1 tablespoon baking powder
1 teaspoon ground cinnamon
3/4 teaspoon salt
1/4 teaspoon cream of tartar
4 cups fresh whole strawberries, *divided*
2-1/2 cups heavy whipping cream

1. In a small bowl, combine the egg yolks, water, oil and 1 teaspoon vanilla; set aside. In a mixing bowl, combine the flour, 1 cup sugar, baking powder, cinnamon and salt. Gradually add egg yolk mixture, beating just until smooth.

2. In another mixing bowl, beat egg whites until foamy. Add cream of tartar; beat until soft peaks form. Fold into batter. Gently spoon batter into an ungreased 10-in. tube pan. Cut through batter with a knife to remove air pockets.

3. Bake on the lowest rack at 325° for 60-70 minutes or until top springs back when lightly touched and cracks feel dry. Immediately invert cake; cool completely. Run a knife around sides and center tube of pan. Invert cake onto serving plate and remove from pan.

4. Slice off the top 1/2 in. of the cake; set aside. With a knife, cut a tunnel about 1-1/2 in. deep in top of cake, leaving a 3/4-in. shell. Remove cake from tunnel and save for another use. Chop half of the strawberries; set aside.

5. In a mixing bowl, beat whipping cream until soft peaks form. Gradually add the remaining sugar and vanilla, beating until stiff peaks form. Combine 1-1/2 cups cream mixture and chopped berries; fill the tunnel. Replace cake top.

6. Frost cake with the remaining cream mixture. Refrigerate. Just before serving, cut the remaining strawberries in half and use to garnish the cake. **Yield:** 12 servings.

This cake goes a long way. While it's not overly sweet or heavy, its rich taste makes just one piece satisfying. Here's a serving alternative if your family doesn't care for strawberries—peaches are equally delicious.

Shirley Noe
Lebanon Junction, Kentucky

Fresh Strawberry Pie

Bottom Layer:
- 2 cups sliced fresh strawberries
- 1 pastry shell (9 inches), baked and cooled

Middle Layer:
- 2 cups halved fresh strawberries, mashed
- 1 cup sugar
- 3 tablespoons cornstarch

Top Layer:
- 2 cups halved fresh strawberries
- 1 cup heavy whipping cream
- 2 tablespoons sugar
- 1/4 teaspoon almond extract, optional

Each year we wait for "strawberry time" here in the Upper Peninsula of Michigan. We believe our strawberries are the best in the country! After picking them at a nearby farm, I can't wait to get home to make this pie.

Mary Egan
Carney, Michigan

1. For bottom layer, place sliced strawberries in the pie shell.

2. For middle layer, combine mashed strawberries, sugar and cornstarch in a saucepan. Bring to a boil; cook and stir for 2 minutes or until thickened. Cool for 15 minutes; pour over bottom layer.

3. For top layer, arrange strawberry halves on top of pie. Refrigerate for 2-3 hours. Just before serving, whip cream with sugar and almond extract if desired until stiff peaks form. Spread over pie or dollop on individual servings. **Yield:** 6-8 servings.

Raspberry Ribbon Cheesecake

2 cups chocolate wafer crumbs (about 32 wafers)
1/3 cup butter, melted
3 tablespoons sugar

Raspberry Sauce:
2-1/2 cups fresh *or* frozen raspberries, thawed
2/3 cup sugar
2 tablespoons cornstarch
2 teaspoons lemon juice

Filling/Topping:
3 packages (8 ounces *each*) cream cheese, softened

1/2 cup sugar
2 tablespoons all-purpose flour
1 teaspoon vanilla extract
2 egg whites
1 cup heavy whipping cream
2 to 3 tablespoons orange juice
1-1/2 cups fresh *or* frozen raspberries, thawed

Here's a mouth-watering dessert that tastes wonderful with its chocolate cookie crust, rich creamy cheesecake and tangy raspberry center and topping...it also looks lovely!

Peggy Frazier
Indianapolis, Indiana

1. Combine the first three ingredients; press into bottom and 1-1/2 in. up sides of a greased 9 in. springform pan. Refrigerate for 1 hour or until firm.

2. Puree raspberries in a blender or food processor. Press through a sieve; discard seeds. Add enough water if necessary to measure 1 cup. In a saucepan, combine sugar and cornstarch. Stir in raspberry juice until smooth. Bring to a boil; cook and stir for 2 minutes or until thickened. Remove from the heat; stir in lemon juice and set aside.

3. In a mixing bowl, beat the cream cheese, sugar, flour and vanilla until fluffy. Add egg whites; beat on low just until blended. Stir in cream. Pour half into crust. Top with 3/4 cup raspberry sauce (cover and refrigerate remaining sauce). Carefully spoon remaining filling over sauce. Place pan on a baking sheet. Bake at 375° for 35-40 minutes or until center is nearly set. Remove from the oven; immediately run a knife around pan to loosen crust. Cool on wire rack 1 hour.

4. Refrigerate overnight. Remove sides of pan. Add orange juice to chilled raspberry sauce; gently fold in raspberries. Spoon over cheesecake. Refrigerate leftovers. **Yield:** 12-16 servings.

Oat-Fashioned Strawberry Dessert

Thanks to this dessert, our house is a popular place in summertime. I make it for family get-togethers, picnics and potlucks, too. It's a treat on a breakfast or brunch buffet also. We like it best with whipped cream or a scoop of vanilla ice cream on top.

Linda Forrest
Belleville, Ontario

4 cups sliced fresh
  strawberries
1-1/4 cups whole wheat flour
1-1/4 cups quick-cooking oats
2/3 cup packed brown sugar
1/4 teaspoon baking soda
1/8 teaspoon salt
2/3 cup cold butter
2 tablespoons sugar
1/4 to 1/2 teaspoon ground
  cinnamon

1. Drain strawberries on paper towels; set aside. In a large bowl, combine the flour, oats, brown sugar, baking soda and salt. Cut in butter until mixture resembles coarse crumbs. Reserve 1-1/2 cups for topping. Pat remaining crumb mixture into a greased 9-in. square baking pan.

2. In a bowl, combine sugar and cinnamon; stir in strawberries. Spoon over the prepared crust. Sprinkle with the reserved crumb mixture. Bake at 350° for 35-40 minutes or until golden brown. Serve warm. **Yield:** 9 servings.

Blueberry Sour Cream Pound Cake

I used to sell several lines of kitchenware through home parties. This recipe came from the hostess at one of those parties. It's been a favorite ever since!

Juanita Miller
Arnett, Oklahoma

1 cup butter, softened
3 cups sugar
6 eggs, *separated*
1 teaspoon vanilla extract
1 teaspoon almond extract
1 teaspoon butter flavoring
3 cups all-purpose flour
1/4 teaspoon baking soda
1 cup (8 ounces) sour
  cream
1-1/2 cups fresh *or* frozen
  blueberries

1. In a mixing bowl, cream butter and sugar. Add egg yolks, one at a time, beating well after each addition. Beat in extracts and butter flavoring. Combine flour and baking soda; add to creamed mixture alternately with the sour cream. In a large mixing bowl, beat egg whites until stiff peaks form. Fold egg whites into batter, then fold in berries.

2. Spoon into a greased 10-in. tube pan. Bake at 350° for 60-70 minutes or until a toothpick inserted near the center comes out clean. Cool for 10 minutes before removing from pan to a wire rack to cool completely. **Yield:** 16-20 servings.

Blueberry Cream Pie

1-1/3 cups crushed vanilla
    wafers (about 20 wafers)
2 tablespoons sugar
5 tablespoons butter,
    melted
1/2 teaspoon vanilla extract

Filling:
  1/4 cup sugar
  3 tablespoons all-purpose
    flour
Dash salt

1 cup half-and-half cream
3 egg yolks, beaten
3 tablespoons butter
1 teaspoon vanilla extract
1 tablespoon confectioners'
    sugar

Topping:
  5 cups fresh blueberries,
    divided
2/3 cup sugar
1 tablespoon cornstarch

1. Combine the first four ingredients; press into the bottom and sides of an ungreased 9-in. pie pan. Bake at 350° for 8-10 minutes or until crust just begins to brown. Cool.

2. In a saucepan, combine the sugar, flour and salt. Gradually whisk in cream until smooth; cook and stir over medium-high heat until thickened and bubbly. Reduce heat; cook and stir 2 minutes longer. Remove from the heat. Stir a small amount of hot filling into egg yolks; return all to pan, stirring constantly. Bring to a gentle boil; cook and stir 2 minutes longer. Remove from the heat. Gently stir in butter and vanilla. Cool for 5 minutes, stirring occasionally. Pour into crust; sprinkle with confectioners' sugar. Refrigerate for 30 minutes or until set.

3. Meanwhile, crush 2 cups of blueberries in a medium saucepan; bring to a boil. Boil and stir for 2 minutes. Press berries through sieve. Reserve 1 cup juice, adding water if necessary to measure 1 cup. Discard pulp.

4. In a saucepan, combine sugar and cornstarch. Gradually stir in blueberry juice until smooth. Bring to a boil; cook and stir for 2 minutes or until thickened. Remove from the heat; cool 15 minutes. Gently stir in remaining berries; carefully spoon over filling. Chill for 3 hours or until set. Store in the refrigerator. **Yield:** 6-8 servings.

Whenever I ask my family which pie they'd like me to make, everyone requests this refreshing dessert.

Kim Erickson
Sturgis, Michigan

Broccoli & Cauliflower

Savory Cauliflower Pie, p. 91

Bacon-Broccoli Cheese Ball

Needing a quick appetizer one night when dinner was running late, I combined a few leftovers into this easy cheese ball. For variety, you can shape it into a log, or substitute your favorite herbs for the pepper.

Tamara Rickard
Bartlett, Tennessee

1 package (8 ounces)
  cream cheese, softened
1 cup (4 ounces) finely
  shredded cheddar cheese
1/2 teaspoon pepper

1 cup finely chopped
  broccoli florets
6 bacon strips, cooked and
  crumbled
Assorted crackers

1. In a mixing bowl, beat the cream cheese, cheddar cheese and pepper until blended. Stir in broccoli. Shape into a ball and roll in bacon. Cover and refrigerate.

2. Remove from the refrigerator 15 minutes before serving. Serve with crackers. **Yield:** 2-1/2 cups.

Basil Broccoli & Tomato Platter

5 fresh tomatoes, peeled
  and sliced
1 red onion, thinly sliced
  and separated into rings
2 pounds fresh broccoli,
  cut into florets, cooked

Dressing:
1/2 cup vegetable oil

1/2 cup red wine vinegar
3 tablespoons fresh minced
  basil *or* 1 tablespoon
  dried basil
1 tablespoon fresh minced
  parsley *or* 1 teaspoon
  dried parsley flakes
1-1/2 teaspoons salt
Pepper to taste

1. In a large shallow dish or 13-in. x 9-in. x 2-in. pan, layer tomatoes and onion along one side; place broccoli on the other side.

2. In a small bowl, combine dressing ingredients; pour over vegetables. Cover and chill for several hours, occasionally spooning dressing over vegetables. Serve vegetables on lettuce-lined platter if desired. **Yield:** 6-8 servings.

My family especially loves this at the end of summer, during the peak of fresh tomato season.

Pauline Barker
Springfield, Missouri

Broccoli Cheese Soup

2 cups sliced fresh carrots
1 cup sliced celery
2 cups broccoli florets
1-1/2 cups chopped onions
1/2 cup butter
3/4 cup all-purpose flour
1 can (10-1/2 ounces) condensed chicken broth, undiluted
1 quart milk
1/2 pound process American cheese, cut into cubes

1. In a large saucepan, bring 2 quarts water to a boil. Add the carrots, celery and broccoli; cover and boil for 5 minutes. Drain and set aside.

2. In the same saucepan, saute onions in butter. Stir in flour until smooth. Gradually add chicken broth and milk. Bring to a boil over medium heat; cook and stir for 2 minutes or until thickened. Add vegetables; heat until tender. Add cheese; heat until cheese is melted. **Yield:** 6-8 servings (2 quarts).

This simple soup has basic ingredients, but it tastes so good. The green broccoli florets and the brilliant orange carrots make this creamy soup a colorful addition to any table.

Evelyn Massner
Oakville, Iowa

Marinated Vegetable Salad

2 cups sugar
1 cup cider vinegar
1 tablespoon salt
1 tablespoon ground
   mustard
1 cup vegetable oil
1 teaspoon celery seed
1/2 teaspoon Italian
   seasoning

Vegetables:
1 large head cauliflower,
   cut into florets
1 large bunch broccoli, cut
   into florets
4 carrots, thinly sliced
2 cups sliced celery
1 pint cherry tomatoes,
   halved
1/2 cup sliced radishes
1/2 medium green pepper,
   sliced
2 green onions, thinly sliced
1 can (6 ounces) pitted
   ripe olives, drained and
   sliced

*The combination of
ingredients in this salad gives
it a unique tangy flavor.
Perhaps that's why I get
requests for the recipe
whenever I serve this dish to
company or bring it to a
potluck dinner.*

Betty Olason
Hensel, North Dakota

1. In a saucepan, bring the sugar, vinegar, salt and mustard to a boil. Cook and stir for 1 minute. Let stand until cooled. Add oil, celery seed and Italian seasoning; mix well. Cover and refrigerate.

2. Combine all vegetables in a large bowl; add dressing and toss. Cover and refrigerate several hours, stirring occasionally. **Yield:** 16-20 servings.

Hot Broccoli Dip

1/2 cup finely chopped onion
1/2 cup finely chopped celery
2 tablespoons butter
1 package (16 ounces) process American cheese, cut into cubes

2 cups chopped fresh broccoli, blanched
1/2 teaspoon dried rosemary, crushed
1 loaf (1 pound) round bread
Raw vegetables, optional

So many friends ask about the special flavor of this dip. The mystery is rosemary! I especially like to serve this hot dip during the holidays, but my family loves it year-round.

Betty Reinholt
Culver, Indiana

1. In a small saucepan, saute onion and celery in butter until tender. Add cheese and cook over low heat until melted. Stir in broccoli and rosemary.

2. Cut top off bread; scoop out center. Cut center piece into cubes. Pour dip into center of bread. Serve with bread cubes and/or raw vegetables if desired. **Yield:** 3 cups.

Cream of Cauliflower Soup

2 medium onions, chopped
2 medium carrots, grated
2 celery ribs, sliced
2 garlic cloves, minced
1/4 cup plus 6 tablespoons butter, *divided*
1 medium head cauliflower, chopped
5 cups chicken broth
1/4 cup minced fresh parsley
1 teaspoon salt

1 teaspoon coarsely ground pepper
1/2 teaspoon dried basil
1/2 teaspoon dried tarragon
6 tablespoons all-purpose flour
1 cup milk
1/2 cup heavy whipping cream
1/4 cup sour cream
Fresh tarragon, optional

Generally, my husband isn't a soup fan—but his spoon's poised and ready for this version. I adapted the rich and creamy concoction from a recipe I tasted at a local restaurant...and it's since become a popular item on my "menu."

Carol Reaves
San Antonio, Texas

1. In a soup kettle or Dutch oven, saute the onions, carrots, celery and garlic in 1/4 cup butter until tender. Add the cauliflower, broth, parsley, salt, pepper, basil and tarragon. Bring to a boil. Reduce heat; cover and simmer for 30 minutes or until the vegetables are tender.

2. Meanwhile, in a saucepan, melt the remaining butter. Stir in flour until smooth. Gradually stir in the milk and whipping cream. Bring to a boil; cook and stir for 2 minutes or until thickened. Add to cauliflower mixture. Cook for 10 minutes or until thickened, stirring frequently. Remove from the heat; stir in sour cream. Garnish with tarragon if desired. **Yield:** 8 servings.

My mother gets the credit for this delicious dish, which is a mainstay at our house. It can be an appetizer or side dish... and is wonderful served with turkey, roast beef and ham.

Sandra Furman-Krajewski
Amsterdam, New York

Breaded Cauliflower

1 small head cauliflower, broken into florets (about 5 cups)
4 egg yolks
1 teaspoon garlic powder
1 teaspoon onion powder
1 teaspoon minced fresh parsley
1/2 teaspoon sugar

1/2 teaspoon salt
1/4 teaspoon pepper
1 cup seasoned bread crumbs
3 tablespoons grated Parmesan cheese
3/4 cup butter
Minced fresh parsley, optional

1. Place cauliflower and a small amount of water in a skillet. Bring to a boil. Reduce heat; cover and simmer for 8 minutes or until crisp-tender. Drain and set aside.

2. In a bowl, whisk egg yolks and seasonings. Place bread crumbs and Parmesan cheese in a large resealable plastic bag. Add a few florets at a time to the egg mixture; toss to coat. Using a slotted spoon, transfer cauliflower to crumb mixture; toss to coat.

3. In a skillet, melt the butter over medium-high heat. Cook cauliflower in batches until golden brown, about 4 minutes. Sprinkle with parsley if desired. **Yield:** 4-6 servings.

Sesame Broccoli

1 cup water
1 pound fresh broccoli, cut into spears
1 tablespoon sesame seeds
4 teaspoons olive oil, divided

1 tablespoon sugar
1 tablespoon lemon juice
1 tablespoon soy sauce

1. In a large saucepan, bring water to a boil. Add broccoli. Reduce heat; cover and simmer for 5-7 minutes or until crisp-tender.

2. Meanwhile, in a small skillet, saute sesame seeds in 1 teaspoon oil until lightly browned. Remove from the heat. Stir in the sugar, lemon juice, soy sauce and remaining oil. Drain broccoli; toss with sesame seed mixture. **Yield:** 8 servings.

For a time-saving addition to supper, I season broccoli spears with lemon, soy sauce and sesame seeds. It's a nice change from plain broccoli.

Myra Innes
Auburn, Kansas

Cauliflower Spinach Salad

- 2 cups cauliflowerets
- 1 can (11 ounces) mandarin oranges, well drained
- 1/4 cup chopped green pepper
- 2 large radishes, sliced
- 4 cups torn fresh spinach
- 1 can (5 ounces) evaporated milk
- 1/3 cup orange juice concentrate

In a large bowl, combine first five ingredients. Pour milk in a small bowl; gradually whisk in orange juice concentrate. Drizzle over salad and toss to coat. Refrigerate leftovers. **Yield:** 8-10 servings.

This delightful and different spinach salad has an orange-flavored dressing and a nice crunch from the cauliflower and radishes.

Marjorie Carey
Freeport, Florida

Picante Broccoli Chicken Salad

- 1/2 cup mayonnaise
- 1/4 cup picante sauce
- 1 garlic clove, minced
- 1/2 to 1 teaspoon chili powder
- 2 cups cubed cooked chicken
- 2 cups broccoli florets
- 1 cup diced fresh tomato
- 1/2 cup shredded cheddar cheese
- 1/2 cup chopped onion
- 1/4 cup julienned green pepper
- 1/4 cup julienned sweet red pepper
- Flour tortillas, warmed

In a large bowl, combine the first four ingredients. Add the chicken, broccoli, tomato, cheese, onion and peppers; toss to coat. Refrigerate for at least 30 minutes before serving. Serve with tortillas. **Yield:** 6-8 servings.

Since our family likes things spicy, I often add a fresh jalapeno pepper to this salad. It's a simple, savory way to use up leftover chicken. Plus, it's so eye-catching, it could double as the main dish!

Krista Shumway
Billings, Montana

End of Summer Vegetable Bake

1 small head cauliflower, broken into small florets (about 5 cups)

1 medium bunch broccoli, cut into small florets (about 4 cups)

1 medium onion, chopped

2 garlic cloves, minced

1 tablespoon butter

2 medium tomatoes, chopped

3/4 teaspoon dried basil

3/4 teaspoon dried oregano

3/4 teaspoon salt

1/4 teaspoon pepper

1/4 teaspoon hot pepper sauce

4 eggs

1/3 cup half-and-half cream

1-1/2 cups (6 ounces) shredded Swiss cheese, *divided*

1/4 cup shredded Parmesan cheese

When my husband worked as a deputy agricultural commissioner, he'd bring me bushels of vegetables from area farms. This pretty side dish is the result—it's easy to fix but impressive enough for company.

Judy Williams
Hayden, Idaho

1. Place the cauliflower and broccoli in a saucepan with a small amount of water. Bring to a boil. Reduce heat; cover and simmer for 5-10 minutes or until crisp-tender. Drain and set aside.

2. In a large skillet, saute onion and garlic in butter until tender. Stir in the tomatoes, seasonings, cauliflower and broccoli. Cook, uncovered, until heated through, about 4 minutes, stirring occasionally. Remove from the heat and set aside.

3. In a large bowl, beat eggs and cream; stir in 1 cup Swiss cheese, Parmesan cheese and the vegetable mixture. Transfer to a greased shallow 2-qt. baking dish. Sprinkle with remaining Swiss cheese.

4. Bake, uncovered, at 375° for 25-30 minutes or until a knife inserted near the center comes out clean. Let stand for 10 minutes before serving. **Yield:** 12 servings.

Freezing Broccoli

When buying a large amount of fresh broccoli, wash it, blanch it in boiling water for a couple minutes and freeze in freezer bags. It always tastes garden-fresh.

Cauliflower Ham Chowder

2 cups cubed peeled
  potatoes
2 cups cauliflowerets
1 small onion, finely diced
1 cup chicken broth
3 cups milk
2-1/2 cups cubed fully cooked
  ham

1 teaspoon salt
1/2 teaspoon pepper
Dash ground nutmeg
1/2 to 1 cup instant potato
  flakes
Minced fresh parsley

1. In a saucepan, bring the potatoes, cauliflower, onion and chicken broth to a boil. Reduce heat; cover and cook until tender. Stir in the milk, ham, salt, pepper and nutmeg; heat through.

2. Stir in potato flakes; simmer for 5-10 minutes or until soup is as thick as desired. Sprinkle with parsley. **Yield:** 6-8 servings (2 quarts).

Soup is always good for warming the tummy and the heart, and this is one of our family's favorites. With a busy household, it's a simple but nutritious meal to have on hand!

Lois Buch
Clarinda, Iowa

Broccoli Cauliflower Salad

1 medium head cauliflower,
  broken into florets
  (about 7-1/2 cups)
1 medium bunch broccoli,
  cut into florets (about 4
  cups)
2 cups seedless red grapes
6 green onions with tops,
  sliced
2 cups (8 ounces) shredded
  part-skim mozzarella
  cheese

2 cups mayonnaise
1/4 cup grated Parmesan
  cheese
2 tablespoons sugar
2 tablespoons cider vinegar
1/2 to 1 pound sliced bacon,
  cooked and crumbled
Leaf lettuce
Additional red grapes, optional

1. In a large bowl, combine the cauliflower, broccoli, grapes, onions and mozzarella cheese. Combine the mayonnaise, Parmesan cheese, sugar and vinegar; pour over vegetable mixture and toss to coat.

2. Cover and refrigerate for at least 2 hours. Just before serving, stir in bacon. Transfer to a lettuce-lined bowl. Garnish with grapes if desired. **Yield:** 15-20 servings.

This salad has been to as many family gatherings as I have! It holds well...and leftovers are still tasty a day later.

Linda Kangas
Outlook, Saskatchewan

Since our son is a broccoli grower, our friends keep supplying us with recipes using broccoli. To this family favorite, add a tossed salad, rolls, fruit and cookies, and you have an easy but delicious supper full of nutrition.

Dorothy Child
Malone, New York

Broccoli and Crab Bisque

1 cup sliced leeks (white part only)
1 cup sliced fresh mushrooms
1 cup fresh broccoli florets
1 garlic clove, minced
1/4 cup butter
1/4 cup all-purpose flour
1/4 teaspoon dried thyme, crushed
1/8 teaspoon pepper

1 bay leaf
2 cans (10-1/2 ounces *each*) condensed chicken broth, undiluted
1 cup half-and-half cream
3/4 cup shredded Swiss cheese
1 package (6 ounces) frozen crabmeat, thawed, drained and flaked

1. In a saucepan, cook the leeks, mushrooms, broccoli and garlic in butter until broccoli is crisp-tender. Remove from the heat; stir in flour and seasonings until blended. Stir in broth and cream.

2. Bring to a boil; cook and stir for 2 minutes or until thickened. Add cheese; stir until melted. Add crabmeat and heat through (do not boil). Remove bay leaf before serving.
Yield: 4-5 servings (5 cups).

Creamy Cauliflower Salad

6 to 7 cups cauliflowerets
1 celery rib, thinly sliced
1/3 cup chopped green pepper
1/3 cup chopped sweet red pepper
1 cup (8 ounces) sour cream

1/2 cup ranch salad dressing
2 teaspoons Dijon mustard
1/2 teaspoon salt
1/8 teaspoon pepper
2 bacon strips, cooked and crumbled

Paprika

In a bowl, combine the cauliflower, celery and peppers. In a small bowl, combine the sour cream, salad dressing, mustard, salt and pepper; stir into vegetable mixture. Add bacon. Cover and refrigerate for at least 2 hours. Sprinkle with paprika.
Yield: 10-12 servings.

My family really enjoys this salad. It has a very tasty dressing, and it's different from the usual picnic fare.

Emma Magielda
Amsterdam, New York

Wild Rice Floret Bake

1 medium onion, chopped
3 tablespoons butter
2 tablespoons all-purpose flour
1/2 teaspoon salt
Dash pepper
2 cups milk
1 cup (8 ounces) sour cream
1 cup (4 ounces) shredded cheddar cheese, *divided*
4 cups cooked wild rice, *divided*
6 cups chopped cooked broccoli (about 1 large bunch)
5 cups chopped cooked cauliflower (about 1 small head)
6 bacon strips, cooked and crumbled

1. In a saucepan, saute the onion in butter until tender. Stir in the flour, salt and pepper until blended. Gradually add milk. Bring to a boil; cook and stir for 2 minutes or until thickened and bubbly. Remove from the heat; stir in sour cream and 1/2 cup cheese until smooth.

2. Place 2 cups wild rice in a greased 13-in. x 9-in. x 2-in. baking dish. Top with broccoli and cauliflower. Place remaining wild rice lengthwise down the center of dish. Pour the sauce over all. Sprinkle with remaining cheese.

3. Cover and bake at 350° for 20 minutes. Uncover; sprinkle with bacon. Bake 10-15 minutes longer or until bubbly. **Yield:** 8-10 servings.

My mom used to make this hearty dish for family get-togethers. Now I do the same when our five grown children come to visit.

Donna Torgerson
Park Rapids, Minnesota

Color-Flower

To help cauliflower retain its color while cooking, add a small amount of nonfat dry milk powder to the cooking water.

Broccoli Orange Salad

1 egg
1/4 cup sugar
1-1/2 teaspoons honey
1 teaspoon ground mustard
1/2 teaspoon cornstarch
2 tablespoons water
2 tablespoons cider vinegar
2 tablespoons mayonnaise
2 tablespoons sour cream
4-1/2 teaspoons butter
4 cups broccoli florets
  (about 1 medium bunch)
1 cup salted cashews
1 cup cubed Swiss cheese
1 can (11 ounces)
  mandarin oranges, well
  drained
1/2 cup raisins
6 bacon strips, cooked and
  crumbled
1/2 cup chopped red onion,
  optional

Every time I take this sweet, orangy salad to a potluck, I pass around the recipe, too.

Cathy Lavers
Scotsburn, Nova Scotia

1. In a heavy saucepan, combine the egg, sugar, honey, mustard and cornstarch with a whisk until smooth. Gradually whisk in water and vinegar. Cook and stir over medium heat until mixture is thickened and a thermometer reads 160°. Remove from the heat; stir in the mayonnaise, sour cream and butter until blended. Cool.

2. Meanwhile, in a large bowl, combine the broccoli, cashews, cheese, oranges, raisins, bacon and onion if desired. Just before serving, add dressing and toss to coat. **Yield:** 8-10 servings.

Broccoli-Stuffed Potatoes

2 tablespoons butter
2 tablespoons all-purpose
  flour
1 cup milk
1/4 teaspoon ground mustard
1/4 teaspoon salt
1/4 teaspoon pepper

1/2 cup shredded cheddar
  cheese
3 cups chopped fresh
  broccoli, cooked
1 cup chopped fully cooked
  ham
4 to 6 baking potatoes,
  baked

This is one of my favorite light suppers...an easy spur-of-the-moment meal that satisfies even the heartiest appetites.

Dia Steele
Comanche, Texas

In a small saucepan, melt butter. Stir in flour until smooth. Gradually add milk, mustard, salt and pepper. Bring to a boil over medium heat; cook and stir for 2 minutes or until thickened. Reduce heat; add cheese, stirring until melted. Fold in broccoli and ham. Serve over hot baked potatoes. **Yield:** 4-6 servings.

Creamy Floret Bake

1 large head cauliflower,
  broken into florets
  (4 cups)
1 medium bunch broccoli,
  cut into florets (4 cups)
1/4 cup butter
1/4 cup all-purpose flour
2 cups half-and-half cream

2 tablespoons grated
  orange peel
1/2 teaspoon salt
1/4 teaspoon ground nutmeg
1/4 teaspoon white pepper
1/4 cup shredded cheddar
  cheese

1. In a saucepan, bring 1 in. of water to a boil; add cauliflower. Reduce heat; cover and simmer for 10-12 minutes or until crisp-tender.

2. In another saucepan, bring 1 in. of water to a boil; add broccoli. Reduce heat; cover and simmer for 8-10 minutes or until crisp-tender. Drain vegetables and rinse with cold water.

3. Melt butter in a saucepan. Stir in flour until smooth. Gradually add cream. Bring to a boil; cook and stir for 2 minutes or until thickened. Stir in the orange peel, salt, nutmeg and pepper.

4. Arrange cauliflower and broccoli in alternate rows in a 3-qt. or 13-in. x 9-in. x 2-in. baking dish. Top with cream sauce and cheese. Bake, uncovered, at 325° for 20-25 minutes or until heated through. **Yield:** 12 servings.

My family loves to come over for special dinners because of the tasty side dishes I prepare. This one is always a winner! The creamy orange sauce complements the tender broccoli and cauliflower beautifully.

Patricia Potter
Manassas, Virginia

Lamb Broccoli Strudel

1 pound ground lamb *or* pork
1 medium onion, chopped
2 cups chopped fresh broccoli, blanched
1 cup (4 ounces) shredded part-skim mozzarella cheese
1/2 cup sour cream
1/4 cup dry bread crumbs
1 garlic clove, minced
1 teaspoon seasoned salt
1/2 teaspoon pepper
20 sheets phyllo dough (14 inches x 9 inches)
1/2 cup butter, melted

1. In a skillet, cook lamb and onion over medium heat until meat is no longer pink; drain and cool. In a large bowl, combine the broccoli, cheese, sour cream, bread crumbs, garlic, seasoned salt and pepper. Mix in meat and onion.

2. Place 1 sheet of phyllo dough on a piece of waxed paper. Brush with butter; continue layering with 9 more sheets of dough, brushing each with butter. Keep remaining phyllo dough covered with plastic wrap and a damp towel to prevent it from drying out. Spoon half of the meat mixture on dough. Roll up jelly-roll style, starting with the short end.

3. Place roll seam side down on a greased baking sheet. Repeat with remaining dough and filling. Brush tops of rolls with remaining butter. Bake at 350° for 45-50 minutes or until golden brown. Cool for 10 minutes before slicing. **Yield:** 6 servings.

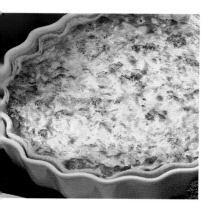

Broccoli Pie

1 large onion, chopped
3 tablespoons vegetable oil
4 eggs, lightly beaten
4 cups chopped fresh broccoli, cooked
2 cups (8 ounces) shredded part-skim mozzarella cheese
1 carton (15 ounces) ricotta cheese
1/3 cup grated Parmesan cheese
1/4 teaspoon salt
Dash ground nutmeg
1 unbaked pie pastry (9 inches)

1. In a skillet, saute onion in oil until tender, about 5 minutes. Transfer to a bowl; add eggs, broccoli, cheeses, salt and nutmeg.

2. Pour into pie shell. Bake at 350° for 50-55 minutes or until a knife inserted near the center comes out clean. Let stand for 5 minutes before serving. **Yield:** 6-8 servings.

Savory Cauliflower Pie

- 3 cups seasoned croutons, crushed
- 1/2 cup butter, melted, *divided*
- 1 small head cauliflower, cut into small florets (about 5 cups)
- 1 cup chopped onion
- 1/2 cup thinly sliced carrots
- 1 garlic clove, minced
- 1/2 teaspoon salt
- 1/4 to 1/2 teaspoon dried oregano
- 1 cup (4 ounces) shredded cheddar cheese, *divided*
- 2 eggs
- 1/4 cup milk

1. In a bowl, combine croutons and 1/4 cup butter. Press onto the bottom and up the sides of an ungreased 9-in. pie plate. Bake at 375° for 8 minutes or until lightly browned; set aside.

2. In a large skillet, saute the cauliflower, onion, carrots, garlic, salt and oregano in remaining butter over medium heat for 10 minutes, stirring frequently. Sprinkle 1/2 cup cheese into prepared crust. Top with cauliflower mixture and remaining cheese.

3. In a bowl, beat the eggs and milk. Pour over pie. Bake, uncovered, at 375° for 30 minutes or until a knife inserted near the center comes out clean and the cauliflower is tender. **Yield:** 6-8 servings.

If you're looking for a meatless main dish or a hearty side to take to a church potluck or family gathering, this pie is the perfect choice.

Debbie Hart
Ft. Wayne, Indiana

Cauliflower And Ham Casserole

1 tablespoons chopped onion

3 tablespoons butter, *divided*

2 tablespoons all-purpose flour

1/2 teaspoon salt, optional

Pepper to taste

1 cup milk

1/2 cup shredded cheddar cheese

1 medium head cauliflower, cut into florets, cooked and drained

2 cups cubed fully cooked ham

1 jar (4-1/2 ounces) sliced mushrooms, drained

1 jar (2 ounces) diced pimientos, drained

6 saltines, crumbled

My mother made this recipe many times while I was growing up. I remember leaning on the table to watch her.

Rosemary Flexman
Waukesha, Wisconsin

1. In a saucepan, saute onion in 2 tablespoons butter until tender. Stir in the flour, salt if desired and pepper until smooth. Gradually add milk. Bring to a boil over medium heat; cook and stir for 2 minutes or until thickened. Remove from the heat; add cheese, stirring until melted. Fold in the cauliflower, ham, mushrooms and pimientos. Pour into a greased 2-qt. baking dish.

2. In a small saucepan, brown cracker crumbs in remaining butter; sprinkle over top. Cover and bake at 350° for 20 minutes. Uncover and bake 5-10 minutes longer or until heated through. **Yield:** 6 servings.

Turkey Broccoli Hollandaise

1 cup fresh broccoli florets
1 package (6 ounces)
  stuffing mix
1 envelope Hollandaise
  sauce mix

2 cups cubed cooked turkey
  or chicken
1 can (2.8 ounces)
  french-fried onions

This delectable dish is a great way to use extra turkey. The original recipe called for Thanksgiving leftovers, but my family loves it so much that I prepare this version all year long.

Pamela Yoder
Elkhart, Indiana

1. In a saucepan, bring broccoli and 1 in. of water to a boil. Reduce heat; cover and simmer for 5-8 minutes or until crisp-tender. Meanwhile, prepare stuffing and sauce mixes according to package directions.

2. Spoon stuffing into a greased 11-in. x 7-in. x 2-in. baking dish. Top with turkey. Drain broccoli; arrange over turkey. Spoon sauce over the top; sprinkle with onions. Bake, uncovered, at 325° for 25-30 minutes or until heated through. **Yield:** 6 servings.

Broccoli Fish Bundles

18 fresh broccoli spears
  (about 1-1/2 pounds)
6 cubes Monterey Jack
  cheese (1-1/2 inches)
6 sole *or* flounder fillets
  (about 2 pounds)
1/8 teaspoon lemon-pepper
  seasoning, optional

1/3 cup butter, melted
2 teaspoons lemon juice
1 garlic clove, minced
1/4 teaspoon salt
1/8 teaspoon pepper

1. In a saucepan, place broccoli in a small amount of water. Bring to a boil. Reduce heat; cover and simmer for 2-3 minutes or until crisp-tender. Rinse in cold water; drain.

2. For each bundle, place a cheese cube on three spears. Wrap with a fish fillet and fasten with a toothpick if necessary. Place on a greased foil-lined baking sheet. Sprinkle with lemon-pepper if desired. Bake at 350° for 15-25 minutes or until fish flakes easily with a fork.

3. Meanwhile, combine the butter, lemon juice, garlic, salt and pepper. Transfer fish bundles to a serving platter; remove toothpicks. Drizzle with butter mixture. **Yield:** 6 servings.

These bundles take a little time to assemble, but they're worth it! They're always popular at a shower or buffet...and they're great for an everyday dinner, too. This flavorful dish goes nicely with rice or a saucy pasta.

Frances Quinn
Farmingdale, New York

Chicken and Broccoli Roll-Ups

6 boneless skinless chicken breast halves, pounded thin
2 tablespoons vegetable oil
6 slices Swiss cheese
6 to 12 spears fresh broccoli, blanched

Sauce:
1 cup chopped onion
2 tablespoons butter

2 tablespoons all-purpose flour
1/2 cup chicken broth
1/2 cup milk
1/4 to 1/2 teaspoon dried basil
1/4 teaspoon celery salt
1/4 teaspoon white pepper

1. In a skillet, brown chicken breasts in oil on one side. On each unbrowned side, place 1 piece of Swiss cheese and 1 to 2 spears of broccoli. Roll up (secure with a toothpick if desired); set aside.

2. In a saucepan, saute onion in butter until tender. Stir in flour until blended. Gradually add broth and milk; add the basil, celery salt and pepper. Bring to a boil over medium heat; cook and stir for 2 minutes or until thickened.

3. Place half of sauce in the bottom of greased 11-in. x 7-in. x 2-in. baking dish. Place chicken rolls over sauce. Cover with remaining sauce. Cover and bake at 350° for 20 minutes. Uncover and bake 10 minutes longer or until chicken is no longer pink. **Yield:** 6 servings.

Broccoli Muffins

1-3/4 cups all-purpose flour
1 cup quick-cooking oats
1/4 cup sugar
2 teaspoons baking powder
1/4 teaspoon salt
1 cup milk

1/3 cup vegetable oil
1 egg, lightly beaten
1 cup chopped fresh broccoli, blanched
1/2 cup shredded cheddar cheese

1. In a large bowl, combine the flour, oats, sugar, baking powder and salt. In a small bowl, whisk together the milk, oil and egg; stir into dry ingredients just until moistened. Fold in broccoli and cheese.

2. Spoon into greased or paper-lined muffin cups. Bake at 400° for 18-20 minutes or until top springs back when lightly touched. Cool for 5 minutes before removing from pan to a wire rack. **Yield:** 1 dozen.

Vegetable Stew

1-1/2 pounds lean boneless
    lamb *or* pork, cut into
    1-inch cubes
  2 tablespoons vegetable oil
  1 medium onion, chopped
  2 medium potatoes, peeled
    and cubed
  1 medium leek, sliced
  6 cups beef broth
  2 tablespoons tomato paste
  1 teaspoon salt
1/2 teaspoon dried thyme
1/4 teaspoon pepper
  4 cups chopped cabbage
  2 to 3 cups cauliflowerets
  3 carrots, sliced
  1 celery rib, sliced
1-1/2 cups fresh green beans
Chopped fresh parsley
Cornstarch and water, optional

1. In a Dutch oven, brown meat in oil over medium high. Add onion and cook until tender; drain. Add the next seven ingredients. Cover and simmer until the meat is tender, about 1 hour.

2. Add the cabbage, cauliflower, carrots, celery, beans and parsley; cover and simmer until the vegetables are tender, about 30 minutes. If desired, thicken with cornstarch dissolved in water. **Yield:** about 8-10 servings (3-1/2 quarts).

Everyone in my family welcomes a dinner that centers around stew. This particular stew is so colorful, you can bring the pot right to the table and serve it from there!

Kenneth Wrigley
Langley, British Columbia

Cabbage

Cabbage Fruit Salad, p. 100

Scalloped Cabbage

5 to 6 cups shredded cabbage

2 medium onions, finely chopped

1 medium green pepper, finely chopped

1/4 cup butter

2 cups (8 ounces) shredded sharp cheddar cheese

2 cups coarsely crushed sour cream and chive croutons, *divided*

1 cup milk *or* half-and-half cream

1. In a large saucepan, cook cabbage in boiling salted water for 4-5 minutes or until almost tender; drain. In a smaller saucepan, saute onions and green pepper in butter until tender. Combine the cabbage, onion mixture, cheese and 1-1/2 cups croutons.

2. Spoon into a 13-in. x 9-in. x 2-in. baking dish. Pour milk over top; do not stir. Sprinkle with remaining croutons. Bake, uncovered, at 350° for 20-25 minutes or until bubbly. **Yield:** 6-8 servings.

Creamed Cabbage Soup

2 cans (14-1/2 ounces *each*) chicken broth

2 celery ribs, chopped

1 medium head cabbage (3 pounds), shredded

1 medium onion, chopped

1 medium carrot, chopped

1/4 cup butter

3 tablespoons all-purpose flour

1 teaspoon salt

1/4 teaspoon pepper

2 cups half-and-half cream

1 cup milk

2 cups cubed fully cooked ham

1/2 teaspoon dried thyme

Minced fresh parsley

1. In a Dutch oven, combine the broth, celery, cabbage, onion and carrot; bring to a boil. Reduce heat; cover and simmer for 15-20 minutes or until vegetables are tender.

2. Meanwhile, melt butter in a medium saucepan. Stir in the flour, salt and pepper until blended. Combine cream and milk; gradually add to flour mixture, stirring constantly. Bring to a boil; cook and stir for 2 minutes or until thickened. Gradually stir into vegetable mixture. Add ham and thyme and heat through. Garnish with parsley. **Yield:** 8-10 servings.

Cheddar Cabbage Wedges

1 medium head cabbage (3 pounds)
1/2 cup chopped green pepper
1/4 cup chopped onion
1/4 cup butter
1/4 cup all-purpose flour
1/2 teaspoon salt
1/8 teaspoon pepper
2 cups milk
3/4 cup shredded cheddar cheese
1/2 cup mayonnaise
3 tablespoons chili sauce

1. Cut the cabbage into eight wedges, leaving a portion of the core on each wedge. In a Dutch oven, cook cabbage wedges in boiling salted water for 10-15 minutes or until crisp-tender. Drain; remove core. Place the wedges in a greased shallow 3-qt. baking dish.

2. In a medium saucepan, saute the green pepper and onion in butter until tender. Stir in the flour, salt and pepper until blended. Gradually add milk. Bring to a boil; cook and stir for 2 minutes or until thickened. Pour over cabbage.

3. Bake, uncovered, at 375° for 15 minutes. In a small bowl, combine the cheese, mayonnaise and chili sauce; spoon over wedges. Bake 5 minutes longer or until heated through. **Yield:** 8 servings.

Whether it's a simple meal or an elaborate Sunday dinner that you are fixing, this side dish adds so much to it. I enjoying making this recipe, and my husband, John, loves to eat it!

Karren Fairbanks
Salt Lake City, Utah

Cabbage Fruit Salad

4 cups shredded cabbage

2 medium oranges, peeled and cut into bite-size pieces

2 medium red apples, chopped

1 cup seedless red grape halves

1/4 cup dried currants *or* raisins

1/2 cup mayonnaise

1/4 cup milk

1 tablespoon lemon juice

1 tablespoon sugar

1/8 teaspoon salt

1/2 cup chopped pecans, toasted

This salad goes well with all fish and meats—it's especially good at barbecues.

Florence McNulty
Montebello, California

In a large bowl, toss the cabbage, oranges, apples, grapes and currants; cover and refrigerate. In a small bowl, combine the mayonnaise, milk, lemon juice, sugar and salt; cover and refrigerate. Just before serving, stir dressing and pecans into salad. **Yield:** 6-8 servings.

Shredding Cabbage

To shred cabbage by hand, cut cabbage into wedges. Place cut side down on a cutting board. With a large sharp knife, cut into thin slices.

Spinach Slaw

8 cups shredded iceberg
 lettuce
5 cups shredded spinach
4 cups shredded red cabbage
3 cups shredded green
 cabbage

1 cup mayonnaise
1/4 cup honey
3/4 to 1 teaspoon garlic
 powder
1/2 teaspoon salt
1/4 teaspoon pepper

In a large bowl, toss the lettuce, spinach and cabbages; cover and refrigerate. In a small bowl, combine remaining ingredients; cover and refrigerate. Just before serving, pour dressing over the salad and toss to coat. **Yield:** 12-16 servings.

Even people who don't normally enjoy cabbage like it in this salad, thanks to the honey's sweetness.

GaleLynn Peterson
Long Beach, California

Sweet-Sour Red Cabbage

2 tablespoons cider vinegar
1 tablespoon brown sugar
1/4 teaspoon caraway seed
1/4 teaspoon celery seed

2 cups shredded red
 cabbage
1/2 cup thinly sliced onion
Salt and pepper to taste

1. In a small bowl, combine the vinegar, brown sugar, caraway seed and celery seed; set aside. Place cabbage and onion in a saucepan; add a small amount of water.

2. Cover and steam until tender, about 15 minutes. Add vinegar mixture and toss to coat. Season with salt and pepper. Serve warm. **Yield:** 2 servings.

The first time I bought a red cabbage, I didn't quite know what to do with it. But after some experimenting, I came up with this recipe. It has now become my fall "comfort food."

Karen Gorman
Gunnison, Colorado

Stuffed Whole Cabbage

My husband's great about taste-testing my new recipes— like this one I experimented with before getting just right!

Wyn Jespersen
Suffield, Connecticut

1 can (28 ounces) diced
  tomatoes, undrained
1 can (6 ounces) tomato
  paste
1 garlic clove, minced
1-1/2 teaspoons dried oregano
1 teaspoon dried thyme
1 teaspoon brown sugar
1/2 teaspoon salt

Filling:
  1 pound ground beef

1 medium onion, chopped
1 large head cabbage
  (4 pounds)
3/4 cup cooked rice
1 egg, beaten
1 teaspoon salt
1/2 teaspoon pepper
2-1/4 cups water, *divided*
3 tablespoons cornstarch
2 tablespoons shredded
  Parmesan cheese

1. Combine the first seven ingredients; set aside. In a skillet, cook beef and onion over medium heat until meat is no longer pink; drain.

2. Leaving a 1-in. shell and the core intact, cut out and chop the inside of the cabbage. To beef, add 1 cup chopped cabbage, 1 cup sauce, rice, egg, salt and pepper; mix well. Spoon into cabbage shell.

3. Place 2 cups water, the remaining chopped cabbage and the remaining sauce in a Dutch oven; mix well. Carefully add stuffed cabbage meat side up. Cover and bring to a boil. Reduce heat; cover and simmer 1-1/2 hours or until whole cabbage is tender. Remove cabbage to a serving platter and keep warm.

4. Combine the cornstarch and remaining water until smooth; stir into Dutch oven. Bring to a boil; cook and stir for 2 minutes or until thickened. Pour over the cabbage; sprinkle with Parmesan cheese. Cut into wedges to serve. **Yield:** 8 servings.

Red Cabbage Casserole

1 tablespoon shortening
8 cups shredded red cabbage
1 medium onion, chopped
1/2 cup lemon juice *or* cider vinegar
1/4 cup sugar
1 teaspoon salt
1 to 2 medium apples, chopped
1/4 cup red currant jelly
Lemon slices, optional

1. In a Dutch oven, melt shortening. Add the cabbage, onion, lemon juice, sugar and salt; mix well.

2. Cover and cook over medium heat for 10-15 minutes or until cabbage is crisp-tender, stirring occasionally. Add apples; cook 10-15 minutes longer or until cabbage and apples are tender. Stir in jelly until melted. Garnish with lemon slices if desired. **Yield:** 8-10 servings.

When you want to spend time with your guests instead of in the kitchen, try this dish...it's so easy. With its color and eye appeal, I serve it on special days like Christmas or Easter. I'd also recommend it for potlucks.

Julie Murray
Sunderland, Ontario

Unstuffed Cabbage

1 pound ground beef
1 cup chopped onion
1 small head cabbage, (1 pound), shredded
1 can (28 ounces) Mexican-style tomatoes, undrained
1 tablespoon brown sugar
1 tablespoon cider vinegar
1/4 teaspoon salt
1/8 teaspoon pepper
Hot cooked rice

1. In a Dutch oven, cook beef and onion over medium heat until meat is no longer pink; drain. Stir in cabbage. Cover and cook for 5 minutes or until cabbage is crisp-tender.

2. Stir in the tomatoes, brown sugar, vinegar, salt and pepper. Cook 10 minutes longer, stirring occasionally. Serve over rice. **Yield:** 4-6 servings.

This one-dish wonder hits the spot every time! It packs all the flavor of traditional stuffed cabbage with a lot less hassle.

Diana Filban
Cut Bank, Montana

Beef and Cabbage Stew

1 pound ground beef
1/2 cup chopped onion
2 cans (16 ounces *each*) kidney beans, rinsed and drained
1 can (14-1/2 ounces) beef broth
1 can (14-1/2 ounces) crushed tomatoes
4 cups chopped cabbage
1/2 teaspoon dried basil
1/2 teaspoon dried marjoram
1/2 teaspoon dried thyme
1/2 teaspoon salt
1/8 teaspoon pepper

This hearty stew is quick to make. Just cook the ground beef and combine it with a few canned items, fresh cabbage and seasoning. While it's simmering, you can finish up the rest of the meal.

Sharon Downs
St. Louis, Missouri

1. In a Dutch oven, cook beef and onion over medium heat until meat is no longer pink; drain. In a small bowl, mash 1/4 cup beans with 1/4 cup beef broth. Add to Dutch oven with remaining beans and broth. Stir in the tomatoes, cabbage and seasonings.

2. Bring to a boil. Reduce heat; cover and simmer for 30 minutes or until the cabbage is tender. **Yield:** 6-8 servings.

——— Removing Core from Cabbage ———

Cut the cabbage in half or quarters. Make a V-shaped cut around core and remove.

Creamy Noodles & Cabbage

6 tablespoons butter
1 small head cabbage (1 pound), chopped
1 medium onion, chopped
1/4 teaspoon salt
1/4 teaspoon pepper
1 tablespoon all-purpose flour

2 cups half-and-half cream
1 package (12 ounces) egg noodles *or* fettuccine, cooked and drained
1 cup (4 ounces) shredded Parmesan cheese
1/2 cup crumbled cooked bacon

This quick-fix, comforting dish makes a great side to a beef or pork entree.

Gail Nero
Canton, Georgia

1. In a Dutch oven, melt butter. Add the cabbage, onion, salt and pepper. Cook and stir until vegetables are crisp-tender, about 10 minutes. Combine flour and cream until smooth. Stir into vegetables. Bring to a boil; cook and stir for 1 minute or until thickened.

2. Stir in noodles and Parmesan cheese; mix well. Pour into serving dish and sprinkle with bacon. Serve immediately.
Yield: 10-12 servings.

Dilly Corned Beef And Cabbage

1 corned beef brisket (2-1/2 to 3-1/2 pounds)
1/4 cup honey
3 teaspoons Dijon mustard, *divided*

1 medium head cabbage (3 pounds)
2 tablespoons butter
1 tablespoon minced fresh dill *or* 1 teaspoon dill weed

One year, when St. Patrick's Day was near, I wanted to serve something other than plain cabbage—so I decided to try this recipe. It's now become a family tradition for us come every March 17th.

June Bridges
Franklin, Indiana

1. Place brisket with its seasoning packet in a Dutch oven; add enough water to cover. Cover and simmer 2-1/2 hours or until tender. Remove the brisket and place on a broiling pan; reserve cooking liquid in Dutch oven. Combine the honey and 1 teaspoon mustard; brush half over meat.

2. Broil 4 in. from the heat for 3 minutes. Brush with the remaining honey mixture; broil 2 minutes longer or until glazed. Meanwhile, cut cabbage into eight wedges; simmer in cooking liquid for 10-15 minutes or until tender.

3. Combine the butter, dill and remaining mustard; serve over the cabbage wedges and sliced corned beef. **Yield:** 6-8 servings.

Old-Fashioned Cabbage Rolls

1 medium head cabbage (3 pounds)
1/2 pound ground beef
1/2 pound ground pork
1 can (15 ounces) tomato sauce, *divided*
1 small onion, chopped
1/2 cup uncooked long grain rice

1 tablespoon dried parsley flakes
1/2 teaspoon salt
1/2 teaspoon dill weed
1/8 teaspoon cayenne pepper
1 can (14-1/2 ounces) diced tomatoes, undrained
1/2 teaspoon sugar

1. In a Dutch oven, cook cabbage in boiling water for 2-3 minutes, just until leaves fall off head. Set aside 12 large leaves for rolls. Cut out the thick vein from bottom of each reserved leaf, making a V-shaped cut. Set aside remaining cabbage.

2. In a small bowl, combine the beef, pork, 1/2 cup tomato sauce, onion, rice, parsley, salt, dill and cayenne. Place about 1/4 cup meat mixture on each cabbage leaf; overlap cut ends of leaf. Fold in sides, beginning from the cut end. Roll up completely to enclose filling.

3. Slice remaining cabbage; place in Dutch oven. Arrange the cabbage rolls seam side down over sliced cabbage. Combine the tomatoes, sugar and remaining tomato sauce; pour over the rolls. Cover and bake at 350° for 1-1/2 hours or until tender and meat thermometer reads 160°. **Yield:** 6 servings.

Smoked Sausage Skillet

1 pound smoked kielbasa *or* Polish sausage, sliced into 1/4-inch pieces
3 cups shredded cabbage
1 celery rib, finely chopped
1 tablespoon vegetable oil

2 tablespoons Dijon mustard
1/2 teaspoon garlic salt
1/4 teaspoon rubbed sage
2 cups cooked pasta

In a large skillet, saute the sausage, cabbage and celery in oil for 5 minutes. Add the mustard, garlic salt and sage. Cook and stir over medium heat for 4-6 minutes or until vegetables are tender. Stir in noodles; cook until heated through. **Yield:** 4 servings.

Hearty New England Dinner

2 medium carrots, sliced
1 medium onion, sliced
1 celery rib, sliced
1 boneless chuck roast
(about 3 pounds)
1 teaspoon salt, *divided*
1/4 teaspoon pepper
1 envelope onion soup mix
2 cups water
1 tablespoon cider vinegar
1 bay leaf
1/2 small head cabbage, cut
into wedges
3 tablespoons butter
2 tablespoons all-purpose
flour
1 tablespoon dried minced
onion
2 tablespoons prepared
horseradish

1. Place the carrots, onion and celery in a 5-qt. slow cooker. Place the roast on top; sprinkle with 1/2 teaspoon salt and pepper. Add the soup mix, water, vinegar and bay leaf. Cover and cook on low for 7-9 hours or until beef is tender.

2. Remove beef and keep warm; discard bay leaf. Add cabbage. Cover and cook on high for 30-40 minutes or until cabbage is tender.

3. Meanwhile, melt butter in a small saucepan; stir in flour and onion. Add 1-1/2 cups cooking liquid from the slow cooker. Stir in horseradish and remaining salt; bring to a boil. Cook and stir over low heat until thick and smooth, about 2 minutes. Serve with roast and vegetables. **Yield:** 6-8 servings.

This favorite slow-cooker recipe came from a friend. At first, my husband was a bit skeptical about a roast that wasn't fixed in the oven, but he loves the old-fashioned goodness of this version. The horseradish adds zip.

Claire McCombs
San Diego, California

Carrots

Chocolate Chip Carrot Bread, p. 119

Apricot-Orange Glazed Carrots

Looking for an easy way to dress up cooked carrots, I hit on this delicious recipe. The fruity glaze complements the natural sweetness of the carrots. I've found this versatile side dish can be used with almost any meat.

Joan Huggins
Waynesboro, Mississippi

8 medium carrots, sliced
1/2 cup dried apricots, sliced
1/2 cup orange juice
1 tablespoon butter
1-1/2 teaspoons brown sugar
1/2 teaspoon salt
1/4 teaspoon grated orange peel
1/8 teaspoon ground ginger

1. Place 1 in. of water in a large saucepan; add carrots. Bring to a boil. Reduce heat; cover and simmer for 9-11 minutes or until crisp-tender. Drain and set aside.

2. In the same pan, combine the remaining ingredients; cook and stir until lightly thickened. Return carrots to the pan; stir until glazed and heated through. **Yield:** 6 servings.

Carrots and Pineapple

2 cups baby carrots
1 can (20 ounces) pineapple chunks
4 teaspoons cornstarch
1/2 teaspoon ground cinnamon
1/2 cup packed brown sugar
1 tablespoon butter

A sweet pineapple sauce makes the baby carrots seem extra-special. It's also quick-to-fix and goes well with beef, pork or chicken.

Cora Christian
Church Hill, Tennessee

1. In a saucepan, bring 1 in. of water to a boil; place carrots in a steamer basket over water. Cover and steam for 8-10 minutes or until crisp-tender. Drain pineapple, reserving juice; set pineapple aside.

2. In a saucepan, combine cornstarch and cinnamon. Add the brown sugar, butter and reserved juice. Bring to a boil; cook and stir for 2 minutes or until thickened. Stir in the carrots and pineapple; heat through. **Yield:** 4 servings.

Confetti Carrot Fritters

6 cups water
2-1/2 cups finely chopped carrots
1/4 cup all-purpose flour
1/4 teaspoon salt
1/4 teaspoon pepper
2 eggs, *separated*
3 tablespoons milk
2 tablespoons finely chopped onion
2 tablespoons minced fresh parsley
Vegetable oil for deep-fat frying

Mustard Sauce:
1 tablespoon minced fresh parsley
1 tablespoon red wine vinegar
1 tablespoon Dijon mustard
1 teaspoon finely chopped green onion
1/4 cup olive oil

1. In a saucepan, bring water to a boil. Add carrots; cover and boil for 3 minutes. Drain and immediately place carrots in ice water. Drain and pat dry.

2. In a large bowl, combine flour, salt and pepper. Combine egg yolks and milk; stir into flour mixture until smooth. Stir in the onion, parsley and carrots. In a mixing bowl, beat egg whites on high speed until stiff peaks form; fold into batter.

3. In an electric skillet, heat 1/4 in. of oil over medium heat. Drop batter by 1/3 cupfuls; press lightly to flatten. Fry until golden brown, about 2 minutes on each side. Remove to paper towels to drain.

4. For mustard sauce, in a small bowl, combine the parsley, vinegar, mustard and green onion. Slowly whisk in oil until blended. Serve with the fritters. **Yield:** 9 servings.

Crispy, sweet and savory, these delicate fritters are a fun twist on the traditional fruit-filled variety. They're yummy served with a mustard dipping sauce, but our kids enjoy them with a drizzle of warm maple syrup, too.

Peggy Camp
Twain, California

Creamy Carrot Parsnip Soup

8 cups chopped carrots

6 cups chopped peeled parsnips

4 cups chicken broth

3 cups water

2 teaspoons sugar

1 teaspoon salt

1 medium onion, chopped

4 garlic cloves, minced

1 teaspoon grated fresh horseradish

1 teaspoon grated fresh gingerroot

3 tablespoons butter

2 cups buttermilk

2 tablespoons sour cream

Fresh dill sprigs, optional

This creamy concoction tastes like it's fresh from the garden. A hint of horseradish and ginger sparks every steaming spoonful.

Phyllis Clinehens
Maplewood, Ohio

1. In a Dutch oven, combine the carrots, parsnips, broth, water, sugar and salt; bring to a boil. Reduce heat; cover and cook for 25-30 minutes or until vegetables are tender. In a skillet, saute the onion, garlic, horseradish and ginger in butter until tender. Add to the carrot mixture. Cool slightly.

2. Transfer soup to a blender in batches; cover and process until smooth. Return to the pan. Stir in buttermilk; heat through (do not boil). Garnish servings with sour cream and dill if desired. **Yield:** 12 servings (3 quarts).

Pickled Carrots

1 pound carrots, cut into
3-inch julienne strips
3/4 cup water
2/3 cup white vinegar
3/4 cup sugar

1 cinnamon stick
(3 inches), broken
3 whole cloves
1 tablespoon mustard seed

1. Place 1 in. of water in a saucepan; add carrots. Bring to a boil. Reduce heat; cover and simmer for 3-4 minutes or until crisp-tender. Drain and rinse in cold water. Place in a bowl and set aside.

2. In a saucepan, combine the water, vinegar, sugar, cinnamon, whole cloves and mustard seed. Bring to a boil. Reduce heat; simmer, uncovered, for 10 minutes. Cool; pour over the carrots. Cover and refrigerate for 8 hours or overnight. Discard cloves and cinnamon. Serve carrots with a slotted spoon. **Yield:** 6-8 servings.

The trick to pickled carrots is cooking them just long enough to retain a harvest-fresh "snap." These tangy treats are terrific for perking up a relish tray or serving with a sandwich.

Cecilia Grondin
Grand Falls, New Brunswick

Baked Stuffed Carrots

12 medium carrots, peeled
1/4 cup mayonnaise
4 teaspoons grated onion
2 teaspoons prepared
horseradish
1/8 teaspoon ground nutmeg

Salt and pepper to taste
1/4 cup dry bread crumbs
2 tablespoons butter,
melted, *divided*
1/8 teaspoon paprika

1. Place carrots in a skillet; add 1 in. of water. Bring to a boil. Reduce heat; cover and simmer for 10-15 minutes or until crisp-tender. Drain.

2. Cut a thin lengthwise slice out of each carrot. Scoop out carrot, leaving a 1/4-in. shell; set shells aside. Place the carrot pulp in a food processor or blender; cover and process until finely chopped. Transfer to a bowl; add the mayonnaise, onion, horseradish, nutmeg, salt and pepper. Spoon into carrot shells.

3. Place in a greased 13-in. x 9-in. x 2-in. baking dish. Combine crumbs, 1 tablespoon butter and paprika; sprinkle over carrots. Drizzle with remaining butter. Bake, uncovered, at 375° for 20-25 minutes or until tender. **Yield:** 6 servings.

This interesting preparation is a much more impressive side dish than plain cooked carrots. When we were raising our children, we grew our own carrots. Now we get them from a nearby farmers market.

Roma Steckling
Aitkin, Minnesota

Carrot Mushroom Stir-Fry

This savory combination of carrots with mushrooms is irresistible.

Jacqueline Thompson Graves
Lawrenceville, Georgia

6 to 8 medium carrots (1 pound), thinly sliced

2 tablespoons butter, optional

2 teaspoons olive oil

1 jar (6 ounces) sliced mushrooms, drained

5 green onions with tops, thinly sliced

1 tablespoon lemon juice

1/2 teaspoon salt, optional

1/4 teaspoon pepper

In a skillet, stir-fry carrots in butter if desired and oil for 7 minutes over medium heat. Add mushrooms and onions; cook and stir for 4-6 minutes or until vegetables are tender. Stir in lemon juice, salt if desired and pepper. **Yield:** 7 servings.

Scalloped Carrots

6 cups water

12 medium carrots, sliced 1/4 inch thick (about 4 cups)

1 medium onion, finely chopped

1/2 cup butter, *divided*

1/4 cup all-purpose flour

1 teaspoon salt

1/4 teaspoon ground mustard

1/4 teaspoon celery salt

Dash pepper

2 cups milk

2 cups (8 ounces) shredded cheddar cheese

3 slices whole wheat bread, cut into small cubes

A cookbook my husband gave me as a wedding gift included this recipe—he remembers having the dish as a child at church dinners. Now I make it whenever I need a special vegetable side. It's rich and cheesy even after reheating.

Joyce Tornholm
New Market, Iowa

1. In a saucepan, bring water to a boil; add carrots. Return to a boil; cover and cook for 4 minutes. Drain and immediately place the carrots in ice water; drain and pat dry.

2. In another saucepan, saute onion in 1/4 cup butter. Stir in the flour, salt, mustard, celery salt and pepper until blended. Gradually add milk. Bring to a boil; cook and stir for 2 minutes or until thickened.

3. In a greased 11-in. x 7-in. x 2-in. baking dish, layer half of the carrots, cheese and white sauce. Repeat layers. Melt remaining butter; toss with bread cubes. Sprinkle over top. Bake, uncovered, at 350° for 35-40 minutes or until hot and bubbly. **Yield:** 4-6 servings.

Savory Chicken Vegetable Strudel

2 cups diced cooked chicken

1/2 cup shredded carrots

1/2 cup finely chopped fresh broccoli

1/3 cup finely chopped sweet red pepper

1 cup (4 ounces) shredded sharp cheddar cheese

1/2 cup mayonnaise

2 garlic cloves, minced

1/2 teaspoon dill weed

1/4 teaspoon salt

1/4 teaspoon pepper

2 tubes (8 ounces *each*) refrigerated crescent rolls

1 egg white, beaten

2 tablespoons slivered almonds

1. In a bowl, combine the first 10 ingredients. Unroll crescent dough and place in a greased 15-in. x 10-in. x 1-in. baking pan; press seams and perforations together, forming a 15-in. x 12-in. rectangle (dough will hang over edges of pan).

2. Spread filling lengthwise down the center of the dough. On each long side, cut 1-1/2-in. wide strips 3-1/2 in. into center. Starting at one end, alternate strips, twisting twice and laying at an angle across filling. Seal ends. Brush dough with egg white; sprinkle with almonds.

3. Bake at 375° for 30-35 minutes or until golden brown. Cut into slices; serve warm. **Yield:** 12 servings.

If you're looking for a way to sneak vegetables into the meal, try this one that looks fancy without the fuss. Now that our two sons are grown, I make it for my husband and me. It is definitely a recipe for company as well.

Michele Barneson
Washburn, Wisconsin

Chicken Carrot Fried Rice

3/4 pound boneless skinless chicken breasts, cubed

4 tablespoons soy sauce, *divided*

2 garlic cloves, minced

1-1/2 cups chopped fresh broccoli

3 green onions, sliced

2 tablespoons vegetable oil, *divided*

3 large carrots, shredded

4 cups cold cooked rice

1/4 teaspoon pepper

A friend shared this colorful stir-fry when my children were small. It quickly won over those picky eaters! To cut down on prep time, I make the rice ahead and often marinate the chicken beforehand.

Peggy Spieckermann
Joplin, Missouri

1. In a bowl, combine the chicken, 1 tablespoon soy sauce and garlic; set aside. In a large skillet or wok, stir-fry the broccoli and green onions in 1 tablespoon oil for 5 minutes. Add carrots; stir-fry 4 minutes longer or until crisp-tender. Remove and set aside.

2. In the same skillet, stir-fry chicken in remaining oil until no longer pink and juices run clear. Add the rice, pepper, vegetables and remaining soy sauce. Stir-fry until heated through. **Yield:** 4-6 servings.

Shredded Carrots Shortcut

To save time later, shred and freeze carrots in 1-cup portions in resealable plastic freezer bags. Then when a recipe calls for shredded carrots, just pull a bag from the freezer.

Carrots in Almond Sauce

1 pound carrots, julienned
1/2 cup thinly sliced green onions
1/4 cup butter
1 teaspoon cornstarch
1/2 cup water
1/2 teaspoon chicken bouillon granules
1/2 teaspoon dill weed
1/8 teaspoon pepper
1/4 cup sliced almonds, toasted

1. Place 1 in. of water in a large saucepan; add carrots. Bring to a boil. Reduce heat; cover and simmer for 3-4 minutes or until crisp-tender. Drain. Transfer to a serving bowl and keep warm.

2. In the same pan, saute onions in butter until tender. Combine cornstarch and water until smooth; stir into onions. Add the bouillon, dill and pepper. Bring to a boil over medium heat; cook and stir for 1 minute or until thickened and bubbly. Stir in almonds. Pour over carrots; stir to coat. **Yield:** 6 servings.

Here's an easy way to add elegance and flavor to a plain vegetable. The combination of tender carrots and crunchy nuts is different and delightful. Plus, the touch of dill lends just the right zip.

Carol Anderson
Salt Lake City, Utah

Oven-Roasted Carrots

2 pounds baby carrots
4 small onions, quartered
6 garlic cloves, peeled
2 tablespoons olive oil
2 teaspoons white wine vinegar
1 to 2 teaspoons dried thyme
1/2 teaspoon salt
1/8 teaspoon pepper

1. Place the carrots, onions and garlic in two greased 15-in. x 10-in. x 1-in. baking pans. Drizzle with oil and vinegar. Sprinkle with thyme, salt and pepper; gently toss to coat.

2. Cover and bake at 450° for 20 minutes; stir. Bake, uncovered, for 10 minutes; stir again. Bake 10 minutes longer or until carrots are crisp-tender. **Yield:** 8 servings.

My seven children and 15 grandchildren really look forward to carrots when they're prepared this flavorful way. As a cook at our local school, I served two generations of children, plus relatives and friends from all over our area.

Marlene Schott
Devine, Texas

Cottontail Carrots

2 pounds carrots, julienned
1/4 cup apple juice
1/4 cup butter

2 tablespoons brown sugar
1 teaspoon salt, optional
Minced fresh parsley

In a 2-qt. microwave-safe casserole, combine carrots and apple juice. Cover and microwave on high for 10-12 minutes or until carrots are crisp-tender, stirring once. Add the butter, brown sugar and salt if desired; toss to coat. Sprinkle with parsley. **Yield:** 12 servings.

Editor's Note: This recipe was tested in a 700-watt microwave.

Carrot Pancakes

1-1/4 cups all-purpose flour
   2 tablespoons finely chopped pecans
   2 teaspoons baking powder
   1 teaspoon ground cinnamon
1/4 teaspoon salt
1/4 teaspoon ground ginger
   1 egg, lightly beaten
1/3 cup packed brown sugar

1 cup milk
1 cup grated carrots
1 teaspoon vanilla extract

Cream Cheese Spread:
   4 ounces cream cheese, softened
1/4 cup confectioners' sugar
   2 tablespoons milk
1/2 teaspoon vanilla extract
Dash ground cinnamon

1. In a bowl, combine the first six ingredients. Combine the egg, brown sugar, milk, carrots and vanilla. Stir into the dry ingredients just until moistened. Pour batter by 1/4 cupfuls onto a greased hot griddle. Turn when bubbles form on top of pancake; cook until second side is golden brown.

2. Meanwhile, place the cream cheese, confectioners' sugar, milk and vanilla in a blender or food processor; cover and process until smooth. Transfer to a bowl; sprinkle with cinnamon. Serve with pancakes. **Yield:** 4 servings.

Chocolate Chip Carrot Bread

3 cups all-purpose flour
1 cup sugar
1 cup packed brown sugar
2 to 3 teaspoons ground cinnamon
2 teaspoons baking powder
1 teaspoon baking soda
1 teaspoon salt
1 teaspoon ground ginger
1/4 to 1/2 teaspoon ground cloves
3 eggs
3/4 cup orange juice
3/4 cup vegetable oil
1 teaspoon vanilla extract
2 cups grated carrots
1 cup (6 ounces) semisweet chocolate chips

1. In a large bowl, combine the first nine ingredients. In a small bowl, beat the eggs, orange juice, oil and vanilla. Stir into the dry ingredients just until moistened. Fold in the carrots and chocolate chips.

2. Transfer to two greased 8-in. x 4-in. x 2-in. loaf pans. Bake at 350° for 55-60 minutes or until a toothpick inserted near the center comes out clean. Cool for 10 minutes before removing from pans to wire racks. **Yield:** 2 loaves.

My family likes sweet breads, and this loaf incorporates many of their favorite ingredients. Coming up with flavorful recipes that are a little out of the ordinary is a favorite pastime.

Sharon Setzer
Philomath, Oregon

Eliminate Peeling

Before grating carrots, simply wash them thoroughly with a brush. There's no need to peel them!

Surprise Carrot Cake

3 eggs
1-3/4 cups sugar
3 cups shredded carrots
1 cup vegetable oil
2 cups all-purpose flour
2 teaspoons baking soda
2 teaspoons ground cinnamon
1 teaspoon salt
1/2 cup chopped pecans

Filling:
1 package (8 ounces) cream cheese, softened
1/4 cup sugar
1 egg

Frosting:
1 package (8 ounces) cream cheese, softened
1/4 cup butter, softened
2 teaspoons vanilla extract
4 cups confectioners' sugar

A cousin gave me this recipe. It's a wonderful potluck pleaser with its "surprise" cream cheese center. My husband and our two young children love it, too! It's a great way to use up the overabundance of carrots from my garden.

Lisa Bowen
Little Britian, Ontario

1. In a mixing bowl, beat eggs and sugar. Add carrots and oil; beat until blended. Combine the flour, baking soda, cinnamon and salt. Add to carrot mixture; mix well. Stir in pecans. Pour 3 cups batter into a greased and floured 10-in. fluted tube pan.

2. In a mixing bowl, beat cream cheese and sugar. Add egg; mix well. Spoon over batter. Top with remaining batter.

3. Bake at 350° for 55-60 minutes or until a toothpick inserted near the center comes out clean. Cool for 10 minutes before removing from pan to a wire rack to cool completely.

4. For frosting, in a small mixing bowl, beat the cream cheese, butter and vanilla until smooth. Gradually add confectioners' sugar. Frost cake. Store in the refrigerator. **Yield:** 12-16 servings.

Carrot Fruitcake

1-1/2 cups vegetable oil
  2 cups sugar
  4 eggs
  3 cups all-purpose flour
  2 teaspoons baking powder
  2 teaspoons baking soda
  2 teaspoons ground
    cinnamon
  1 teaspoon salt
  3 cups finely shredded
    carrots
1-1/2 cups coarsely chopped
    nuts
  1 cup *each* raisins, chopped
    dates and mixed candied
    fruit

Start a new holiday tradition with this flavorful golden fruitcake.

Judy Jungwirth
Athol, South Dakota

1. In a large mixing bowl, combine oil and sugar. Add eggs, one at a time, beating well after each addition. Combine the flour, baking powder, baking soda, cinnamon and salt; add to the egg mixture. Beat until smooth. Stir in remaining ingredients.

2. Pour into two greased and floured 9-in. x 5-in. x 3-in. loaf pans. Bake at 350° for 1 hour or until a toothpick inserted near the center comes out clean. Cool for 10 minutes before removing from pans to wire racks to cool completely. **Yield:** 2 loaves.

Maple Carrot Cupcakes

  2 cups all-purpose flour
  1 cup sugar
  1 teaspoon baking powder
  1 teaspoon baking soda
  1 teaspoon ground
    cinnamon
1/2 teaspoon salt
  4 eggs
  1 cup vegetable oil
1/2 cup maple syrup
  3 cups grated carrots
    (about 6 medium)

Frosting:
  1 package (8 ounces)
    cream cheese, softened
1/4 cup butter, softened
1/4 cup maple syrup
  1 teaspoon vanilla extract
Chopped walnuts, optional

I come from a family of cooks and was inspired to cook and bake ever since I was young. This recipe is handed down from Grandmom and is always requested at special gatherings.

Lisa Ann DiNunzio
Vineland, New Jersey

1. In a large bowl, combine the first six ingredients. In another bowl, beat eggs, oil and syrup. Stir into dry ingredients just until moistened. Fold in carrots. Fill greased or paper-lined muffin cups two-thirds full.

2. Bake at 350° for 20-25 minutes or until a toothpick comes out clean. Cool for 5 minutes. Removing from pans to wire racks.

3. For frosting, combine cream cheese, butter, syrup and vanilla in a mixing bowl; beat until smooth. Frost cooled cupcakes. Sprinkle with nuts if desired. **Yield:** 1-1/2 dozen.

Corn

Corn and Chicken Dinner, p. 134

Spicy Corn and Black Bean Relish

2-1/2 cups fresh *or* frozen corn, cooked
1 can (15 ounces) black beans, rinsed and drained
3/4 to 1 cup chopped seeded anaheim chili peppers
1/8 to 1/4 cup chopped seeded jalapeno peppers
1/4 cup white vinegar
2 tablespoons vegetable oil
1 tablespoon Dijon mustard
1 teaspoon chili powder
1 teaspoon ground cumin
3/4 teaspoon salt
1/2 teaspoon pepper

In a large bowl, combine corn, beans and peppers. Combine remaining ingredients in a small bowl; pour over corn mixture and toss to coat. Cover and refrigerate. **Yield:** 6-8 servings.

Editor's Note: When cutting or seeding hot peppers, use rubber or plastic gloves to protect your hands. Avoid touching your face.

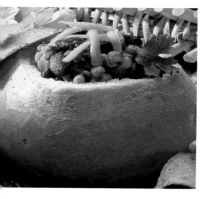

Taco Soup

1 pound ground beef
1/4 cup chopped onion
2 cups fresh *or* frozen corn
1 can (14-1/2 ounces) diced tomatoes, undrained
1 can (16 ounces) kidney beans, rinsed and drained
1 can (8 ounces) tomato sauce
1 envelope taco seasoning
Corn chips, shredded cheddar cheese *and/or* sour cream, optional

1. In a large saucepan, cook beef and onion over medium heat until meat is no longer pink; drain. Add the corn, tomatoes, beans, tomato sauce and taco seasoning. Bring to a boil.

2. Reduce heat; cover and simmer for 15 minutes, stirring occasionally. Serve with corn chips, cheese and/or sour cream if desired. **Yield:** 4-6 servings (1-1/2 quarts).

Fiesta Corn Salad

- 2 cups fresh *or* frozen corn
- 3 medium tomatoes, chopped
- 1 can (2-1/4 ounces) sliced pitted ripe olives, drained
- 1/4 cup sliced green olives
- 2 tablespoons taco seasoning mix
- 1/4 cup vegetable oil
- 1/4 cup cider vinegar
- 1/4 cup water

In a large bowl, combine the corn, tomatoes and olives. In a small bowl, combine seasoning mix, oil, vinegar and water; pour over corn mixture and mix well. Chill several hours before serving. **Yield:** 8-10 servings.

This salad is great for potlucks since it travels well and goes with everything.

Marian Platt
Sequim, Washington

Fresh Corn Salad

8 ears fresh corn, husked and cleaned
1/2 cup vegetable oil
1/4 cup cider vinegar
1-1/2 teaspoons lemon juice
1/4 cup minced fresh parsley
2 teaspoons sugar
1 teaspoon salt, optional
1/2 teaspoon dried basil
1/8 to 1/4 teaspoon cayenne pepper
2 large tomatoes, seeded and coarsely chopped
1/2 cup chopped onion
1/3 cup chopped green pepper
1/3 cup chopped sweet red pepper

People who prefer food with some tang find this corn salad particularly appealing. It's a pretty dish besides— and very economical.

Carol Shaffer
Cape Girardeau, Missouri

1. In a large saucepan, cook corn in enough boiling water to cover for 3-5 minutes or until tender. Drain; cool and set aside. In a large bowl, combine the oil, vinegar, lemon juice, parsley, sugar, salt if desired, basil and cayenne pepper.

2. Cut cooled corn off the cob (should measure 4 cups). Add the corn, tomatoes, onion and peppers to the oil mixture. Mix well. Cover and chill for several hours or overnight. **Yield:** 10 servings.

—— Cutting Kernels from Corncobs ——

Stand one end of the cob on a cutting board. Starting at the top, run a sharp knife down the cob, cutting deeply to remove whole kernels. One medium cob yields 1/3 to 1/2 cup kernels.

Corny Lettuce Salad

3 cups shredded lettuce
3/4 cup cooked fresh *or*
   frozen corn, cooled
2 tablespoons sugar
2 tablespoons cider vinegar
1-1/2 teaspoons poppy seeds

1/2 teaspoon grated onion
1/4 teaspoon salt
1/4 teaspoon ground mustard
1/4 cup vegetable oil
1/4 cup finely chopped sweet
   red pepper

In a salad bowl, toss the lettuce and corn. In a small bowl, combine the sugar, vinegar, poppy seeds, onion, salt and mustard; gradually whisk in oil. Pour over salad and toss to coat. Sprinkle with red pepper. **Yield:** 4 servings.

It takes no time to toss together the corn, lettuce and red peppers in my Corny Lettuce Salad. People love the sweet and tangy homemade dressing and the nutty crunch of poppy seeds. I've taken it to potlucks and picnics, and it's gone in no time!

Ruth Lee
Troy, Ontario

Corny Tomato Dumpling Soup

1 pound ground beef
3 cups fresh *or* frozen corn
1 can (28 ounces) diced
   tomatoes, undrained
2 cans (14-1/2 ounces
   each) beef broth
1 cup chopped onion
1 garlic clove, minced
1-1/2 teaspoons dried basil
1-1/2 teaspoons dried thyme
1/2 teaspoon dried rosemary,
   crushed
Salt and pepper to taste

Corn Dumplings:
   1 cup all-purpose flour
1/2 cup cornmeal
2-1/2 teaspoons baking powder
1/2 teaspoon salt
   1 egg
2/3 cup milk
   1 cup fresh *or* frozen corn
1/2 cup shredded cheddar
   cheese
   1 tablespoon minced fresh
   parsley

1. In a large saucepan or Dutch oven, cook beef over medium heat until no longer pink; drain. Stir in the corn, tomatoes, broth, onion, garlic and seasonings. Bring to a boil. Reduce heat; cover and simmer for 30-45 minutes.

2. For dumplings, combine the flour, cornmeal, baking powder and salt in a bowl. In another bowl, beat egg; stir in the milk, corn, cheese and parsley. Stir into dry ingredients just until moistened. Drop by tablespoonfuls onto simmering soup. Cover and simmer for 15 minutes or until a toothpick inserted in a dumpling comes out clean (do not lift cover while simmering). **Yield:** 8 servings (about 2 quarts).

I have a big garden on our farm and enjoy cooking with my harvest. In this savory tomato soup, corn stars in both the broth and dumplings. It has a fresh-picked flavor. Ground beef makes it a hearty first course or satisfying light main dish.

Jackie Ferris
Tiverton, Ontario

Double Corn Bake

1 pound ground beef
1/3 cup chopped onion
1/3 cup ketchup
1/2 teaspoon salt
1/2 teaspoon chili powder
1/4 teaspoon dried oregano
1-1/2 cups fresh *or* frozen corn

1 package (8-1/2 ounces) corn bread mix
3 tablespoons butter, melted, *divided*
1 tablespoon cornstarch
1 can (14-1/2 ounces) diced tomatoes, undrained

1. In a skillet, cook beef and onion over medium heat until meat is no longer pink; drain. Add the ketchup, salt, chili powder and oregano; cook for 5 minutes. Cool slightly. With a spoon, press meat mixture into the bottom and up the sides of a greased 10-in. pie plate. Spoon corn into crust.

2. Prepare corn bread batter according to package directions; stir in 2 tablespoons melted butter. Spread over corn.

3. Bake at 425° for 20 minutes. Meanwhile, combine the cornstarch and remaining butter in a saucepan until smooth. Stir in tomatoes. Bring to a boil; cook and stir for 2 minutes or until thickened. Cut pie into wedges and serve with sauce. **Yield:** 6-8 servings.

Grilled Sweet Corn

8 large ears sweet corn in husks
6 tablespoons butter, softened
1 tablespoon minced fresh parsley

1 to 2 teaspoons chili powder
1 teaspoon garlic salt
1/2 to 1 teaspoon ground cumin

1. Carefully peel back husks from corn to within 1 in. of bottom; remove silk. Combine remaining ingredients; spread over corn. Rewrap corn in husks and secure with kitchen string. Place in a large kettle; cover with cold water. Soak for 20 minutes; drain.

2. Grill corn, covered, over medium heat for 25-30 minutes or until tender, turning often. **Yield:** 8 servings.

Cazuela

6 chicken drumsticks *or* thighs
Butternut squash, peeled and cut into 24 1 inch cubes
6 small potatoes, peeled
6 pieces of fresh *or* frozen corn on the cob (2 inches *each*)
3 carrots, cut into 1-inch chunks
4 cans (10-3/4 ounces *each*) chicken broth
Hot cooked rice
Hot pepper sauce to taste
Salt and pepper to taste
Minced fresh cilantro to taste

1. In a large Dutch oven, place the chicken, squash, potatoes, corn, carrots and broth; bring to a boil. Reduce heat; cover and simmer for 25 minutes or until chicken and vegetables are tender.

2. Serve over rice in a shallow soup bowl; add hot pepper sauce, salt, pepper and cilantro to taste. **Yield:** 6-8 servings.

I learned to make Cazuela while we were living in Chile for a few months. We grow extra butternut squash and corn in our garden just for this favorite recipe.

Louise Schmid
Marshall, Minnesota

Crowd-Pleasing Corn on the Cob

Fill a 3-pound coffee can with hot water; melt a stick of butter and add to the water. Everyone can quickly and neatly butter their cooked ear of corn by simply dipping it into the can.

Corn and Sausage Chowder

3 ears fresh corn, husked and cleaned

4 cups heavy whipping cream

2 cups chicken broth

4 garlic cloves, minced

10 fresh thyme sprigs

1 bay leaf

1-1/2 medium onions, finely chopped, *divided*

1/2 pound hot Italian sausage links

2 teaspoons minced jalapeno peppers with seeds

1/2 teaspoon ground cumin

2 tablespoons butter

2 medium potatoes, peeled and cut into 1/2-inch cubes

2 tablespoons all-purpose flour

Salt and pepper to taste

1-1/2 teaspoons snipped fresh chives

I've had several cooking "teachers" over the years— my Irish grandmother, my mother and the restaurant that my husband and I operated in Manitoba at one time!

Joanne Watts
Kitchener, Ontario

1. Using a small sharp knife, cut corn from cobs; set corn aside. In a large saucepan, combine the corncobs, cream, broth, garlic, thyme, bay leaf and 1/2 cup onions. Heat almost to boiling. Reduce heat; cover and simmer for 1 hour, stirring occasionally.

2. Remove and discard corncobs. Strain cream mixture through a sieve set over a large bowl, pressing solids with back of spoon. Discard solids and reserve corn broth.

3. In a large skillet, cook sausage over medium heat until browned. Cool and cut into 1/2-in. slices. In a large saucepan, cook jalapenos, cumin and remaining onions in butter for 5 minutes. Set aside 1/4 cup corn stock. Add remaining corn stock along with potatoes and sausage to saucepan. Bring to a boil. Reduce heat; cover and cook for 25 minutes or until potatoes are tender.

4. Combine flour with reserved corn stock until smooth. Stir into chowder. Bring to a boil; cook and stir for 2 minutes or until thickened. Add corn and cook just until tender, about 5 minutes. Discard bay leaf. Season with salt and pepper. For a thinner chowder, add additional chicken broth. Sprinkle with chives before serving. **Yield:** 8 servings (2 quarts).

Editor's Note: When cutting or seeding hot peppers, use rubber or plastic gloves to protect your hands. Avoid touching your face.

Corn Balls

1 cup chopped celery	3 eggs, beaten
1/2 cup chopped onion	1/2 cup water
1/2 cup butter, cubed	1/2 teaspoon salt
3-1/2 cups herb-seasoned stuffing croutons	1/4 teaspoon pepper
3 cups cooked whole kernel corn	

1. In a saucepan, saute celery and onion in butter until tender; set aside to cool. In a bowl, combine the croutons, corn, eggs, water, salt, pepper and onion mixture. Shape into 8-10 balls.

2. Place in an ungreased shallow baking dish. Bake, uncovered, at 375° for 25-20 minutes or until lightly browned. **Yield:** 8-10 servings.

Whenever I serve my Corn Balls, it's just about certain someone will ask for the recipe—I've gotten more requests for it than any other I've ever tried. I usually make them when we have company as a nice change-of-pace side dish. They're great with ham, steak or roast beef.

Sharon Knicely
Harrisonburg, Virginia

Colossal Cornburger

1 egg, beaten	1 teaspoon Worcestershire sauce
1 cup fresh corn, cooked	2 pounds ground beef
1/2 cup coarsely crushed cheese crackers	1 teaspoon salt
1/4 cup sliced green onions	1/2 teaspoon pepper
1/4 cup chopped fresh parsley	1/2 teaspoon rubbed sage

1. In a medium bowl, combine the egg, corn, crackers, green onions, parsley and Worcestershire sauce; set aside. In a large bowl, combine ground beef and seasonings.

2. On waxed paper, pat half of beef mixture at a time into an 8-1/2-in. circle. Spoon corn mixture onto one circle of meat to within 1 in. of the edge. Top with second circle of meat; seal edges.

3. Invert onto a well-greased wire grill basket; peel off waxed paper. Grill over medium heat for 25-30 minutes or until burger is no longer pink and a meat thermometer reads 160°, turning once. Cut into wedges to serve. **Yield:** 6 servings.

Editor's Note: For oven method, place burger in a baking pan. Bake at 350° for 40-45 minutes or until no longer pink and a meat thermometer reads 160°.

It's been such a long time since I added this recipe to my file that I don't even remember where it came from! Cooking's something I thoroughly enjoy—and, when I'm finished, my husband always wonders which truck ran through our kitchen!

Louise Schmid
Marshall, Minnesota

Fresh Corn Cakes

Corn's always been the basis of my favorite recipes—in fact, these corn cakes were one of the first things I made for my husband. For dinner, they're nice with fresh fruit salad and ham. They're also great with breakfast sausage and orange juice.

Gaynelle Fritsch
Welches, Oregon

1 cup all-purpose flour
1/2 cup yellow *or* blue cornmeal
1 tablespoon sugar
1 tablespoon baking powder
1/2 teaspoon salt
2 eggs, *separated*
1 cup milk
1/2 cup butter, melted

1 cup cooked fresh *or* frozen corn
4 green onions, thinly sliced
1/2 medium sweet red pepper, finely chopped
1 can (4 ounces) chopped green chilies
Butter *or* vegetable oil for frying
Maple syrup, optional

1. In a medium bowl, combine flour, cornmeal, sugar, baking powder and salt. In a small bowl, beat egg yolks; blend in milk and butter. Add to dry ingredients; stir until just mixed (batter may be slightly lumpy). Stir in the corn, green onions, red pepper and green chilies; set aside. In a small mixing bowl, beat egg whites until stiff peaks form. Gently fold into batter.

2. For each pancake, pour about 1/4 cup batter onto a lightly greased hot griddle; turn when bubbles form on tops of cakes. Cook second side until golden brown. Serve immediately with syrup if desired. **Yield:** 20 pancakes.

Corny Meat Roll

This mild-flavored meat loaf features a fresh corn and parsley filling. It slices nicely into colorful swirls.

Velma Bonds
Worth, West Virginia

1-1/2 pounds lean ground beef
1 teaspoon salt
1/4 teaspoon pepper

Filling:
1-1/2 cups fresh corn *or* frozen corn, thawed

1 cup soft bread crumbs
1 egg, beaten
1/4 cup minced fresh parsley
1/2 teaspoon salt
1/8 teaspoon pepper

1. In a bowl, combine beef, salt and pepper. On a piece of heavy-duty foil, pat beef mixture into a 12-in. x 10-in. rectangle. Combine the filling ingredients. Spoon over beef to within 1 in. of edges. Roll up jelly-roll style, starting with a short side and peeling foil away while rolling. Seal seam and ends.

2. Place seam side down in a greased 13-in. x 9-in. x 2-in. baking dish. Bake, uncovered, at 350° for 1 hour or until meat is no longer pink and a meat thermometer reads 160°. Using two large spatulas, carefully transfer meat loaf to a serving platter. **Yield:** 6 servings.

Corn-Stuffed Peppers

4 **medium green peppers**

1 **can (10-3/4 ounces) condensed cream of celery soup, undiluted**

2-1/2 **cups frozen shredded hash browns, thawed**

2 **cups fresh *or* frozen corn**

1/2 **cup shredded cheddar cheese**

1/4 **cup chopped onion**

1 **jar (2 ounces) chopped pimientos, drained**

2 **tablespoons snipped chives**

1/2 **teaspoons salt**

1. Slice tops off peppers and reserve; remove seeds. In a bowl, combine the remaining ingredients. Spoon filling into peppers and replace tops.

2. Place in an 8-in. square baking dish; cover with foil. Bake at 350° for 45-60 minutes or until heated through. **Yield:** 4 servings.

I created this recipe—and haven't had any complaints yet! The peppers can be served alone as a meal or alongside pork chops, steak or hamburgers.

Suzanne Hubbard
Greeley, Colorado

Better Buttered Corn

For a sweet treat, make herb butter to spread on corn on the cob or dollop on fresh cut corn. Simply combine 2 sticks of softened butter with 1 teaspoon chopped fresh basil or 1/2 teaspoon dried basil.

Corn and Chicken Dinner

3 garlic cloves, minced, *divided*

1/2 cup butter, *divided*

3 pounds chicken legs and thighs (about 8 pieces)

3 ears fresh corn, husked, cleaned and cut into thirds

1/4 cup water

2 teaspoons dried tarragon, *divided*

1/2 teaspoon salt

1/4 teaspoon pepper

2 medium zucchini, sliced into 1/2-inch pieces

2 tomatoes, seeded and cut into chunks

My interests are reading, gardening...and growing most of the ingredients I use in this dinner! There's something for every taste in this recipe. It would be great as a meal-in-one dish for a picnic or a reunion. My family became "fans" of this meal from the start!

Doralee Pinkerton
Milford, Indiana

1. In a Dutch oven or large skillet, saute 2 garlic cloves in 2 tablespoons butter. Add the chicken and brown on both sides. Reduce heat. Add corn and water. Sprinkle with 1 teaspoon tarragon, salt and pepper. Cover and simmer for 20-25 minutes or until chicken is tender.

2. Meanwhile, in a small saucepan, melt remaining butter. Add remaining garlic and tarragon; simmer for 3 minutes. Layer zucchini and tomatoes over the chicken mixture. Drizzle seasoned butter over all; cover and cook for 3-5 minutes. **Yield:** 6-8 servings.

Creamy Sweet Corn

2 cups fresh *or* frozen corn
1/4 cup half-and-half cream
2 tablespoons butter
1 tablespoon sugar
1/2 teaspoon salt

In a saucepan, combine all ingredients. Bring to a boil over medium heat. Reduce heat; simmer, uncovered, for 6-8 minutes or until heated through. **Yield:** 4 servings.

I use cream to dress up fresh or frozen corn. The simple side dish tastes rich and takes just minutes to simmer.

Florence Jacoby
Granite Falls, Minnesota

Pork Chops with Corn Dressing

1 egg, beaten
2 cups soft bread crumbs
1-1/2 cups cooked whole kernel corn
1/4 cup water
1/2 cup chopped green pepper
1 small onion, chopped
1 teaspoon Worcestershire sauce
2 tablespoons vegetable oil
6 butterfly pork chops (about 1 inch thick)
Salt and pepper to taste
1 can (10-3/4 ounces) condensed cream of mushroom soup, undiluted
2/3 cup milk

1. In a bowl, combine the egg, bread crumbs, corn, water, green pepper, onion and Worcestershire sauce; set aside. In a large ovenproof skillet or a Dutch oven, heat oil over medium-high heat. Lightly brown pork chops on both sides. Season with salt and pepper. Top with corn dressing mixture. Add enough water to cover bottom of pan.

2. Bake, uncovered, at 350° for about 1 hour or until pork is tender and a meat thermometer reads 160°. Add additional water to pan if necessary. Remove pork chops and dressing to a serving platter; keep warm. Skim fat from pan drippings. Stir in soup and milk. Cook and stir over medium heat until hot and bubbly. Serve with pork chops. **Yield:** 6 servings.

As a new bride, I came across the original version of this recipe in a newspaper. I changed it around some and tried it out on my groom. It became a family favorite— not to mention a great, easy main course for unexpected company!

June Hassler
Sultan, Washington

Corn and Spinach Souffle

1-3/4 cups fresh *or* frozen corn, cooked
1-1/4 cups chopped cooked spinach, well drained
1/4 cup butter
2 tablespoons all-purpose flour

1-1/2 teaspoons salt
3/4 cup evaporated milk
3 eggs, lightly beaten
1 tablespoon chopped pimientos
2 teaspoons dried minced onion

1. Combine corn and spinach; set aside. In a saucepan, melt butter over low heat. Stir in flour and salt until smooth. Gradually add milk. Bring to a boil; cook and stir for 2 minutes or until thickened. Cool. Combine the eggs, pimientos and onion; fold into cooled butter mixture. Fold in corn and spinach.

2. Pour into a greased 8-in. x 4-in. x 2-in. loaf pan. Bake, uncovered, at 350° for 45-50 minutes or until done. Slice to serve. **Yield:** 8 servings.

Corn Tortilla Pizzas

1-1/4 pounds ground beef
1 small onion, chopped
1/2 cup chopped green pepper
3 cans (6 ounces *each*) tomato paste
1-1/4 cups water
1 cup salsa
2 cups fresh *or* frozen corn
1-1/2 cups chopped fresh tomatoes
3/4 cup chopped ripe olives

1 envelope taco seasoning
3 teaspoons garlic powder
1-1/2 teaspoons dried parsley flakes
1/2 teaspoon dried oregano
1/8 teaspoon salt
1/4 teaspoon pepper
32 corn *or* flour tortillas (6 inches)
8 cups (2 pounds) shredded part-skim mozzarella cheese

1. In a large skillet, cook beef, onion and green pepper over medium heat until meat is no longer pink; drain. In a bowl, combine tomato paste and water until blended; add salsa. Stir into meat mixture. Stir in corn, tomatoes, olives and seasonings.

2. Place tortillas on ungreased baking sheets. Spread each with 1/4 cup meat mixture to within 1/2 in. of edge and sprinkle with 1/4 cup of cheese.

3. Bake at 375° for 5-7 minutes or until the cheese is melted. **Yield:** 32 pizzas.

Egg and Corn Quesadilla

1 medium onion, chopped
1 medium green pepper, chopped
1 garlic clove, minced
2 tablespoons olive oil
3 cups fresh *or* frozen corn
1 teaspoon minced chives
1/2 teaspoon dried cilantro flakes
1/2 teaspoon salt
1/4 teaspoon pepper
4 eggs, beaten
4 flour tortillas (10 inches)
1/2 cup salsa
1 cup (8 ounces) sour cream
1 cup (4 ounces) shredded cheddar cheese
1 cup (4 ounces) shredded part-skim mozzarella cheese
Additional salsa and sour cream, optional

1. In a skillet, saute onion, green pepper and garlic in oil until tender. Add the corn, chives, cilantro, salt and pepper. Cook until heated through, about 3 minutes. Stir in eggs; cook until completely set, stirring occasionally. Remove from the heat.

2. Place one tortilla on a lightly greased baking sheet or pizza pan; top with a third of the corn mixture, salsa and sour cream. Sprinkle with a fourth of the cheeses. Repeat layers twice. Top with the remaining tortilla and cheeses.

3. Bake at 350° for 10 minutes or until the cheese is melted. Cut into wedges. Serve with salsa and sour cream if desired. **Yield:** 6-8 servings.

For a deliciously different breakfast or brunch, try this excellent quesadilla. It's also great for a light lunch or supper. Corn is a natural in Southwestern cooking and a tasty addition to this unique egg dish.

Stacy Joura
Stoneboro, Pennsylvania

Enchilada Casserole

1 pound ground beef
1 can (10 ounces) enchilada sauce
1 cup salsa
6 flour tortillas (10 inches)
2 cups fresh *or* frozen corn
4 cups (16 ounces) shredded cheddar cheese

I get great reviews every time I serve this—even from my father who usually doesn't like Mexican food.

Nancy VanderVeer
Knoxville, Iowa

1. In a skillet, cook ground beef over medium heat until no longer pink; drain. Stir in enchilada sauce and salsa; set aside.

2. Place two tortillas, overlapping as necessary, in the bottom of a greased 13-in. x 9-in. x 2-in. baking dish. Cover with one-third of the meat mixture; top with 1 cup corn. Sprinkle with 1-1/3 cups cheese. Repeat layers once, then top with remaining tortillas, meat and cheese.

3. Bake, uncovered, at 350° for 30 minutes or until heated through. **Yield:** 6-8 servings.

Dessert Corn Crepes

1 cup fresh corn
3 tablespoons cornstarch
1/3 cup all-purpose flour
3/4 cup plus 1 tablespoon milk
2 eggs, beaten
2 tablespoons butter, melted
1/2 teaspoon salt

11 tablespoons apricot jam
Confectioners' sugar

Lemon Cream:
1 cup (8 ounces) sour cream
1/4 cup confectioners' sugar
1 to 2 tablespoons grated
lemon peel

1. Place corn in a blender; cover and process until smooth. In a large mixing bowl, whisk cornstarch, flour and milk until smooth. Stir in the eggs, pureed corn, butter and salt until blended. Cover and refrigerate for 1 hour.

2. Heat a lightly greased 8-in. nonstick skillet; pour 3 tablespoons batter into the center of skillet. Lift and tilt pan to evenly coat bottom. Cook until top appears dry; turn and cook 15-20 seconds longer. Remove to a wire rack. Repeat with remaining batter, greasing skillet as needed. When cool, stack crepes with waxed paper or paper towels in between.

3. Spread 1 tablespoon apricot jam over each crepe. Fold in half, then fold in half again, making triangles. Dust with confectioners' sugar. In a small bowl, combine the lemon cream ingredients. Serve with crepes. **Yield:** 11 crepes.

Although I'm in my 80's, I still love to cook. I often serve these crepes as a unique dessert. You can replace apricot jam with your favorite filling.

Mildred Pavek
Eagle River, Wisconsin

Delicious Corn Pudding

4 eggs, *separated*
2 tablespoons butter,
    melted and cooled
1 tablespoon sugar
1 tablespoon brown sugar
1 teaspoon salt

1/2 teaspoon vanilla extract
Dash *each* ground cinnamon and
    nutmeg
2 cups fresh *or* frozen corn
1 cup half-and-half cream
1 cup milk

1. In a mixing bowl, beat yolks until lemon-colored, 5-8 minutes. Add butter, sugars, salt, vanilla, cinnamon and nutmeg; mix well. Add corn. Stir in cream and milk. In a small bowl, beat egg whites on high speed until stiff; fold into yolk mixture.

2. Pour into a greased 1-1/2-qt. baking dish. Bake, uncovered, at 350° for 35 minutes or until a knife inserted near the center comes out clean. Cover loosely with foil during the last 10 minutes of baking if top browns too quickly. **Yield:** 8 servings.

This comforting dish has been part of family meals for years, and it's been shared at many gatherings.

Paula Marchesi
Rocky Point, Long Island, New York

Greens

Spinach Salad, p. 144

Basil Garden Salad

A combination of crisp and buttery lettuce are coated with a tangy red wine vinaigrette in this fresh-tasting salad.

Bobbie Talbott
Veneta, Oregon

2 cups torn leaf lettuce
1 cup torn Bibb lettuce
3 green onions with tops, sliced
1 medium tomato, peeled and diced
6 fresh mushrooms, sliced

9 fresh basil leaves, thinly sliced
2 tablespoons red wine vinegar
3 tablespoons olive oil
1/4 teaspoon pepper
1/2 teaspoon salt, optional
1/2 teaspoon sugar, optional

In a large salad bowl, combine the lettuce, onions, tomato, mushrooms and basil. In a jar with a tight-fitting lid, combine the vinegar, oil, pepper and salt and sugar if desired; shake well. Pour over the salad and toss to coat. Serve immediately. **Yield:** 6 servings.

Curly Endive Salad

4 cups torn curly endive, Belgian endive *and/or* escarole
1/4 cup chopped red onion
24 whole pimiento-stuffed olives
2 tablespoons olive oil
1 tablespoon red wine vinegar

3 tablespoons minced fresh oregano *or* 3 teaspoons dried oregano
1 tablespoon minced fresh mint *or* 1 teaspoon dried mint flakes
1/4 teaspoon salt
1/8 teaspoon pepper
2 ounces crumbled feta cheese

My wife grows herbs in our tiny city garden. I use oregano and mint to season this refreshing unique salad I created.

Roger Burch
Staten Island, New York

In a salad bowl, toss the endive, onion and olives. In a jar with a tight-fitting lid, combine the oil, vinegar, oregano, mint, salt and pepper; shake well. Drizzle over salad and toss to coat. Top with cheese. **Yield:** 4 servings.

Red Pepper Salad with Parsley Dressing

1/3 cup finely chopped onion
1/3 cup olive oil
1/4 cup minced fresh parsley
2 tablespoons red wine vinegar
2 tablespoons sour cream
1 teaspoon salt
1 teaspoon sugar
1/4 to 1/2 teaspoon pepper
6 cups torn Boston lettuce
2 cups watercress, stems removed
3-1/2 cups sliced fresh mushrooms
1 teaspoon lemon juice
2 large sweet red peppers, cut into 1-inch pieces

1. In a jar with a tight-fitting lid, combine the first eight ingredients; shake well. Refrigerate until serving.

2. In a salad bowl, combine the lettuce and watercress. Toss the mushrooms with lemon juice; add to greens. Top with red peppers. Drizzle with dressing; toss to coat. **Yield:** 8 servings.

A tangy sour cream dressing tops this colorful combination of veggies. I get rave reviews whenever I toss together this recipe.

Mary-Lynne Mason
Janesville, Wisconsin

Spinach Salad

1 pound fresh spinach, torn

1 can (14 ounces) bean sprouts, drained

1 can (8 ounces) sliced water chestnuts, drained, sliced

4 hard-cooked eggs, sliced

1/4 cup green onions, including tops, sliced

1/2 pound bacon, cooked and crumbled

1 cup fresh mushrooms, sliced

Dressing:

3/4 cup sugar

1/4 cup white vinegar

1/4 cup vegetable oil

1/3 cup ketchup

2 teaspoons salt

1 teaspoon Worcestershire sauce

There are so many people who turn up their noses at the mention of spinach. But not one person I've served this salad to has said they didn't like it. And it's so nutritious, too.

Linda McCoy
Greensburg, Indiana

In a large serving bowl, combine the first seven ingredients. For the dressing, in a jar with a tight-fitting lid, combine all the dressing ingredients; shake well. Just before serving, drizzle dressing over salad; toss until well coated. Serve immediately. **Yield:** 8 cups.

Watercress Dip

1 tablespoon lemon juice
1 tablespoon prepared
  horseradish
1 garlic clove, minced
1/2 teaspoon salt
1/4 teaspoon white pepper

1 bunch watercress,
  trimmed (about 6 cups)
4 green onions, cut into
  fourths
1 package (8 ounces)
  cream cheese, cubed
Tortilla chips

In a food processor or blender, combine the first seven ingredients; cover and process until finely chopped. Add cream cheese; process until creamy and blended. Refrigerate until serving. Serve with chips. **Yield:** 1-3/4 cups.

This dip is similar to mock guacamole. A bit of horseradish gives it some zip.

Taste of Home Test Kitchen
Greendale, Wisconsin

Wilted Endive Salad

2 bacon strips, diced
1 tablespoon olive oil
2 garlic cloves, minced
2 tablespoons finely
  chopped green onion
2 tablespoons tarragon
  vinegar

2 tablespoons minced fresh
  tarragon *or* 2 teaspoons
  dried tarragon
1 teaspoon salt
1/4 teaspoon pepper
1 bunch curly endive, torn
4 slices bread, cubed and
  toasted

1. In a skillet, cook bacon over medium heat until crisp. Using a slotted spoon, remove to paper towels to drain. Add oil to drippings; saute garlic and onion until tender. Stir in the vinegar, tarragon, salt and pepper.

2. In a large bowl, toss the endive, bread cubes and bacon. Pour the warm dressing over salad and serve immediately. **Yield:** 4-6 servings.

The blend of seasonings, greens and warm bacon dressing makes this salad a sure hit. My guess is that it'll be a favorite at your next gathering.

Mildred Davis
Hagerstown, Maryland

Sweet Potato Kale Soup

If you're looking for a healthier dish with a difference, try this one. White kidney beans, sweet potatoes, kale and plenty of garlic flavor this brothy blend. It's the perfect winter soup and has soothed me through many a cold.

Tamar Holmes
San Diego, California

4 ounces fresh kale
1 large onion, chopped
3-1/2 teaspoons Italian seasoning
2 teaspoons olive oil
3 cans (14-1/2 ounces *each*) vegetable broth

2 cans (15 ounces *each*) white kidney *or* cannellini beans, rinsed and drained
1 pound sweet potatoes, peeled and cubed
12 garlic cloves, minced
1/2 teaspoon salt
1/4 teaspoon pepper

1. Cut out and discard the thick vein from each kale leaf. Coarsely chop kale; set aside. In a large saucepan or Dutch oven, saute onion and Italian seasoning in oil until onion is tender.

2. Stir in the broth, beans, sweet potatoes and kale. Bring to a boil. Reduce heat; simmer, uncovered, for 10 minutes. Stir in the garlic, salt and pepper. Simmer 10-15 minutes longer or until potatoes are tender. **Yield:** 8 servings (2 quarts).

Orange-Onion Lettuce Salad

2 heads Bibb lettuce, torn
3 medium navel oranges, peeled and sectioned
1 small red onion, sliced and separated into rings
1/4 cup vegetable oil

2 tablespoons white vinegar
2 teaspoons sugar
2 teaspoons poppy seeds
1/8 teaspoon salt
Dash pepper

Attractive and a little different, this pretty salad is a standard for special occasions at our house.

Grace Yaskovic
Branchville, New Jersey

Arrange lettuce on six salad plates. Top with oranges and onion rings. In a small bowl, combine the remaining ingredients. Drizzle over salads; serve immediately. **Yield:** 6 servings.

Layered Ham And Spinach Salad

16 cups torn fresh spinach
1 teaspoon sugar
1 teaspoon pepper
1/4 teaspoon salt
6 hard-cooked eggs, chopped
1-1/2 cups cubed fully cooked ham
1 medium red onion, sliced
1 envelope ranch salad dressing mix
1-1/2 cups mayonnaise
1 cup (8 ounces) sour cream
2 cups (8 ounces) shredded Swiss cheese
1/2 pound sliced bacon, cooked and crumbled

1. Place two-thirds of the spinach in a 4-qt. salad bowl. Sprinkle with half of the sugar, pepper and salt. Top with eggs, ham and remaining spinach. Sprinkle with remaining sugar, pepper and salt. Arrange onion slices on top.

2. In a bowl, combine the dressing mix, mayonnaise and sour cream. Spread over onions. Sprinkle with cheese and bacon. Refrigerate until serving. **Yield:** 8-10 servings.

Here's a delicious salad that's sure to be a favorite with your family and friends. It's very easy to make.

Beverly Sprague
Baltimore, Maryland

Smoked Turkey and Apple Salad

5 tablespoons olive oil
2 tablespoons cider vinegar
1 tablespoon Dijon mustard
1 teaspoon lemon-pepper seasoning
1/2 teaspoon salt, optional

Salad:
1 bunch watercress *or* romaine, torn into bite-size pieces
1 medium carrot, julienned
10 cherry tomatoes, halved
8 ounces smoked turkey, julienned
4 unpeeled apples, sliced
1/3 cup chopped walnuts, toasted

An eye-catching dish, this refreshing salad is a great main course for a summer lunch or light dinner. The dressing's Dijon flavor goes nicely with the turkey, and the apples add crunch.

Carolyn Popwell
Lacey, Washington

Whisk together dressing ingredients; set aside. Just before serving, arrange salad greens on a platter or individual plates. Top with the carrot, tomatoes, turkey and apples. Drizzle dressing over salad; toss to coat. Sprinkle with walnuts. **Yield:** 8 servings.

Sausage Kale Soup

1 pound uncooked Italian
  sausage links
3/4 cup chopped onion
1 bacon strip, diced
2 garlic cloves, minced
2 cups water

1 can (14-1/2 ounces)
  chicken broth
2 cups diced potatoes
2 cups thinly sliced fresh
  kale
1/3 cup heavy whipping
  cream

1. Place the sausages in an ungreased 15-in. x 10-in. x 1-in. baking pan; pierce casings. Bake at 325° for 15-20 minutes or until fully cooked. Drain; set aside to cool.

2. Meanwhile, in a saucepan, saute onion and bacon for 3 minutes or until onion is tender. Add garlic; saute for 1 minute. Add the water, broth and potatoes; bring to a boil. Reduce heat; cover and simmer for 20 minutes or until potatoes are tender.

3. Cut sausages in half lengthwise, then into 1/4-in. slices. Add the kale, cream and sausage to soup; heat through (do not boil). **Yield:** 8 servings (2 quarts).

This zesty Italian soup is sure to become a favorite with your guests—just as it has with mine. The spicier the seasoning in the sausage, the better the soup.

Nancy Dyer
Grover, Oklahoma

Washing and Storing Lettuce & Greens

Remove and discard any brown, wilted or damaged outer leaves. Cut off or out core. Separate leaves, except for iceberg.

For sandy, gritty greens, such as arugula or escarole, swish leaves in a sink or bowl of cold water, then lift and allow the sand and grit to sink to the bottom. Repeat in clean water if necessary. Rinse other greens gently in cool water.

Pat greens dry with a clean towel or paper towel. Store in a covered container or plastic bag and refrigerate for at least 30 minutes before serving to crisp the greens. Place a piece of paper towel in the bottom of the container or bag to absorb excess moisture. Store in the refrigerator crisper drawer for about 1 week.

White Beans and Spinach

8 cups torn fresh spinach
2 tablespoons water
2 garlic cloves, minced
1/4 teaspoon salt

Dash cayenne pepper
Dash ground nutmeg
3/4 cup white kidney *or* cannellini beans, rinsed and drained

In a large skillet, combine the spinach, water and garlic; cover and cook over medium heat for 3 minutes or until tender, stirring occasionally. Sprinkle with the salt, cayenne and nutmeg. Gently stir in beans; heat through. **Yield:** 2 servings.

Tomato Spinach Soup

2 large yellow onions, cubed
2 tablespoons olive oil
1 can (28 ounces) diced tomatoes, undrained
1 quart water
4 beef bouillon cubes
1 cup sliced fresh mushrooms

3/4 teaspoon Italian seasoning
1/2 teaspoon dried basil
1/2 teaspoon salt
1/8 teaspoon pepper
4 cups loosely packed spinach leaves
Grated Parmesan *or* shredded cheddar cheese, optional

In a Dutch oven, saute onions in oil over medium heat for 10 minutes or until tender. Add the next eight ingredients; bring to a boil. Reduce heat; cover and simmer for 30 minutes. Stir in spinach; simmer for 3-5 minutes or until tender. Garnish individual servings with cheese if desired. **Yield:** 8-10 servings (2-1/2 quarts).

White Beans with Rigatoni

- 8 ounces rigatoni *or* large tube pasta
- 1/2 cup chopped onion
- 1 garlic clove, minced
- 1 tablespoon olive oil
- 1 package (8 ounces) sliced fresh mushrooms
- 1 can (15 ounces) white kidney *or* cannellini beans, rinsed and drained
- 1 can (14-1/2 ounces) diced tomatoes, undrained
- 2 tablespoons minced fresh sage
- 1/2 teaspoon salt
- 1/4 teaspoon pepper
- 2 cups chopped kale
- 1/4 cup shredded Parmesan cheese

1. Cook pasta according to package directions. In a large saucepan, saute onion and garlic in oil until tender. Stir in the mushrooms; cook about 5 minutes longer or until mushrooms are almost tender.

2. Stir in the beans, tomatoes, sage, salt and pepper. Bring to a boil. Reduce heat; simmer, uncovered, for 5 minutes. Stir in the kale. Return to boil. Cover and cook for 3-4 minutes or until kale is wilted and tender. Drain pasta; add to bean mixture and heat through. Sprinkle with Parmesan cheese.
Yield: 5 servings.

My husband and I are fans of canned beans...especially when they're combined with pasta. This quick-to-fix recipe makes a wonderful after-work meal served with whole wheat rolls and a salad with light vinaigrette dressing.

Carol Gaus
Itasca, Illinois

Grilled Chicken Over Spinach

1 to 2 tablespoons olive oil
1 tablespoon cider vinegar
1 garlic clove, minced
1 teaspoon dried thyme
1/2 teaspoon dried oregano
1/2 teaspoon cayenne pepper
1/4 teaspoon salt
Dash pepper
4 boneless skinless chicken breast halves (1 pound)

Sauteed Spinach:
1 green onion, finely chopped
1 to 2 garlic cloves, minced
1 to 2 tablespoons olive oil
1/2 pound fresh mushrooms, sliced
1 package (10 ounces) fresh spinach, torn

I find with two young children to keep me busy, it's essential to have a few "ready-in-minutes" meals. This is a recipe I've pieced together and added my own touches to. It really satisfies my family.

Michelle Krzmarzick
Redondo Beach, California

1. In a bowl, combine the first eight ingredients. Spoon over chicken. Grill, uncovered, over medium heat for 7 minutes on each side or until juices run clear.

2. In a large skillet, saute onion and garlic in oil for 1 minute. Stir in mushrooms; saute for 3-4 minutes or until tender. Add spinach; saute for 2 minutes or until wilted. Transfer to a serving platter; top with chicken. **Yield:** 4 servings.

Popeye Special

1 pound ground beef
1/2 pound fresh mushrooms, sliced
1/2 pound fresh spinach, torn
6 green onions, sliced
1/4 cup chopped celery
1/4 cup chopped sweet red pepper
1 teaspoon garlic salt
1/2 teaspoon pepper
6 eggs, beaten

In a large skillet, cook beef and mushrooms over medium heat until meat is no longer pink; drain. Add the spinach, onions, celery, red pepper, garlic salt and pepper. Cook and stir for 1 minute. Add eggs; cook and stir just until the eggs are set. Serve immediately. **Yield:** 4-6 servings.

This recipe is a family favorite that I created—and named—myself. The spinach packs it with a real "Popeye punch," and the other vegetables combined with the ground beef make it a hearty meal.

Marcy Cella
L'Anse, Michigan

Spinach Artichoke Pie

3 tablespoons vegetable oil, *divided*
1/4 cup dry bread crumbs
1/2 pound fresh mushrooms, sliced
1 pound fresh spinach, chopped and cooked
1 jar (6-1/2 ounces) marinated artichoke hearts, drained and quartered
1 cup day-old bread cubes
1-1/4 cups shredded cheddar cheese, *divided*
1 jar (4 ounces) diced pimientos, drained
2 eggs, beaten
1/4 to 1/2 teaspoon garlic powder

1. Brush the bottom and sides of a 9-in. pie plate with 2 tablespoons oil; sprinkle with bread crumbs. Set aside. In a skillet, saute mushrooms in remaining oil; drain. Remove from the heat. Squeeze spinach dry; add to mushrooms. Stir in the artichokes, bread cubes, 1 cup of cheese, pimientos, eggs and garlic powder; stir well.

2. Spoon into the prepared pie plate. Bake, uncovered, at 350° for 30 minutes. Sprinkle with remaining cheese. Bake 5-10 minutes longer or until the cheese is melted. Let stand for 10 minutes before cutting. **Yield:** 6-8 servings.

Spinach is an abundant vegetable grown here in our state. I make this side dish often when that popular green is in season.

Lori Coleman
Glassboro, New Jersey

Potatoes

Parmesan Potato Soup, p. 158

Creamy Potato Salad

Mildly seasoned with onion and dill, Mom's delightfully different potato salad is pretty, too, with the red potatoes left unpeeled. Of course, that also means it's quicker to make than traditional potato salad!

Pat Cole
Polebridge, Montana

7-1/2 cups cubed red potatoes (about 2-1/2 pounds)
1 hard-cooked egg, chopped
3 celery ribs, chopped
3/4 cup chopped onion
2 tablespoons finely chopped green pepper
3/4 cup mayonnaise
1/4 cup sour cream
1 to 1-1/2 teaspoons salt
1/4 teaspoon pepper
1/8 to 1/4 teaspoon dill weed
Sliced hard-cooked egg, paprika and fresh dill sprigs, optional

1. Place potatoes in a large saucepan or Dutch oven; cover with water. Bring to a boil. Reduce heat; cover and cook for 20-30 minutes or until tender. Drain and cool.

2. Place potatoes in a large bowl. Add the chopped egg, celery, onion and green pepper. In a small bowl, combine the mayonnaise, sour cream, salt, pepper and dill. Pour over potato mixture; toss gently to coat. Cover and refrigerate until serving. Garnish with egg, paprika and dill if desired. **Yield:** 12 servings.

Red, White and Green Salad

1 pound small red potatoes, cooked and cubed
2 large tomatoes, diced
1 pound green beans, cut into 2-inch pieces and cooked
7 tablespoons olive oil
5 tablespoons white wine vinegar
3/4 teaspoon salt
1/2 teaspoon pepper

This is a great summertime salad—crisp, refreshing...and easy to prepare! Try it at your next family picnic.

Jodie McCoy
Tulsa, Oklahoma

In a large bowl, combine the potatoes, tomatoes and beans. In a small bowl, combine the oil, vinegar, salt and pepper. Pour dressing over vegetables; toss to coat. Refrigerate for several hours before serving. **Yield:** 8-10 servings.

Baked German Potato Salad

12 medium red potatoes
  (about 3 pounds)
8 bacon strips
2 medium onions, chopped
3/4 cup packed brown sugar
1/3 cup cider vinegar
1/3 cup sweet pickle juice
2/3 cup water, *divided*
2 teaspoons dried parsley
  flakes
1 teaspoon salt
1/2 to 3/4 teaspoon celery
  seed
4-1/2 teaspoons all-purpose
  flour

1. Place potatoes in a large saucepan and cover with water. Bring to a boil. Reduce heat; cover and cook for 15-30 minutes or until tender. Drain and cool slightly. Peel and slice into an ungreased 2-qt. baking dish; set aside.

2. In a skillet, cook bacon over medium heat until crisp. Remove to paper towels; drain, reserving 2 tablespoons drippings. Crumble bacon and set aside. Saute onions in drippings until tender. Stir in the brown sugar, vinegar, pickle juice, 1/2 cup water, parsley, salt and celery seed. Simmer, uncovered, for 5-10 minutes.

3. Meanwhile, combine flour and remaining water until smooth; stir into onion mixture. Bring to a boil; cook and stir for 2 minutes or until thickened. Pour over potatoes. Add bacon; gently stir to coat. Bake, uncovered, at 350° for 30 minutes or until heated through. **Yield:** 8-10 servings.

What makes this German potato salad so different is that it's sweet instead of tangy. During the holidays, my family has an annual ham dinner, and I always prepare it. The tastes blend very well.

Julie Myers
Lexington, Ohio

Parmesan Potato Soup

4 medium baking potatoes
(about 2 pounds)
3/4 cup chopped onion
1/2 cup butter, cubed
1/2 cup all-purpose flour
1/2 teaspoon dried basil
1/2 teaspoon seasoned salt
1/4 teaspoon celery salt
1/4 teaspoon garlic powder
1/4 teaspoon onion salt
1/4 teaspoon pepper
1/4 teaspoon rubbed sage
1/4 teaspoon dried thyme
4-1/2 cups chicken broth
6 cups milk
3/4 to 1 cup grated Parmesan
cheese
10 bacon strips, cooked and
crumbled

Even my husband, who's not much of a soup eater, likes this. Our two boys do, too. With homemade bread and a salad, it's a satisfying meal.

Tami Walters
Kingsport, Tennessee

1. Pierce potatoes with a fork; bake in the oven or microwave until tender. Cool, peel and cube; set aside.

2. In a large Dutch oven, saute onion in butter until tender. Stir in flour and seasonings until blended. Gradually add broth, stirring constantly. Bring to a boil; cook and stir for 2 minutes or until thickened. Add potatoes; return to a boil. Reduce heat; cover and simmer for 10 minutes. Reduce heat; add milk and cheese, stirring until cheese is melted. Heat through. Stir in bacon. **Yield:** 10-12 servings.

No-Sprout Solution

To keep potatoes from sprouting before using them, place an apple in the bag with the potatoes.

Sweet Potato Salad

3 pounds sweet potatoes, cooked, peeled and cubed
1/2 cup chopped onion
1 cup chopped sweet red pepper
1-1/4 cups mayonnaise
1-1/2 teaspoons salt
1/2 teaspoon pepper
1/4 teaspoon hot pepper sauce

In a large bowl, combine the sweet potatoes, onion and red pepper. In a small bowl, blend remaining ingredients; add to potato mixture and toss to coat. Cover and refrigerate. **Yield:** 10-12 servings.

My mother used to make this potato salad. We all liked it back then—and now my family likes it, too!

Mrs. Willard Wilson
Woodsfield, Ohio

Potato Tossed Salad

1/2 cup olive oil
2 tablespoons lemon juice
2 teaspoons dried oregano
1 garlic clove, minced
1/4 teaspoon salt
1/2 pound small red potatoes, cooked, peeled and sliced
6 cups torn mixed salad greens
2 small tomatoes, cut into wedges
1 small cucumber, thinly sliced
1 small red onion, thinly sliced into rings
1/2 cup crumbled feta cheese

1. In a small bowl, whisk together the first five ingredients. Add potatoes and toss gently. Cover and refrigerate for 1 hour. Drain, reserving dressing.

2. Place salad greens in a large bowl. Arrange the tomatoes, cucumber, onion, cheese and potatoes on top. Drizzle with the reserved dressing. **Yield:** 8 servings.

Instead of serving potato salad plus a tossed salad, I combine the two into one unique and colorful recipe that's met with many compliments. The red potatoes take on added flavor as they marinate.

Priscilla Weaver
Hagerstown, Maryland

Au Gratin Potatoes

12 medium red *or* white potatoes, unpeeled
1 teaspoon salt
1/2 teaspoon pepper

1/2 teaspoon garlic *or* onion salt
2 cups (8 ounces) shredded cheddar cheese
1 cup heavy whipping cream

1. Place potatoes in a large saucepan and cover with water. Bring to a boil. Reduce heat; cover and cook for 30-40 minutes or until tender. Drain and refrigerate several hours or overnight.

2. Peel potatoes and coarsely shred. Combine the salt, pepper and garlic salt. In a greased 13-in. x 9-in. x 2-in. baking dish, layer potatoes and salt mixture. Sprinkle with cheese; pour cream over all. Bake, uncovered, at 350° for 1 hour or until golden. **Yield:** 12-15 servings.

Taco Tater Skins

6 large russet potatoes
1/2 cup butter, melted
2 tablespoons taco seasoning
1 cup (4 ounces) shredded cheddar cheese

15 bacon strips, cooked and crumbled
3 green onions, chopped
Salsa *and/or* sour cream, optional

1. Pierce potatoes several times with a fork. Bake potatoes at 375° for 1 hour or until tender. Reduce heat to 350°. When cool enough to handle, cut the potatoes lengthwise into quarters. Scoop out pulp, leaving a 1/4-in. shell (save pulp for another use).

2. Combine the butter and taco seasoning; brush over both sides of potato skins. Place skin side down on a greased baking sheet. Sprinkle with the cheese, bacon and onions.

3. Bake for 5-10 minutes or until the cheese is melted. Serve with salsa and/or sour cream if desired. **Yield:** 2 dozen.

Potato Dumplings

5 to 6 medium potatoes

5 tablespoons all-purpose flour

1 egg, beaten

1-1/2 teaspoons salt

1/4 teaspoon ground nutmeg

2 slices white bread, toasted

1/3 cup mashed potato flakes, optional

Melted butter and toasted bread crumbs, optional

1. Place potatoes in a large saucepan and cover with salted water. Bring to a boil. Reduce heat; cover and cook for 15-30 minutes or just until tender. Drain and refrigerate for 2 hours or overnight.

2. Peel and grate potatoes. In a bowl, combine the flour, egg, salt and nutmeg. Add potatoes and mix until a stiff batter is formed, adding additional flour if necessary. Slice toasted bread into 24 squares, 1/2-in. each; shape 2 tablespoons of the potato mixture around two bread squares, forming a 2-in. ball.

3. In a large kettle, bring salted water to a boil; add the test dumpling. Reduce heat; cover and simmer for 15-20 minutes or until dumpling is no longer sticky in the center.

4. If test dumpling falls apart during cooking, add the mashed potato flakes to the batter. Let batter sit for 5 minutes; form remaining dumplings. Add to boiling water; return to a boil and follow the same cooking procedure.

5. Remove dumplings with a slotted spoon to a serving bowl. If desired, drizzle with butter and sprinkle with crumbs. **Yield:** 6-8 servings.

These moist dumplings are an extra-special way to serve potatoes. The bread centers add a comforting touch, and the potato taste really comes through.

Karin Cousineau
Burlington, North Carolina

Swiss Potato Squares

8 medium russet potatoes (about 3 pounds), peeled and cubed
1/3 cup butter, melted
1 tablespoon minced fresh parsley
1-1/2 teaspoons salt
1/4 teaspoon pepper
1-1/2 cups cubed Swiss cheese
1 cup cubed fully cooked ham
1 small onion, grated
1 teaspoon garlic powder
3 eggs
1/2 cup milk
Paprika

To vary these squares, you can substitute cheddar cheese for the Swiss or Canadian bacon for the ham. How ever you make them, they taste wonderful reheated in the microwave. So you can serve the squares warm as leftovers, pack them in a thermal lunch carrier or put them on a potluck table.

Nancy Foust
Stoneboro, Pennsylvania

1. Place potatoes in a large saucepan and cover with water. Bring to a boil. Reduce heat; cover and cook for 20-25 minutes or until very tender. Drain well. Mash with the butter, parsley, salt and pepper.

2. Spread about 4 cups of the potato mixture onto the bottom and up the sides of a greased 8-in. square baking dish. Combine the cheese, ham, onion and garlic powder; spoon into potato shell. Combine eggs and milk; pour over all. Top with remaining potato mixture. Sprinkle with paprika.

3. Bake, uncovered, at 400° for 45-50 minutes or until golden. Let stand for 5 minutes before cutting. **Yield:** 8-9 servings.

Whiter Potatoes

To prevent potatoes from darkening when boiling, add a small amount of milk to the water.

Gourmet Potato Soup With Croutons

3 cups diced peeled potatoes
1/2 cup diced celery
1/2 cup diced onion
1 chicken bouillon cube
  or 1 teaspoon chicken
  bouillon granules
1-1/2 cups water
2 cups milk
1 cup (8 ounces) sour cream
1 tablespoon all-purpose
  flour
1 tablespoon minced fresh
  chives

Croutons:
8 cups cubed day-old French
  bread (1-1/2-inch pieces)
Oil for deep-frying
1/2 cup grated Parmesan
  cheese
1 tablespoon minced fresh
  parsley
1/2 teaspoon paprika
1/2 teaspoon garlic salt
1/4 teaspoon pepper

During the long Wisconsin winters, my family lives on homemade soups because they are economical and freeze well. And, as with most soups, this one is even better the next day.

Sherrie Pfister
Hollandale, Wisconsin

1. In a Dutch oven, cook the potatoes, celery, onion and bouillon in water until vegetables are tender, about 20 minutes. Add milk. In a bowl, combine sour cream and flour. Blend in 1/2 cup of hot soup; stir into pan. Add chives and simmer just until thickened.

2. Meanwhile, for croutons, heat oil in a deep-fat fryer to 375°. Fry bread cubes, a few at a time, until golden brown. Drain on paper towel.

3. In a medium bowl, combine the remaining ingredients. Add croutons and toss to coat. Ladle soup into bowls and top with croutons. **Yield:** 6-8 servings (2 quarts).

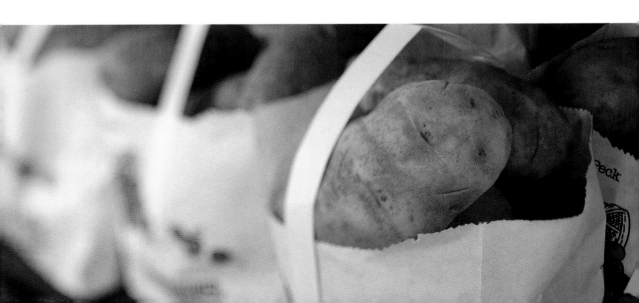

Spiced Potatoes

Red pepper flakes give a little zip to this buttery potato dish. It's especially good with fresh fish.

Mary Fitch
Lakewood, Colorado

6 to 8 medium unpeeled red potatoes, sliced
1/2 cup butter, melted
1 tablespoon dried oregano

1 garlic clove, minced
1/2 teaspoon crushed red pepper flakes

1. Place potatoes in an ungreased 11-in. x 7-in. x 2-in. baking dish. Combine the butter, oregano, garlic and red pepper flakes; pour over potatoes.

2. Bake, uncovered, at 450° for 30 minutes or until potatoes are tender, stirring every 10 minutes. **Yield:** 4-6 servings.

Grilled Three-Cheese Potatoes

6 large potatoes, sliced 1/4 inch thick
2 medium onions, chopped
1/3 cup grated Parmesan cheese
1 cup (4 ounces) shredded sharp cheddar cheese, *divided*
1 cup (4 ounces) shredded part-skim mozzarella cheese, *divided*

1 pound sliced bacon, cooked and crumbled
1/4 cup butter, cubed
1 tablespoon minced chives
1 to 2 teaspoons seasoned salt
1/2 teaspoon pepper

While this is delicious grilled, I've also cooked it in the oven at 350° for an hour. Add cubed ham to it and you can serve it as a full-meal main dish.

Margaret Hanson-Maddox
Montpelier, Indiana

1. Divide the potatoes and onions equally between two pieces of heavy-duty foil (about 18 in. square) coated with nonstick cooking spray.

2. Combine Parmesan cheese and 3/4 cup each cheddar and mozzarella; sprinkle over potatoes and onions. Top with the bacon, butter, chives, seasoned salt and pepper. Bring opposite ends of foil together over filling and fold down several times. Fold unsealed ends toward filling and crimp tightly.

3. Grill, covered, over medium heat for 35-40 minutes or until potatoes are tender. Remove from the grill. Open foil carefully and sprinkle with remaining cheeses. **Yield:** 6-8 servings.

Potato Frittata

4 medium potatoes,
   peeled, quartered and
   sliced
1 cup chopped onion
1 medium green pepper,
   chopped
1 to 2 tablespoons
   vegetable oil
3/4 cup diced fully cooked
   ham *or* cooked bulk pork
   sausage
10 eggs
1 teaspoon paprika
Salt and pepper to taste
3 slices process American
   cheese, cut diagonally

1. In a large skillet, saute the potatoes, onion and green pepper in oil until potatoes are tender. Add the meat and heat through. In a bowl, beat eggs, paprika, salt and pepper. Pour over potato mixture. Do not stir. Cover and cook over medium-low heat for 10-15 minutes or until eggs are nearly set.

2. Broil 6 in. from the heat for 2 minutes or until top is lightly browned. Arrange cheese slices on top; let stand for 5 minutes before serving. **Yield:** 6-8 servings.

Years ago, I took a trip to Spain to visit my nephew who was in the Air Force. While touring the small towns and villages, we could always buy a fresh slice of potato frittata. It was so tasty and filling, I just had to make my own version of it when I returned home!

Helen Clavelouix
Newark, Delaware

Waste Not, Want Not

When it's time to use up potatoes, prepare a huge batch of mashed potatoes and freeze individual portions. They're a quick addition to any meal with no waste.

Pleasing Potato Pizza

3 **large potatoes, peeled and cubed**

1 **tube (10 ounces) refrigerated pizza crust**

1/4 **cup milk**

1/2 **teaspoon salt**

1 **pound sliced bacon, diced**

1 **large onion, chopped**

1/2 **cup chopped sweet red pepper**

1-1/2 **cups (6 ounces) shredded cheddar cheese**

1-1/2 **cups (6 ounces) shredded part-skim mozzarella cheese**

Sour cream, optional

I first heard of this delicious and distinctive pizza when a friend tried it at a restaurant. It sounded great so I experimented to come up with my own recipe. The way the slices disappear, there's no doubt about their popularity. Guests are always excited when my potato pizza is on the menu.

Barbara Zimmer
Wanless, Manitoba

1. Place potatoes in a saucepan and cover with water. Bring to a boil. Reduce heat; cover and cook for 20-25 minutes or until very tender.

2. Meanwhile, unroll the pizza crust onto an ungreased 14-in. pizza pan; flatten dough and build up edges slightly. Prick dough several times with a fork. Bake at 350° for 15 minutes or until lightly browned. Cool on a wire rack.

3. Drain potatoes and transfer to a mixing bowl. Mash with milk and salt until smooth. Spread over crust. In a skillet, partially cook the bacon over medium heat. Add onion and red pepper; cook until bacon is crisp and vegetables are tender. Using a slotted spoon, remove to paper towels and drain well. Sprinkle over potatoes. Top with cheeses. Bake at 375° for 20 minutes or until cheese is melted. Serve with sour cream if desired. **Yield:** 8 slices.

Bacon Potato Pancakes

5 to 6 medium uncooked red potatoes, peeled and shredded (about 3 cups)
5 bacon strips, cooked and crumbled
1/2 cup chopped onion
2 eggs, beaten
2 tablespoons all-purpose flour
Salt and pepper to taste
Dash ground nutmeg
Oil for frying

1. Rinse and thoroughly drain potatoes. In a bowl, combine the potatoes, bacon, onion, eggs, flour, salt, pepper and nutmeg.

2. In an electric skillet, heat 1/8 in. of oil to 375°. Drop batter by 2 heaping tablespoonfuls into hot oil. Flatten to form patties. Fry until golden brown; turn and cook the other side. Drain on paper towels. **Yield:** 2 dozen.

Potatoes are something I can eat anytime of day and almost any way. This recipe's one I came up with to go along with pigs in blankets several years ago.

Linda Hall
Hazel Green, Wisconsin

Two-Toned Baked Potatoes

6 medium russet potatoes
6 medium sweet potatoes
2/3 cup sour cream, *divided*
1/3 cup milk
3/4 cup shredded cheddar cheese
4 tablespoons minced chives, *divided*
1-1/2 teaspoons salt, *divided*

1. Pierce russet and sweet potatoes several times with a fork. Bake at 400° for 60-70 minutes or until tender. Set sweet potatoes aside.

2. Cut a third off the top of each russet potato; scoop out pulp, leaving skins intact. Place pulp in a bowl; mash with 1/3 cup sour cream, milk, cheese, 2 tablespoons chives and 3/4 teaspoon salt. Set aside.

3. Cut off the tip of each sweet potato; scoop out pulp, leaving skins intact. Mash pulp with remaining sour cream, chives and salt. Stuff mixture into half of each potato skin; spoon russet potato filling into other half. Place on a baking sheet. Bake at 350° for 15-20 minutes or until heated through. **Yield:** 12 servings.

This recipe is doubly wonderful as far as spud lovers are concerned. I have a reputation for trying out new recipes. Everyone is glad I took a chance on this one.

Sherree Stahn
Central City, Nebraska

Cranberry Sweet Potato Muffins

1-1/2 cups all-purpose flour
  1/2 cup sugar
    2 teaspoons baking powder
  3/4 teaspoon salt
  1/2 teaspoon ground
    cinnamon
  1/2 teaspoon ground nutmeg
    1 egg

  1/2 cup milk
  1/2 cup cold mashed sweet
    potatoes (without added
    butter *or* milk)
  1/4 cup butter, melted
    1 cup chopped fresh *or*
    frozen cranberries
Cinnamon-sugar

1. In a bowl, combine the flour, sugar, baking powder, salt, cinnamon and nutmeg. In a small bowl, combine the egg, milk, sweet potatoes and butter; stir into dry ingredients just until moistened. Fold in cranberries.

2. Fill greased or paper-lined muffin cups half full. Sprinkle with cinnamon-sugar. Bake at 375° for 18-22 minutes or until a toothpick comes out clean. Cool in pan 10 minutes before removing to a wire rack. **Yield:** 1 dozen.

Bold autumn flavors of sweet potatoes, cranberries and cinnamon give seasonal appeal to these golden muffins. I recommended them for a change-of-pace treat with a meal, packed into a lunch box or as a snack.

Diane Musil
Lyons, Illinois

Sweet Potato Dessert Squares

1 package (18-1/4 ounces) yellow cake mix, *divided*

1/2 cup butter, melted

1 egg, beaten

Filling:

3 cups cold mashed sweet potatoes (without added milk *or* butter)

2/3 cup milk

1/2 cup packed brown sugar

2 eggs, beaten

1 tablespoon pumpkin pie spice

Topping:

6 tablespoons cold butter

1 cup chopped pecans

1/4 cup sugar

1 teaspoon ground cinnamon

Whipped cream and pecan halves, optional

1. Set aside 1 cup of the cake mix. Combine remaining mix with butter and egg; spread into a greased 13-in. x 9-in. x 2-in. baking pan. Whisk filling ingredients until smooth; pour over crust.

2. For topping, cut butter into reserved cake mix until crumbly. Stir in the pecans, sugar and cinnamon; sprinkle over the filling. Bake at 350° for 60-65 minutes or until a knife inserted near the center comes out clean. Cool. Garnish with whipped cream and pecan halves if desired. **Yield:** 16 servings.

I prepare sweet potatoes every week for my family, mostly as a side dish. But I've found this vegetable also makes desserts even more delightful. These moist, rich squares have a great pecan crunch.

Betty Janway
Ruston, Louisiana

Mashed Potato Cinnamon Rolls

1/2 pound russet potatoes, peeled and quartered
2 packages (1/4 ounce *each*) active dry yeast
2 tablespoons plus 3/4 cup sugar, *divided*
2 cups warm water (110° to 115°)
3/4 cup butter, melted
2 eggs, beaten
3/4 cup sugar
2/3 cup nonfat dry milk powder
1 tablespoon salt
2 teaspoons vanilla extract
8 cups all-purpose flour

Filling:
1/2 cup butter, melted
3/4 cup packed brown sugar
3 tablespoons ground cinnamon

Icing:
2 cups confectioners' sugar
1/4 cup milk
2 tablespoons butter, melted
1/2 teaspoon vanilla extract

A neighbor gave me the recipe for these yummy rolls. They're warm and wonderful to serve for breakfast or as a treat any time of day. I often make extra mashed potatoes with these cinnamon rolls in mind.

Christine Duncan
Ellensburg, Washington

1. Place potatoes in a saucepan and cover with water. Bring to a boil. Reduce heat; cover and cook for 15-20 minutes or until tender. Drain, reserving 1/2 cup cooking liquid; set aside. Mash potatoes; set aside 1 cup. (Save remaining potatoes for another use.)

2. Heat reserved potato liquid to 110°-115°. In a large mixing bowl, dissolve yeast and 2 tablespoons sugar in potato liquid; let stand for 5 minutes. Add warm water, mashed potatoes, butter, eggs, sugar, milk powder, salt, vanilla and 5 cups flour; beat until smooth. Stir in enough remaining flour to form a soft dough.

3. Turn onto a floured surface; knead until smooth and elastic, about 6-8 minutes. Place in a greased bowl; turn once to grease top. Cover and refrigerate overnight.

4. Punch dough down. Turn onto a lightly floured surface; roll each portion into a 12-in. x 8-in. rectangle. Spread butter over dough to within 1/2 in. of edges. Combine brown sugar and cinnamon; sprinkle over the dough.

5. Roll up jelly-roll style, starting with a long side; pinch seams to seal. Cut each into 12 slices; place cut side down in three greased 13-in. x 9-in. x 2-in. baking pans. Cover and let rise until almost doubled, about 45 minutes.

6. Bake at 350° for 25-30 minutes. Combine icing ingredients; drizzle over rolls. **Yield:** 3 dozen.

Fried Sweet Potato Pies

4-1/2 cups self-rising flour
3 tablespoons sugar
1/2 cup shortening
2 eggs
1 cup milk

Filling:
3 cups mashed sweet potatoes
2 cups sugar

3 eggs, lightly beaten
1 can (5 ounces) evaporated milk
1/4 cup butter, melted
3 tablespoons all-purpose flour
1 teaspoon vanilla extract
Oil for frying
Confectioners' sugar, optional

1. In a bowl, combine flour and sugar; cut in shortening until mixture resembles coarse crumbs. Combine eggs and milk; add to crumb mixture, tossing with a fork until a ball forms. Cover and chill several hours.

2. In a large bowl, combine the sweet potatoes, sugar, eggs, milk, butter, flour and vanilla; stir until smooth. Divide the dough into 25 portions. On a floured surface, roll each portion into a 5-in. circle. Spoon 2 tablespoons of filling on half of each circle. Moisten edges with water; fold dough over filling and press edges with a fork to seal. Prick tops with a fork 4-5 times.

3. In an electric skillet, heat 1/2 in. of oil to 375°. Fry pies, a few at a time, for 1 minute on each side or until golden brown. Drain on paper towels. Dust with confectioners' sugar if desired. Store in the refrigerator. **Yield:** 25 pies.

Editor's Note: As a substitute for each cup of self-rising flour, place 1-1/2 teaspoons baking powder and 1/2 teaspoon salt in a measuring cup. Add all-purpose flour to measure 1 cup. For 1/2 cup self-rising flour, place 3/4 teaspoon baking powder and 1/4 teaspoon salt in a 1/2 cup measuring cup. Add all-purpose flour to measure 1/2 cup.

With my dad being a farmer who grew them, sweet potatoes have graced our table for as long as I can recall. These, though, resulted from an experiment at a church bake sale when we had excess pastry. People couldn't get enough!

Marilyn Moseley
Toccoa, Georgia

Rhubarb

Strawberry Rhubarb Sauce, p.176

Rhubarb Steak Sauce

When the aroma of this sauce cooking wafts through the house, my family can't wait to grill steaks! I freeze this sauce in plastic containers and keep some refrigerated ready for use. I not only use it on meat, but I'll also add a dash or two to some soup recipes.

Rose Mundle
Gleichen, Alberta

8 cups chopped fresh *or* frozen rhubarb
4 cups chopped onion
2 cups cider vinegar
2-1/3 cups packed brown sugar

1 teaspoon ground cinnamon
1 teaspoon ground allspice
1/2 teaspoon ground cloves
1 teaspoon salt
1/2 teaspoon pepper

In a large saucepan or Dutch oven, combine all the ingredients. Bring to a boil. Reduce heat and simmer for 1 hour or until thickened, stirring occasionally. Cool. Refrigerate in covered containers. **Yield:** about 7 cups.

Spinach Salad with Rhubarb Dressing

2 cups chopped fresh *or* frozen rhubarb
1/2 cup sugar
1/4 cup cider vinegar
3/4 cup vegetable oil
3 tablespoons grated onion
1-1/2 teaspoons Worcestershire sauce
1/2 teaspoon salt

Salad:
6 cups torn fresh spinach
6 bacon strips, cooked and crumbled
1/2 cup fresh bean sprouts
1/2 cup shredded cheddar cheese
1 to 2 hard-cooked eggs, chopped

Spinach salad is excellent with this tangy topping. It really perks it up. A friend shared a similar salad dressing recipe with me, which I modified a bit. The rhubarb adds rosy color and mouth-watering flavor.

Twila Mitchell
Lindsborg, Kansas

1. In a saucepan, combine the rhubarb, sugar and vinegar; cook over medium heat until the rhubarb is tender, about 6 minutes. Drain, reserving about 6 tablespoons juice; discard pulp.

2. Pour juice into a jar with a tight-fitting lid; add oil, onion, Worcestershire sauce and salt. Shake well. Refrigerate for at least 1 hour. Just before serving, combine salad ingredients in a large bowl. Add the dressing and toss to coat. **Yield:** 6-8 servings.

Rhubarb Chutney

3/4 cup sugar

1/3 cup cider vinegar

1 tablespoon minced garlic

1 teaspoon ground cumin

1 tablespoon minced fresh gingerroot

1/2 teaspoon ground cinnamon

1/4 to 1/2 teaspoon ground cloves

1/4 teaspoon crushed red pepper flakes

4 cups coarsely chopped fresh *or* frozen rhubarb, thawed

1/2 cup chopped red onion

1/3 cup golden raisins

1 teaspoon red food coloring, optional

1. In a large saucepan, combine the sugar, vinegar, garlic, cumin, ginger, cinnamon, cloves and red pepper flakes. Bring to a boil. Reduce heat; simmer, uncovered, for 2 minutes or until sugar is dissolved.

2. Add the rhubarb, onion and raisins. Cook and stir over medium heat for 5-10 minutes or until rhubarb is tender and mixture is slightly thickened. Stir in food coloring if desired. Cool completely. Store in the refrigerator. **Yield:** about 3 cups.

It's always fun to serve a meat or poultry dish with a twist. This tangy-sweet chutney is a wonderfully different garnish. With fine chunks of rhubarb and raisins, it has a nice consistency. It's among our favorite condiments.

Jan Paterson
Anchorage, Alaska

Young vs. Old

Tender, young rhubarb stalks are the easiest to use. They only need to be cut before cooking. Rhubarb with tougher stalks can be peeled with a vegetable peeler to remove fibrous string before they are cut or cooked.

Strawberry Rhubarb Sauce

2-1/2 cups chopped fresh *or* frozen rhubarb (1-inch pieces)
  1 cup water
1/2 cup sugar
  2 tablespoons grated lemon peel
1/4 teaspoon salt
  1 cup sliced fresh *or* frozen unsweetened strawberries
  2 tablespoons lemon juice
1/4 teaspoon ground cinnamon
  3 to 4 drops red food coloring, optional
Pound *or* angel food cake

This versatile sauce brings a sunny new taste to pound cake, ice cream and bread pudding.

Mary Pittman
Shawnee, Kansas

In a saucepan, combine the rhubarb, water, sugar, lemon peel and salt; bring to a boil. Reduce heat; cook, uncovered, for 10-15 minutes or until rhubarb is soft. Remove from the heat and let stand for 5 minutes. Stir in the strawberries, lemon juice and cinnamon. Add food coloring if desired. Cool. Serve over cake. **Yield:** 3 cups.

I received this recipe from a friend about 15 years ago. It's a nice surprise for ketchup lovers and so easy to prepare. The spicy flavor makes this one of the tastiest ketchups I've ever had!

Faith McLillian
Rawdon, Quebec

Rhubarb Ketchup

4 cups diced fresh *or* frozen rhubarb
3 medium onions, chopped
1 cup white vinegar
1 cup packed brown sugar
1 cup sugar

1 can (28 ounces) diced tomatoes, undrained
2 teaspoons salt
1 teaspoon ground cinnamon
1 tablespoon pickling spice

In a large saucepan, combine all the ingredients. Cook for 1 hour or until thickened. Cool. Refrigerate in covered containers. **Yield:** 6-7 cups.

Rhubarb Streusel Muffins

1/2 cup butter, softened
1 cup packed brown sugar
1/2 cup sugar
1 egg
2 cups all-purpose flour
1 teaspoon baking powder
1/2 teaspoon baking soda
1/8 teaspoon salt

1 cup (8 ounces) sour cream
3 cups chopped fresh *or*
   frozen rhubarb, thawed

Topping:
1/2 cup chopped pecans
1/4 cup packed brown sugar
1 teaspoon ground cinnamon
1 tablespoon cold butter

What a pleasure it is to set out a basket of these rhubarb muffins...although the basket doesn't stay full for very long! I have six children and two grandsons, so I do a lot of baking. These snacks are based on a coffee cake recipe.

Sandra Moreside
Regina, Saskatchewan

1. In a mixing bowl, cream butter and sugars. Add egg; beat well. Combine the flour, baking powder, baking soda and salt; add to creamed mixture alternately with sour cream. Fold in rhubarb. Fill paper-lined or greased muffin cups three-fourths full.

2. For topping, combine the pecans, brown sugar and cinnamon in a small bowl; cut in butter until crumbly. Sprinkle over batter. Bake at 350° for 22-25 minutes or until a toothpick comes out clean. Cool for 5 minutes before removing from pans to wire racks. **Yield:** about 1-1/2 dozen.

Rhubarb Marmalade

6 cups chopped fresh *or*
   frozen rhubarb

6 cups sugar
2 medium oranges

1. Combine rhubarb and sugar in a large heavy saucepan. Grind oranges, including the peels, in a food processor; add to rhubarb mixture. Bring to a boil. Reduce heat and simmer, uncovered, stirring often until marmalade sheets from a spoon, about 1 hour.

2. Pour into hot sterilized jars, leaving 1/4-in. headspace. Adjust caps. Process in a boiling-water bath for 10 minutes. **Yield:** about 8 half-pints.

My daughter makes this marmalade every spring when rhubarb's abundant. Our family enjoys her gift...a refreshing departure in flavor from all the berry jams.

Leo Nerbonne
Delta Juction, Alaska

Creamy Rhubarb Crepes

3 eggs
1 cup milk
5 tablespoons butter, melted
1/4 cup sugar
1/4 teaspoon salt
1 cup all-purpose flour
Additional butter

Sauce/Filling:
1 cup sugar
1 tablespoon cornstarch
1/4 teaspoon ground cinnamon
2 cups thinly sliced fresh *or* frozen rhubarb, thawed
1 package (8 ounces) cream cheese, softened
Confectioners' sugar

Fixing rhubarb this way brings a spring zing to the table. I adapted this crepe recipe, which originally featured strawberry jelly, from one I loved as a child. My husband declared it a winner.

Stasha Wampler
Gate City, Virginia

1. In a bowl, whisk the eggs, milk, melted butter, sugar and salt. Beat in flour until smooth; let stand for 30 minutes. Melt 1/2 teaspoon butter in an 8-in. nonstick skillet. Pour 1/4 cup batter into the center of skillet; lift and turn pan to cover bottom. Cook until lightly browned; turn and brown the other side. Remove to a wire rack; cover with paper towel. Repeat with remaining batter, adding butter to skillet as needed.

2. Meanwhile, for sauce, combine the sugar, cornstarch and cinnamon in a saucepan. Stir in rhubarb. Bring to a boil over medium heat; cook and stir for 2 minutes or until slightly thickened and rhubarb is tender. Remove from the heat; cool slightly.

3. For filling, in a mixing bowl, beat cream cheese and 1/4 cup of the rhubarb sauce until smooth and creamy. Place a rounded tablespoonful on each crepe; fold in half and in half again, forming a triangle. Dust with confectioners' sugar. Serve with remaining sauce. **Yield:** 10 crepes.

Rhubarb Cheesecake Dessert

1 cup all-purpose flour
1/2 cup packed brown sugar
1/4 teaspoon salt
1/4 cup cold butter
1/2 cup chopped walnuts
1 teaspoon vanilla extract

Filling:
2 packages (8 ounces *each*)
    cream cheese, softened
3/4 cup sugar
3 eggs
1 teaspoon vanilla extract

Topping:
1 cup sugar
1 tablespoon cornstarch
1/4 teaspoon ground cinnamon
3 cups chopped fresh *or*
    frozen rhubarb, thawed
    and drained
1/4 cup water
3 to 4 drops red food
    coloring, optional

1. In a bowl, combine the flour, brown sugar and salt; cut in butter until mixture resembles coarse crumbs. Stir in walnuts and vanilla. Press into a greased 13-in. x 9-in. x 2-in. baking dish. Bake at 375° for 10 minutes. Cool slightly.

2. In a mixing bowl, beat cream cheese and sugar until light and fluffy. Add eggs and vanilla; mix well. Pour over the crust. Bake for 20-25 minutes or until center is set and edges are light brown. Cool.

3. In a saucepan, combine the sugar, cornstarch and cinnamon; stir in rhubarb and water. Bring to a boil over medium heat; cook and stir for 2 minutes or until thickened. Stir in food coloring if desired. Remove from heat; cool. Pour over filling. Cover and refrigerate for at least 1 hour. **Yield:** 12-15 servings.

After moving to our current home, we were thrilled to discover a huge rhubarb patch. Since I love to bake, I began searching for rhubarb recipes. Each spring, my family looks forward to these sensational squares.

Joyce Krumwiede
Mankato, Minnesota

Cherry Rhubarb Coffee Cake

4 cups chopped fresh *or* frozen rhubarb

2 tablespoons lemon juice

1 cup sugar

1/3 cup cornstarch

1 can (20 ounces) cherry pie filling

Cake:

3 cups all-purpose flour

1 cup sugar

1 teaspoon baking powder

1 teaspoon baking soda

1/2 teaspoon salt

1 cup cold butter

1 cup buttermilk

2 eggs, lightly beaten

1 teaspoon vanilla extract

Crumb Topping:

1-1/2 cups sugar

1 cup all-purpose flour

1/2 cup cold butter

I'm retired now, but when I was working I made this coffee cake for co-workers and also a men's Bible study class. I changed the original recipe from a strawberry-rhubarb combination to one with cherry, which I think gives it a richer flavor.

Kenneth Jacques
Hemet, California

1. In a saucepan, cook rhubarb and lemon juice over medium-low heat for 5 minutes, stirring often to prevent burning. Combine sugar and cornstarch; whisk into rhubarb mixture. Cook and stir 5 minutes longer or until thickened and bubbly. Stir in pie filling; set aside to cool.

2. For cake, combine the flour, sugar, baking powder, baking soda and salt in a large bowl. Cut in butter until mixture resembles fine crumbs.

3. In a mixing bowl, beat the buttermilk, eggs and vanilla. Add to flour mixture; stir just until moistened. Spread a little more than half of the batter into a greased 13-in. x 9-in. x 2-in. baking pan. Spread cooled filling over batter. Drop remaining batter by teaspoonfuls onto filling.

4. For topping, combine sugar and flour. Cut in butter until mixture forms coarse crumbs. Sprinkle over batter. Bake at 350° for 40-45 minutes or until a toothpick inserted near the center comes out clean. Cool in pan on a wire rack. **Yield:** 16-20 servings.

Rhubarb Pudding

8 slices bread, lightly
toasted
1-1/2 cups milk
1/4 cup butter
5 eggs, lightly beaten

3 cups chopped fresh *or*
frozen rhubarb, thawed
1-1/2 cups sugar
1/2 teaspoon ground cinnamon
1/4 teaspoon salt
1/2 cup packed brown sugar

1. Remove crusts from bread; cut bread into 1/2-in. cubes. Place in a greased 1-1/2-qt. baking dish. In a saucepan, heat milk over medium heat until bubbles form around sides of pan; remove from the heat. Stir in butter until melted. Pour over bread; let stand for 15 minutes.

2. In a bowl, combine the eggs, rhubarb, sugar, cinnamon and salt; stir into bread mixture. Sprinkle with brown sugar. Bake at 350° for 45-50 minutes or until set. Serve warm. Refrigerate leftovers. **Yield:** 8 servings.

My mother gave me the recipe for this old-fashioned pudding. It's a great way to use up day-old bread. Nothing enhances this traditional dessert better than garden-grown rhubarb. My family just loves it.

Virginia Andersen
Palermo, North Dakota

Rhubarb Crumble

8 cups chopped fresh *or*
frozen rhubarb
1-1/4 cups sugar, *divided*
2-1/2 cups all-purpose flour
1/4 cup packed brown sugar
1/4 cup quick-cooking oats
1 cup cold butter

Custard Sauce:
6 egg yolks
1/2 cup sugar
2 cups heavy whipping
cream
1-1/4 teaspoons vanilla extract

1. In a saucepan, combine rhubarb and 3/4 cup of sugar. Cover and cook over medium heat for 10 minutes or until the rhubarb is tender, stirring occasionally.

2. Pour into a greased 13-in. x 9-in. x 2-in. baking dish. In a bowl, combine the flour, brown sugar, oats and remaining sugar. Cut in butter until crumbly; sprinkle over rhubarb. Bake at 400° for 30 minutes or until hot and bubbly.

3. Meanwhile, in a saucepan, whisk the egg yolks and sugar; stir in cream. Cook and stir over low heat until a thermometer reads 160° and mixture thickens, about 15-20 minutes. Remove from the heat; stir in vanilla. Serve warm over rhubarb crumble. **Yield:** 12 servings (2-1/2 cups sauce).

When I met my English husband and served him just the crumble, he said it was fantastic but really needed a custard sauce over it. We found a terrific sauce recipe from England, and now the pair is perfect together. I wouldn't eat it any other way.

Amy Freeman
Cave Creek, Arizona

Rhubarb Meringue Pie

1/2 cup butter, softened
1/4 cup sugar
1 teaspoon vanilla extract
1/2 teaspoon salt
1 cup all-purpose flour
3/4 cup quick-cooking oats

Filling:
3 cups diced fresh *or*
frozen rhubarb
1 tablespoon water

1 cup sugar
2 tablespoons all-purpose
flour
1/8 teaspoon salt
3 egg yolks, beaten

Meringue:
3 egg whites
1/2 teaspoon vanilla extract
1/8 teaspoon salt
1/3 cup sugar

*My husband and brother,
former rhubarb haters, now
can't wait for the first stalks
of that plant to appear,
heralding spring and their
favorite pie!*

Theresa Connell
Puyallup, Washington

1. For crust, in a mixing bowl, cream the butter, sugar, vanilla and salt. Add flour and oats; mix well. Press over the bottom and sides of a 9-in. pie plate. Refrigerate while preparing filling.

2. Combine rhubarb and water in a saucepan. Bring to a boil, stirring constantly. Combine the sugar, flour and salt; stir into the rhubarb mixture. Cook and stir over medium-high heat until thickened and bubbly. Reduce heat; cook and stir 2 minutes longer. Remove from the heat. Stir a small amount of hot filling into egg yolks; return all to pan, stirring constantly.

3. Pour filling into crust. Bake at 375° for 25-30 minutes. Reduce temperature to 350°.

4. For meringue, beat egg whites, vanilla and salt in a mixing bowl until soft peaks form. Gradually add sugar, beating until stiff peaks form. Spread evenly over hot filling, sealing edges to crust.

5. Bake at 350° for 12-15 minutes or until the meringue is golden. Cool on a wire rack for 1 hour. Refrigerate for at least 3 hours before serving. Store leftovers in the refrigerator. **Yield:** 6-8 servings.

Rhubarb Granola Crisp

4 cups chopped fresh *or* frozen rhubarb, thawed and drained
1-1/4 cups all-purpose flour, *divided*
1/4 cup sugar
1/2 cup strawberry jam
1-1/2 cups granola cereal
1/2 cup packed brown sugar
1/2 cup chopped pecans
1/2 teaspoon ground cinnamon
1/2 teaspoon ground ginger
1/2 cup cold butter
Ice cream, optional

1. In a bowl, combine the rhubarb, 1/4 cup flour and sugar; stir in jam and set aside. In another bowl, combine the granola, brown sugar, pecans, cinnamon, ginger and remaining flour. Cut in butter until the mixture resembles coarse crumbs.

2. Press 2 cups of the granola mixture into a greased 8-in. square baking dish; spread rhubarb mixture over the crust. Sprinkle with remaining granola mixture.

3. Bake at 375° for 30-40 minutes or until filling is bubbly and topping is golden brown. Serve warm with ice cream if desired. **Yield:** 9 servings.

When my husband and I moved to our house in town, the rhubarb patch had to come along! This is a hit whether I serve it warm with ice cream or cold.

Arlene Beitz
Cambridge, Ontario

Peachy Rhubarb Pie

1 can (8-1/2 ounces) sliced peaches
2 cups chopped fresh *or* frozen rhubarb, thawed and drained
1 cup sugar
1/4 cup flaked coconut
3 tablespoons quick-cooking tapioca
1 teaspoon vanilla extract
Pastry for double-crust pie (9 inches)
1 tablespoon butter

1. Drain peaches, reserving syrup; chop the peaches. Place peaches and syrup in a bowl; add the rhubarb, sugar, coconut, tapioca and vanilla; toss to coat. Let stand for 15 minutes.

2. Line a 9-in. pie plate with the bottom pastry. Add filling; dot with butter. Top with remaining pastry or a lattice crust; flute edges. If using a full top crust, cut slits in it. Bake at 350° for 1 hour or until crust is golden brown and filling is bubbly. Cool on a wire rack. **Yield:** 6-8 servings.

We have an abundance of pieplant in our garden, so I save every rhubarb recipe I come across. My husband especially loves the combination of rhubarb and peaches in this pie.

Phyllis Galloway
Roswell, Georgia

Rhubarb-Filled Cookies

1 cup butter, softened
1 cup sugar
1 cup packed brown sugar
4 eggs
4-1/2 cups all-purpose flour
1 teaspoon baking soda
1 teaspoon salt

Filling:
3-1/2 cups chopped fresh *or* frozen rhubarb, thawed
1-1/2 cups sugar
6 tablespoons water, *divided*
1/4 cup cornstarch
1 teaspoon vanilla extract

I won a blue ribbon at our local fair for these tender cookies. They're so pretty with the filling peeking through the dough. When not just any cookie will do, try making these and watch the smiles appear.

Pauline Bondy
Grand Forks, North Dakota

1. In a mixing bowl, cream butter and sugars. Add eggs, one at a time, beating well after each addition. Combine the flour, baking soda and salt; gradually add to creamed mixture and mix well (dough will be sticky).

2. For filling, combine the rhubarb, sugar and 2 tablespoons water in a large saucepan; bring to a boil. Reduce heat; simmer, uncovered, for 10 minutes or until thickened, stirring frequently. Combine cornstarch and remaining water until smooth; stir into rhubarb mixture. Bring to a boil; cook and stir for 2 minutes or until thickened. Remove from the heat; stir in vanilla.

3. Drop dough by tablespoonfuls 2 in. apart onto ungreased baking sheets. Using the end of a wooden spoon handle, make an indentation in the center of each cookie; fill with a rounded teaspoon of filling. Top with 1/2 teaspoon of dough, allowing some filling to show. Bake at 375° for 8-10 minutes or until lightly browned. **Yield:** about 4-1/2 dozen.

Rhubarb Coconut Cookies

1/2 cup shortening
1-1/3 cups packed brown sugar
1 egg
2 cups all-purpose flour
1/2 teaspoon baking soda
1 teaspoon ground cinnamon
1/2 teaspoon ground cloves
1/2 teaspoon ground nutmeg
1/2 teaspoon salt
1/4 cup milk
1 cup diced fresh *or* frozen rhubarb
1 cup chopped pecans
1 cup raisins
1/2 cup flaked coconut

At our garden club fund-raiser, each group within the club serves a different kind of food. These cookies are made by the rhubarb group...and they are always the first to sell out!

Betty Claycomb
Alverton, Pennsylvania

1. In a mixing bowl, cream shortening and brown sugar. Add egg; beat well. Combine the dry ingredients; add to the creamed mixture alternately with milk. Mix well. Stir in the rhubarb, nuts, raisins and coconut.

2. Drop by tablespoonfuls onto greased baking sheets. Bake at 375° for 12-15 minutes or until golden. Cool on wire racks.
Yield: 3 dozen.

Rhubarb Crumb Cake

1/2 cup shortening
1-1/2 cups packed brown sugar
1 egg
1 teaspoon vanilla extract
2 cups all-purpose flour
1/2 teaspoon baking soda
1/4 teaspoon salt
1 tablespoon orange-flavored breakfast drink mix, optional
1 cup buttermilk
2 cups finely chopped fresh *or* frozen rhubarb

Topping:
1/2 cup sugar
1 teaspoon ground cinnamon
1/2 cup flaked coconut
1/2 cup chopped nuts

When the rhubarb comes up, I'm the first one in our household to get at it. I treat my family to this cake every spring.

John Kosmas
Minneapolis, Minnesota

1. In a mixing bowl, cream shortening and brown sugar. Beat in egg and vanilla. Combine the flour, baking soda, salt and orange drink if desired; add to creamed mixture alternately with buttermilk. Fold in rhubarb.

2. Spread into a greased 13-in. x 9-in. x 2-in. baking pan. For topping, combine sugar and cinnamon; stir in coconut and nuts. Sprinkle over batter. Bake at 350° for 35-40 minutes or until a toothpick inserted near the center comes out clean. Cool in pan on a wire rack. **Yield:** 12-16 servings.

Squash

Grilled Dijon Summer Squash, p. 190

Toasted Zucchini Snacks

2 cups shredded zucchini
1 teaspoon salt
1/2 cup mayonnaise
1/2 cup plain yogurt
1/4 cup grated Parmesan cheese
1/4 cup finely chopped green pepper

4 green onions, thinly sliced
1 garlic clove, minced
1 teaspoon Worcestershire sauce
1/4 teaspoon hot pepper sauce
36 slices snack rye bread

1. Place zucchini in a colander over a plate; sprinkle with salt and toss. Let stand for 1 hour. Rinse and drain well, pressing out excess liquid. Add the next eight ingredients; stir until combined.

2. Spread a rounded teaspoonful on each slice of bread; place on a baking sheet. Bake at 375° for 10-12 minutes or until bubbly. Serve hot. **Yield:** 3 dozen.

Squash and Potatoes

6 bacon strips, diced
1 large potato, peeled and diced
1 small onion, diced
1 medium zucchini, diced
1 medium yellow summer squash, diced

1 tablespoon fresh minced dill *or* 1 teaspoon dill weed
1/2 teaspoon salt
1/8 teaspoon pepper

1. In a large skillet, cook bacon over medium heat until crisp. Using a slotted spoon, remove to paper towels; drain, reserving 2 tablespoons drippings.

2. Add potato to drippings; cook and stir until lightly browned, about 5 minutes. Add the onion, zucchini and yellow squash; cook until tender, about 8 minutes. Return bacon to skillet; sprinkle with the dill, salt and pepper. Cook and stir for about 1 minute. **Yield:** 4-6 servings.

Italian Zucchini Soup

1 pound bulk Italian
    sausage
1 cup chopped onion
2 cups chopped celery
1 medium green pepper,
    chopped
2 to 4 tablespoons sugar
2 teaspoons salt
1/2 teaspoon dried basil
1/2 teaspoon dried oregano
1/2 teaspoon pepper
4 cups diced tomatoes,
    undrained
4 cups diced zucchini
Grated Parmesan cheese,
    optional

1. In a Dutch oven, cook sausage and onion over medium heat until meat is no longer pink; drain excess fat. Add next eight ingredients. Bring to a boil. Reduce heat; cover and simmer for 1 hour.

2. Stir in zucchini and simmer for 10 minutes. Sprinkle with Parmesan cheese if desired. **Yield:** 8 servings (2 quarts).

This recipe was given to me by my neighbor. It's a good way to use a lot of your zucchini and other garden vegetables. It freezes well and is great to have on hand on a cold winter day.

Clara Mae Chambers
Superior, Nebraska

Preparing Squash

Wash squash, then pat dry with paper towels. Use a sharp knife to cut in half and scrape out seeds and fibrous strings. Acorn squash can be cut into decorative rings. Generally winter squash is first cooked, then the flesh is scooped out of the shell. It can be difficult to peel the shell from raw winter squash.

Grilled Dijon Summer Squash

1/4 cup olive oil

2 tablespoons red wine vinegar

1-1/2 teaspoons minced fresh oregano *or* 1/2 teaspoon dried oregano

1-1/2 teaspoons Dijon mustard

1 garlic clove, minced

1/4 teaspoon salt

1/8 teaspoon pepper

2 medium zucchini, cut into 1/2-inch slices

2 medium yellow summer squash, cut into 1/2-inch slices

1 medium red onion, quartered

1 small sweet red pepper, cut into 2-inch pieces

1 small sweet yellow pepper, cut into 2-inch pieces

6 to 8 whole fresh mushrooms

6 cherry tomatoes

A niece gave this mustard-seasoned squash recipe to me. My family loves the zesty flavor and slightly crunchy texture. The kabobs are perfect partners to any grilled meat and reheat easily.

Ruth Lee
Troy, Ontario

1. In a jar with a tight-fitting lid, combine the oil, vinegar, oregano, mustard, garlic, salt and pepper. Place the vegetables in a shallow baking dish. Add marinade and toss to coat. Let stand for 15 minutes. Drain and discard marinade.

2. Arrange vegetables on a vegetable grill rack. Grill, covered, over medium heat for 10-12 minutes or until tender. **Yield:** 8 servings.

Zucchini Garden Chowder

2 medium zucchini, chopped
1 medium onion, chopped
2 tablespoons minced fresh
   parsley
1 teaspoon dried basil
1/3 cup butter
1/3 cup all-purpose flour
1 teaspoon salt
1/4 teaspoon pepper
3 cups water
3 chicken bouillon cubes
1 teaspoon lemon juice

1 can (14-1/2 ounces)
   diced tomatoes, undrained
1 can (12 ounces)
   evaporated milk
1 package (10 ounces)
   frozen corn
1/4 cup grated Parmesan cheese
2 cups (8 ounces) shredded
   cheddar cheese
Pinch sugar, optional
Additional chopped parsley,
   optional

1. In a Dutch oven, saute the zucchini, onion, parsley and basil in butter until vegetables are tender. Stir in flour, salt and pepper until blended. Gradually stir in water. Add the bouillon and lemon juice; mix well. Bring to a boil; cook and stir for 2 minutes or until thickened.

2. Add the tomatoes, milk and corn; bring to a boil. Reduce heat; cover and simmer for 5 minutes or until corn is tender. Just before serving, stir in cheeses until melted. Add sugar and garnish with parsley if desired. **Yield:** 8-10 servings (about 2-1/2 quarts).

Years ago, when my husband and I put in our first garden, a neighbor suggested zucchini since it's easy to grow. Our kids were reluctant to try new things, so I used our squash in this cheesy chowder—it met with solid approval from all of us!

Nanette Jordan
Canton, Michigan

Cheesy Zucchini Saute

1/2 cup chopped onion
1/4 cup butter, cubed
3 cups coarsely shredded
   zucchini
2 teaspoons minced fresh
   basil *or* 1/2 teaspoon
   dried basil

1/2 teaspoon salt
1/8 teaspoon garlic powder
1 cup (4 ounces) shredded
   cheddar cheese
1 cup diced fresh tomato
2 tablespoons sliced ripe
   olives

In a large skillet, saute onion in butter until crisp-tender. Stir in the zucchini, basil, salt and garlic powder. Cook and stir for 4-5 minutes or until zucchini is crisp-tender. Sprinkle with the cheese, tomato and olives. Cover and cook for 4-5 minutes or until cheese is melted. Serve immediately. **Yield:** 6 servings.

Although I no longer have a garden of my own, friends and neighbors keep me amply supplied with squash. As a thank-you, I tell them how to make this refreshing zucchini saute. It's quick, easy and oh, so tasty!

Doris Biggs
Felton, Delaware

Butternut Squash Casserole

5 cups shredded butternut squash	**2 cups ricotta cheese**
Juice and grated peel of 1 lemon	**1 egg, lightly beaten**
1 cup raisins	**3 tablespoons plain yogurt, sour cream *or* buttermilk**
6 to 8 dried apricots, chopped (about 1/3 cup)	**1 teaspoon ground cinnamon**
1 apple, cubed	**1/8 teaspoon ground nutmeg**
	1/2 cup chopped walnuts

1. In a large bowl, toss squash with lemon juice and peel. Place half in the bottom of a greased 11-in. x 7-in. x 2-in. baking dish. Combine the raisins, apricots and apple; sprinkle over squash. In a small bowl, combine the cheese, egg, yogurt, cinnamon and nutmeg; spread over fruit mixture. Cover with remaining squash. Sprinkle with nuts.

3. Cover with foil. Bake at 375° for 35-40 minutes or until heated through. **Yield:** 10-12 servings.

Navy Bean Squash Soup

1 pound dry navy beans, sorted and rinsed	**2 to 2-1/2 pounds butternut squash, peeled, seeded and cubed (about 5 cups)**
2 cans (14-1/2 ounces *each*) chicken broth	
2 cups water	**1 large onion, chopped**
1 meaty ham bone	**1/2 teaspoon salt**
	1/2 teaspoon pepper

1. Place beans in a large saucepan or Dutch oven; add water to cover by 2 in. Bring to a boil; boil for 2 minutes. Remove from the heat; cover and let stand for 1–4 hours or until beans are softened.

2. Drain and rinse beans, discarding liquid. Return beans to pan. Add the broth, water, ham bone, squash, onion, salt and pepper. Bring to a boil. Reduce heat; cover and simmer for 1-1/2 to 1-3/4 hours or until beans are tender.

3. Remove ham bone. Mash the soup mixture, leaving some chunks if desired. Remove ham from bone; cut into chunks. Discard bone and fat. Return meat to the soup; heat through. **Yield:** 12-14 servings (about 3 quarts).

Baked Chicken And Acorn Squash

- 2 small acorn squash (1-1/4 pounds)
- 2 to 4 garlic cloves, minced
- 2 tablespoons vegetable oil, *divided*
- 4 chicken drumsticks (4 ounces *each*)
- 4 chicken thighs (4 ounces *each*)
- 1/4 cup packed brown sugar
- 1 teaspoon salt
- 1 tablespoon minced fresh rosemary *or* 1 teaspoon dried rosemary, crushed
- 1 can (15-1/4 ounces) sliced peaches, undrained

1. Cut squash in half lengthwise; discard seeds. Cut each half widthwise into 1/2-in. slices; discard ends. Place slices in an ungreased 13-in. x 9-in. x 2-in. baking dish. Sprinkle with garlic and drizzle with 1 tablespoon oil.

2. In a large skillet, brown chicken in remaining oil. Arrange chicken over squash. Combine the brown sugar, salt and rosemary; sprinkle over chicken. Bake, uncovered, at 350° for 45 minutes, basting with pan juices twice.

3. Pour peaches over chicken and squash. Bake, uncovered, 15 minutes longer or until chicken juices run clear and peaches are heated through. **Yield:** 4 servings.

This main dish is ideal for harvesttime with its colorful acorn squash and sweet peaches. The fragrance of rosemary-seasoned chicken baking is heavenly.

Connie Svoboda
Elko, Minnesota

Where's the Squash Lasagna

1 pound ground beef
2 large zucchini (about 1 pound), shredded
3/4 cup chopped onion
2 garlic cloves, minced
1 can (14-1/2 ounces) stewed tomatoes
2 cups water
1 can (12 ounces) tomato paste
1 tablespoon minced fresh parsley
1-1/2 teaspoons salt
1 teaspoon sugar
1/2 teaspoon dried oregano
1/2 teaspoon pepper
9 lasagna noodles, cooked, rinsed and drained
1 carton (15 ounces) ricotta cheese
2 cups (8 ounces) shredded part-skim mozzarella cheese
1 cup grated Parmesan cheese

I devised this recipe to hide zucchini from my unsuspecting grandchildren and any others who think they don't like it. It's always a hit at our house.

Norma Brinson
Greenville, North Carolina

1. In a skillet, cook the beef, zucchini, onion and garlic over medium heat until meat is no longer pink; drain. Place tomatoes in a food processor or blender; cover and process until smooth. Stir into beef mixture. Add the water, tomato paste, parsley and seasonings. Bring to a boil. Reduce heat; simmer, uncovered, for 30 minutes, stirring occasionally.

2. Spread 1 cup meat sauce in a greased 13-in. x 9-in. x 2-in. baking dish. Arrange three noodles over sauce. Spread with a third of meat sauce; top with half of ricotta. Sprinkle with a third of mozzarella and Parmesan. Repeat. Top with remaining noodles, meat sauce and cheeses. Cover and bake at 350° for 45 minutes. Uncover; bake 15 minutes longer or until bubbly. Let stand for 15 minutes before cutting. **Yield:** 12 servings.

Sweet and Sour Zucchini

3/4 cup sugar
1 teaspoon salt
1/2 teaspoon pepper
1/3 cup vegetable oil
2/3 cup cider vinegar
2 tablespoons white wine vinegar
5 cups thinly sliced zucchini
1 small onion, chopped
1/2 cup chopped green pepper
1/2 cup chopped celery

In a large bowl, combine first six ingredients. Stir in the vegetables. Cover; refrigerate for several hours or overnight. **Yield:** 6-8 servings.

I have made this many times for potlucks. Everyone loves it, and it travels nicely, too. The recipe is a wonderful way to use up the prolific zucchini that we all have in such abundance in the summertime.

Marian Platt
Sequim, Washington

Zucchini Hamburger Pie

1/2 pound ground beef
1/4 cup minced onion
1 teaspoon salt
1/2 teaspoon garlic salt
1/2 cup diced green pepper
1 teaspoon dried oregano
1 teaspoon dried parsley flakes
1/2 cup dry bread crumbs
1/4 cup grated Parmesan cheese
1 egg, lightly beaten
Pastry for double-crust deep-dish pie (9 to 10 inches)
4 cups sliced zucchini, *divided*
2 medium tomatoes, peeled and thinly sliced

1. In a skillet, cook beef, onion, salt and garlic salt over medium heat until meat is no longer pink; drain well. Add the green pepper, oregano, parsley, bread crumbs, Parmesan cheese and egg; mix well. Set aside.

2. Place bottom pastry in pie plate; layer 2 cups of zucchini in crust. Cover with beef mixture. Cover with tomato slices and remaining zucchini. Roll out remaining pastry to fit top of pie. Place over filling. Trim, seal and flute edges. Cut slits in pastry.

3. Bake at 350° for 1 hour or until crust is lightly browned. Refrigerate leftovers. **Yield:** 6-8 servings.

This is a family favorite handed down from my dear aunt. It is such a hearty pie that it satisfies the appetite well. And my family has always enjoyed the idea of having pie for supper!

Eloise Swisher
Roseville, Illinois

Onion Zucchini Bread

Only two steps and this bread is mixed and ready for the oven! You'll love the flavor of onion and Parmesan cheese. Baked in a round pan, it looks nice on the table whole or sliced in wedges.

Annie Sassard
Ft. McCoy, Florida

3 cups all-purpose flour
3/4 cup chopped onion
1/2 cup grated Parmesan cheese, *divided*
5 teaspoons baking powder
1 teaspoon salt
1/2 teaspoon baking soda
1 cup buttermilk
1/3 cup vegetable oil
2 eggs, lightly beaten
3/4 cup finely shredded zucchini

1. In a bowl, combine the flour, onion, 6 tablespoons Parmesan cheese, baking powder, salt and baking soda. In a small bowl, combine the buttermilk, oil, eggs and zucchini; stir into flour mixture just until blended.

2. Spoon into a greased 9-in. round baking pan. Sprinkle with remaining Parmesan. Bake at 350° for 40 minutes or until a toothpick inserted near the center comes out clean. Cook on a wire rack 10 minutes before removing from the pan. **Yield:** 6-8 servings.

Zucchini Crust Pizza

3 cups shredded zucchini
3/4 cup egg substitute
1/3 cup all-purpose flour
1/2 teaspoon salt
2 cups (8 ounces) shredded part-skim mozzarella cheese
2 small tomatoes, halved and thinly sliced
1/2 cup chopped onion
1/2 cup julienned green pepper
1 teaspoon dried oregano
1/2 teaspoon dried basil
3 tablespoons shredded Parmesan cheese

1. In a bowl, combine zucchini and egg substitute. Add flour and salt; stir well. Spread onto the bottom of a 12-in. pizza pan coated with nonstick cooking spray.

2. Bake at 450° for 8 minutes. Reduce heat to 350°. Sprinkle with the mozzarella, tomatoes, onion, green pepper, oregano, basil and Parmesan cheese. Bake for 15-20 minutes or until onion is tender and cheese is melted. **Yield:** 6 slices.

My mother-in-law shared the recipe for this unique pizza with me. Its quiche-like zucchini crust makes it just right for brunch, lunch or a light supper.

Ruth Denomme
Englehart, Ontario

Golden Squash Rolls

2 packages (1/4 ounce *each*) active dry yeast

1-1/2 cups warm water (110° to 115°)

1/3 cup sugar

2 teaspoons salt

2 eggs

1 cup mashed winter squash

7 to 7-1/2 cups all-purpose flour

2/3 cup butter, melted

2 tablespoons butter, softened

1. In a large mixing bowl, dissolve yeast in water; let stand for 5 minutes. Add the sugar, salt, eggs, squash and 3-1/2 cups flour; beat well. Beat in melted butter. Stir in enough remaining flour to form a soft dough.

2. Turn onto a floured surface; knead until smooth and elastic, about 6-8 minutes. Place in a greased bowl, turning once to grease top. Cover and refrigerate for 2-4 hours. (May refrigerate up to 3 days.)

3. Punch dough down; turn onto a floured surface. Divide dough in half; roll each into a 16-in. circle. Spread with softened butter. Cut each circle into 16 wedges. Roll up from wide end and place with pointed end down on greased baking sheets. Cover and let rise until almost doubled, about 1 hour.

4. Bake at 400° for 15-20 minutes or until golden brown. Remove to wire racks. **Yield:** 2-1/2 to 3 dozen.

These rolls are a big favorite with my family and a "must" at our holiday meals. I adapted the recipe years ago from a potato roll recipe I had, so the texture is quite similar.

Dolores Diercks
Clinton, Iowa

Extra Squash?

Substitute grated squash for carrots in your favorite carrot cake recipe. You won't be able to taste the difference.

Chocolate Zucchini Cake

1 cup butter, softened
1/2 cup vegetable oil
1-1/2 cups sugar
2 eggs, lightly beaten
1/2 cup buttermilk
1 teaspoon vanilla extract
2-1/2 cups all-purpose flour
1/4 cup baking cocoa
1 teaspoon baking soda
1/2 teaspoon baking powder
1/2 teaspoon salt
1/2 teaspoon ground cinnamon
1/4 teaspoon ground cloves
2 cups shredded zucchini
1/2 cup chopped nuts
1/2 cup semisweet chocolate chips

The hint of chocolate in this moist cake is an unexpected flavor and a nice surprise.

Eloise Swisher
Roseville, Illinois

1. In a mixing bowl, beat the butter, oil and sugar. Add the eggs, buttermilk and vanilla; mix well. Combine the flour, cocoa, baking soda, baking powder, salt, cinnamon and cloves; gradually add to creamed mixture. Stir in zucchini.

2. Spread into a greased 13-in. x 9-in. x 2-in. baking pan. Sprinkle with nuts and chocolate chips. Bake at 350° for 35-40 minutes or until a toothpick inserted near the center comes out clean. Cool on wire rack. **Yield:** 12-16 servings.

Plan Ahead

When preparing an autumn oven meal, fill up the extra space with a baking pan of squash. When the squash is cool enough to handle, mash it and freeze it in measured amounts for use throughout the year.

Buttercup Squash Coffee Cake

1/4 cup packed brown sugar
1/4 cup sugar
1/4 cup all-purpose flour
1/4 cup quick-cooking oats
1/4 cup chopped nuts
1-1/2 teaspoons ground cinnamon
3 tablespoons cold butter

Cake:
1/2 cup butter-flavored shortening
1 cup sugar
2 eggs
1 cup mashed cooked buttercup squash
1 teaspoon vanilla extract

2 cups all-purpose flour
2 teaspoons baking powder
1-1/2 teaspoons ground cinnamon
1/2 teaspoon baking soda
1/2 teaspoon salt
1/4 teaspoon ground ginger
1/4 teaspoon ground nutmeg
Pinch ground cloves
1/2 cup unsweetened applesauce

Glaze:
1/2 cup confectioners' sugar
1/4 teaspoon vanilla extract
1-1/2 teaspoons hot water

My father grows a large squash patch, so each fall I get an ample amount of his harvest. I make this treat to share with my co-workers. They rave about the moist cake, the crunchy streusel and the applesauce between the layers.

Mary Jones
Cumberland, Maine

1. Combine the first six ingredients. Cut in butter until crumbly; set aside. In a mixing bowl, cream shortening and sugar. Beat in eggs, one at a time, beating well after each addition. Beat in squash and vanilla. Combine dry ingredients; gradually add to creamed mixture. Spoon half into a greased 9-in. springform pan. Spread applesauce over batter. Sprinkle with half of the streusel. Spoon remaining batter evenly over streusel. Top with remaining streusel.

2. Bake at 350° for 50-55 minutes or until a toothpick inserted in the cake comes out clean. Cool for 10 minutes; remove sides of pan. Combine glaze ingredients; drizzle over coffee cake. **Yield:** 10-12 servings.

APPLESAUCE
JARS FOR $12

Golden Squash Pie

4 eggs
4 cups mashed cooked
  butternut squash
1 cup buttermilk
1/4 cup butter, melted
2 teaspoons vanilla extract
2 cups sugar

2 tablespoons all-purpose
  flour
1 teaspoon salt
1/2 teaspoon baking soda
2 unbaked pastry shells
  (9 inches)
Ground nutmeg, optional

1. In a bowl, combine the eggs, squash, buttermilk, butter and vanilla. Combine the dry ingredients; add to the squash mixture and mix until smooth. Pour into pastry shells. Cover edges loosely with foil.

2. Bake at 350° for 35 minutes. Remove foil. Bake 25 minutes longer or until a knife inserted near the center comes out clean. Cool on a wire rack. Sprinkle with nutmeg if desired. Store in the refrigerator. **Yield:** 2 pies (6-8 servings each).

Pineapple Zucchini Bread

3 eggs
2 cups finely shredded
  zucchini
1 cup vegetable oil
1 can (8 ounces) crushed
  pineapple, drained
2 teaspoons vanilla extract
3 cups all-purpose flour
2 cups sugar

2 teaspoons baking soda
1-1/2 teaspoons ground
  cinnamon
1 teaspoon salt
3/4 teaspoon ground nutmeg
1/2 teaspoon baking powder
1 cup chopped nuts
1 cup raisins *or* dried
  currants, optional

1. In a bowl, combine the eggs, zucchini, oil, pineapple and vanilla. Combine the dry ingredients; stir into egg mixture just until moistened. Fold in nuts and raisins if desired.

2. Pour into two greased 8-in. x 4-in. x 2-in. loaf pans. Bake at 350° for 50-60 minutes or until a toothpick inserted near the center comes out clean. Cool for 10 minutes before removing from pans to wire racks. **Yield:** 2 loaves.

Zucchini Cupcakes

3 eggs
1-1/3 cups sugar
1/2 cup vegetable oil
1/2 cup orange juice
1 teaspoon almond extract
2-1/2 cups all-purpose flour
2 teaspoons ground cinnamon
2 teaspoons baking powder
1 teaspoon baking soda
1 teaspoon salt
1/2 teaspoon ground cloves
1-1/2 cups shredded zucchini

Caramel Frosting:
1 cup packed brown sugar
1/2 cup butter, softened
1/4 cup milk
1 teaspoon vanilla extract
1-1/2 to 2 cups confectioners' sugar

1. In a mixing bowl, beat eggs, sugar, oil, orange juice and extract. Combine dry ingredients; add to the egg mixture and mix well. Add zucchini and mix well.

2. Fill greased or paper-lined muffin cups two-thirds full. Bake at 350° for 20-25 minutes or until a toothpick inserted near the center comes out clean. Cool for 10 minutes before removing to a wire rack.

3. For frosting, combine the brown sugar, butter and milk in a saucepan; bring to a boil over medium heat. Cook and stir for 2 minutes. Remove from the heat; stir in vanilla. Cool to lukewarm. Gradually beat in confectioners' sugar until frosting reaches spreading consistency. Frost cupcakes. **Yield:** 1-1/2 to 2 dozen.

I asked my grandmother for this recipe after trying these irresistible spice cupcakes at her home. I love their creamy caramel frosting. They're such a scrumptious dessert, you actually forget you're eating your vegetables, too!

Virginia Breitmeyer
Craftsbury, Vermont

Tomatoes

Stuffed Garden Tomatoes, p. 209

Tomato-Garlic Dressing

2 cups mayonnaise
1 teaspoon lemon juice

1 teaspoon garlic powder
2 medium tomatoes, cubed

Combine ingredients in a food processor or blender; cover and process until smooth. Chill. **Yield:** about 3 cups.

Smoked Salmon Cherry Tomatoes

30 cherry tomatoes
3 ounces smoked salmon, finely chopped
1/3 cup finely chopped onion
1/3 cup finely chopped green pepper

Salt and pepper to taste
1 package (3 ounces) cream cheese, softened
1 teaspoon milk
Fresh dill sprigs

1. Cut a thin slice off each tomato top; scoop out and discard pulp. Invert tomatoes on paper towels to drain. In a bowl, combine the salmon, onion, green pepper, salt and pepper. Spoon into tomatoes.

2. In a small mixing bowl, beat the cream cheese and milk until smooth. Insert a star tip into a pastry or plastic bag. Pipe a small amount of cream cheese mixture onto tomatoes. Garnish with dill. **Yield:** 2-1/2 dozen.

Four-Tomato Salsa

- 7 plum tomatoes, chopped
- 7 medium tomatoes, chopped
- 3 medium yellow tomatoes, chopped
- 3 medium orange tomatoes, chopped
- 1 teaspoon salt
- 2 tablespoons lime juice
- 2 tablespoons olive oil
- 1 medium white onion, chopped
- 2/3 cup chopped red onion
- 2 green onions, chopped
- 1/2 cup *each* chopped sweet red, orange, yellow and green pepper
- 3 pepperoncinis, chopped
- 3 pickled sweet banana wax peppers, chopped
- 1/2 cup minced fresh parsley
- 2 tablespoons minced fresh cilantro
- 1 tablespoon dried chervil

Tortilla chips

1. In a colander set over a plate, combine the tomatoes and salt. Let drain for 10 minutes. Transfer to a large bowl.

2. Stir in the lime juice, oil, onions, peppers, parsley, cilantro and chervil. Serve with tortilla chips. Refrigerate or freeze leftovers. **Yield:** 14 cups.

Editor's Note: Look for pepperoncinis (pickled peppers) in the pickle and olive section of your grocery store.

A variety of tomatoes, onions and peppers makes this chunky salsa so good. Whenever I try to take a batch to a get-together, it's hard to keep my family from finishing it off first! It's a super snack with tortilla chips or as a relish with meat.

Connie Siese
Wayne, Michigan

Tomato Dill Soup

1 medium onion, thinly sliced
1 garlic clove, minced
2 tablespoons vegetable oil
1 tablespoon butter
1/2 teaspoon salt
Pinch pepper
3 large tomatoes, sliced
1 can (6 ounces) tomato paste
1/4 cup all-purpose flour
2 cups water, *divided*
3/4 cup heavy whipping cream
1 to 2 tablespoons finely minced fresh dill *or* 1 to 2 teaspoons dill weed

Most often, I make this soup ahead and keep it in the fridge. It's particularly good to take out and heat up with tuna or grilled cheese sandwiches, hard rolls or a salad. It would be fine to serve—hot or cold—at a soup supper as well.

Patty Kile
Greentown, Pennsylvania

1. In a large saucepan, cook onion and garlic in oil and butter over low heat until tender. Add the salt, pepper and tomatoes; cook over medium-high heat for 3 minutes. Remove from the heat and stir in tomato paste.

2. In a small bowl, combine flour and 1/2 cup water until smooth. Stir into saucepan. Gradually stir in remaining water. Bring to a boil over medium heat; cook and stir for 2 minutes or until thickened.

3. Place mixture in a sieve over a bowl. With the back of a spoon, press vegetables through the sieve to remove seeds and skins; return puree to pan. Add cream and dill; cook over low heat just until heated through (do not boil). **Yield:** 4 servings (1 quart).

Herbed Tomato And Cheese Salad

A flavorful combination of ingredients and a tangy garlic-laced dressing makes this salad a mouth-watering delight.

Sharon Miller
Olivenhain, California

5 large fresh tomatoes, cut into wedges

1 medium green pepper, chopped

1/2 small red onion, thinly sliced

1-1/2 cups (6 ounces) shredded Monterey Jack cheese

1/4 cup pimiento-stuffed olives, sliced

1/2 teaspoon dried basil

Dressing:

6 tablespoons vegetable oil

2 tablespoons red wine vinegar

2 tablespoons minced fresh parsley

1 tablespoon minced fresh chives

1 garlic clove, minced

1/2 teaspoon salt

1/4 teaspoon pepper

Place tomato wedges in a shallow dish. Cover with the green pepper, onion, cheese and olives. Sprinkle with basil. In a small bowl, whisk together the dressing ingredients. Spoon over salad. **Yield:** 6-8 servings.

Italian Pasta Salad

3/4 cup uncooked spiral pasta

1-1/2 cups halved cherry tomatoes

1 cup sliced fresh mushrooms

1/4 cup chopped sweet red pepper

1/4 cup chopped green pepper

3 tablespoons thinly sliced green onions

1-1/2 cups zesty Italian salad dressing

3/4 cup mayonnaise

1/2 cup grated Parmesan cheese

1/3 cup cubed provolone cheese

1 can (2-1/4 ounces) sliced ripe olives, drained

Leaf lettuce, optional

This zesty recipe combines vegetables and pasta in a creamy dressing. Refreshing and filling, this change-of-pace salad is perfect as a side dish. It's always popular at a potluck.

Tina Dierking
Skohegan, Maine

1. Cook pasta according to package directions; rinse with cold water and drain. Place in a bowl; add the tomatoes, mushrooms, peppers, onions and salad dressing. Cover and refrigerate for at least 4 hours or overnight; drain.

2. In a bowl, combine mayonnaise and Parmesan cheese; stir in provolone cheese and olives. Gently fold into pasta mixture. Serve in a lettuce-lined bowl if desired. **Yield:** 6 servings.

Southwestern Tomato Soup

10 plum tomatoes, halved lengthwise
1 to 2 Anaheim peppers, halved and seeded
1/2 cup chopped onion
2 garlic cloves, minced
1 tablespoon olive oil
2 cans (14-1/2 ounces *each*) chicken broth
1 tablespoon minced fresh cilantro
2 teaspoons ground cumin
1/2 teaspoon sugar
1/2 teaspoon salt
1/4 teaspoon pepper
Vegetable oil for frying
8 corn tortillas (6 inches), cut into 1/4-inch strips
Sour cream, optional

This smooth, flavorful tomato soup is unbeatable when the season's ripest tomatoes are available and the weather starts to cool. Each delicious, fresh-tasting bowlful will warm you from the inside out.

Sherri Jackson
Chillicothe, Ohio

1. Place tomatoes cut side down on a broiler pan; broil 3-4 in. from the heat for 15-20 minutes. Peel and discard skins. Repeat with peppers, broiling for 5-10 minutes.

2. In a skillet, saute onion and garlic in oil until tender. Transfer to a blender or food processor; add the tomatoes and peppers. Cover and process until smooth. Pour into a large saucepan; cook and stir over medium heat for 2 minutes.

3. Press mixture through a strainer with a spoon; discard seeds. Return tomato mixture to the pan. Add the broth, cilantro, cumin, sugar, salt and pepper. Cover and cook on low for 15-20 minutes or until heated through.

4. Meanwhile, heat 1/2 in. of oil in a skillet to 375°. Fry tortilla strips, in batches, for 3-5 minutes or until golden brown; drain on paper towels. Garnish bowls of soup with tortilla strips. Serve with sour cream if desired. **Yield:** 6 servings.

Editor's Note: When cutting or seeding hot peppers, use rubber or plastic gloves to protect your hands. Avoid touching your face.

Too Many Tomatoes?

To quickly use a huge supply of tomatoes, wash and core them, then puree in the blender with lemon juice, onion and celery to taste. This makes a great vegetable juice. Simmer several batches of puree until slightly thickened for spaghetti sauce or until very thick for pizza sauce. Store in the freezer.

Put extra tomatoes in a plastic freezer bag and store in your freezer. To use in soup or sauce, hold the frozen tomatoes under warm water. The skins will slip right off. Drop the whole tomatoes into pot. They'll break up during cooking.

Stuffed Garden Tomatoes

4 medium fresh tomatoes

1 medium carrot, coarsely chopped

8 radishes, coarsely chopped

2 green onions with tops, thinly sliced

1 small cucumber, peeled, seeded and coarsely chopped

1/2 cup fresh *or* frozen peas

1 tablespoon chopped fresh parsley

1/2 teaspoon dried oregano

2 garlic cloves, minced

1/2 teaspoon salt

6 tablespoons butter, *divided*

4 teaspoons grated Parmesan cheese

4 teaspoons seasoned dry bread crumbs

1 teaspoon sugar

1. Cut a thin slice from top of each tomato. Leaving a 1/2-in.-thick shell, scoop out pulp and discard. Invert tomatoes onto paper towels to drain.

2. Meanwhile, in a skillet, saute the carrot, radishes, green onions, cucumber, peas, parsley, oregano, garlic and salt in 4 tablespoons butter until the vegetables are tender.

3. Stuff tomatoes and place in a greased shallow baking dish. Melt remaining butter; stir in the Parmesan cheese, bread crumbs and sugar. Sprinkle over tomatoes. Bake, uncovered, at 400° for 20 minutes or until crumbs are lightly browned. **Yield:** 4 servings.

These stuffed tomatoes make delicious use of vegetables straight from the garden. As a side dish, they're a mouth-watering complement to any meal.

Jessica Gambino
Waveland, Mississippi

Tomato Zucchini Stew

1-1/4 pounds bulk Italian sausage
1-1/2 cups sliced celery (3/4-inch pieces)
8 medium fresh tomatoes (about 4 pounds), peeled and cut into sixths
1-1/2 cups tomato juice
4 small zucchini, sliced into 1/4-inch pieces
2-1/2 teaspoons Italian seasoning
1-1/2 to 2 teaspoons salt
1 teaspoon sugar
1/2 teaspoon garlic salt
1/2 teaspoon pepper
3 cups canned *or* frozen corn
2 medium green peppers, sliced into 1-inch pieces
1/4 cup cornstarch
1/4 cup water
Shredded part-skim mozzarella cheese

This recipe's famous with my friends and the younger friends of my grown daughter and granddaughter. I make it for potlucks and other get-togethers.

Helen Miller
Hickory Hills, Illinois

1. Crumble sausage into a 4-qt. Dutch oven. Cook over medium heat until no longer pink. Add celery and cook for 15 minutes; drain. Add the tomatoes, tomato juice, zucchini and seasonings; bring to a boil. Reduce heat; cover and simmer for 20 minutes. Add corn and peppers; cover and simmer for 15 minutes.

2. Combine cornstarch and water; stir into stew. Bring to a boil; cook and stir for 2 minutes or until mixture thickens. Sprinkle with cheese. **Yield:** 6-8 servings.

Mild Fresh Salsa

3 fresh tomatoes, peeled, seeded and finely chopped
1/2 cup minced fresh cilantro
2 to 3 garlic cloves, minced
1 can (4 ounces) chopped green chilies
1/2 cup sliced green onions
1/2 teaspoon salt
1/4 teaspoon pepper

This quick-and-easy salsa tastes great as an accompaniment to meat dishes as well as with chips.

Rebecca Arce Bell
Holtville, California

In a bowl, combine all ingredients. Chill before serving. **Yield:** 3 cups.

Herbed Cherry Tomatoes

1 pint cherry tomatoes, halved
1/4 cup vegetable oil
3 tablespoons cider vinegar
1/4 cup minced fresh parsley
1-1/2 teaspoons minced fresh basil *or* 1/2 teaspoon dried basil
1-1/2 teaspoons minced fresh oregano *or* 1/2 teaspoon dried oregano
1/2 teaspoon salt
1/2 teaspoon sugar
Leaf lettuce, optional

Place tomatoes in a medium bowl; set aside. In a small bowl, combine oil and vinegar. Add the parsley, basil, oregano, salt and sugar; mix well. Pour over the tomatoes. Cover and refrigerate for at least 3 hours. Drain; serve on lettuce if desired. **Yield:** 4-6 servings.

My recipe's a good one for when you want a fancier salad that's still quick to fix. It's wonderful served with grilled steak, baked potatoes and corn on the cob.

Dianne Bahn
Yankton, South Dakota

─────────More Than One Way to Skin a Tomato─────────

Instead of parboiling tomatoes to remove the skins, rub the tomato all over with the back of a knife. The skin peels right off. You won't have to dirty a pan, wait for water to boil or risk burning your hands.

Tomato-French Bread Lasagna

1 pound ground beef
1/3 cup chopped onion
1/3 cup chopped celery
2 garlic cloves, minced
14 slices French bread
(1/2 inch thick)
4 large tomatoes, sliced
(1/2 inch thick)
1 teaspoon dried basil
1 teaspoon dried parsley
flakes
1 teaspoon dried oregano
1 teaspoon dried rosemary,
crushed

1 teaspoon garlic powder
3/4 teaspoon salt
1/2 teaspoon pepper
2 teaspoons olive oil,
divided
3 tablespoons butter
3 tablespoons all-purpose
flour
1-1/2 cups milk
1/3 cup grated Parmesan
cheese
2 cups (8 ounces) shredded
part-skim mozzarella
cheese

Usually, I make this as a side dish to go with veal cutlets or a roast. You could also serve it as a main dish along with a salad and hot garlic bread if you like.

Patricia Collins
Imbler, Oregon

1. In a skillet, cook the beef, onion, celery and garlic over medium heat until meat is no longer pink; drain and set aside. Toast bread; line the bottom of an ungreased 13-in. x 9-in. x 2-in. baking dish with 10 slices. Top with half of the meat mixture and half of the tomatoes. Combine seasonings; sprinkle half over tomatoes. Drizzle with 1 teaspoon oil. Crumble remaining bread over top. Repeat layers of meat, tomatoes, seasonings and oil.

2. In a saucepan over medium heat, melt the butter; stir in flour until smooth. Gradually stir in milk. Bring to a boil; cook and stir for 2 minutes or until thickened. Remove from the heat; stir in Parmesan. Pour over top. Top with mozzarella.

3. Bake, uncovered, at 350° for 40-45 minutes or until bubbly and cheese is golden brown. Let stand for 10 minutes before serving. **Yield:** 8-10 servings.

BLT Brunch Pie

1-1/4 cups all-purpose flour
   2 teaspoons baking powder
1/2 teaspoon salt
1/2 teaspoon dried basil
1/2 cup shortening
1/2 cup sour cream

Filling:
3/4 cup mayonnaise
1 cup (4 ounces) shredded cheddar cheese
1 can (4-1/2 ounces) mushroom stems and pieces, drained
8 bacon strips, cooked and crumbled
1 tablespoon chopped green pepper
1 tablespoon chopped onion
3 medium tomatoes, peeled and sliced

1. In a bowl, combine the first four ingredients. Cut in shortening until crumbly. Stir in sour cream. Cover and refrigerate for 30 minutes.

2. Press pastry into a 9-in. pie plate; flute edges if desired. Bake at 375° for 10 minutes. Cool completely.

3. In a bowl, combine the mayonnaise, cheddar cheese, mushrooms, bacon, green pepper and onion. Layer half of the tomatoes in crust; top with half of the mayonnaise mixture. Repeat layers.

4. Bake at 350° for 30-35 minutes or until golden brown. Refrigerate leftovers. **Yield:** 6-8 servings.

Editor's Note: Reduced-fat or fat-free mayonnaise is not recommended for this recipe.

My boys can't wait to pick the first ripe tomatoes in our garden to be used in this terrific pie. It has a tempting filling and tomatoes layered in a melt-in-your-mouth crust. And the crust is so easy to make—you just pat the dough into the pan!

Shara Walvoort
Oostburg, Wisconsin

Bruschetta Chicken

1/2 cup all-purpose flour
1/2 cup egg substitute
   4 boneless skinless chicken breast halves (1 pound)
1/4 cup grated Parmesan cheese
1/4 cup dry bread crumbs
   1 tablespoon butter, melted
   2 large tomatoes, seeded and chopped
   3 tablespoons minced fresh basil
   2 garlic cloves, minced
   1 tablespoon olive oil
1/2 teaspoon salt
1/4 teaspoon pepper

My husband and I enjoy serving this tasty chicken to company as well as family. It looks like we fussed, but it's really fast and easy to fix.

Carolin Cattoi-Demkiw
Lethbridge, Alberta

1. Place flour and eggs in separate shallow bowls. Dip chicken in flour, then in eggs; place in a greased 13-in. x 9-in. x 2-in. baking dish. Combine the Parmesan cheese, bread crumbs and butter; sprinkle over chicken. Loosely cover baking dish with foil. Bake at 375° for 20 minutes. Uncover; bake 5-10 minutes longer or until top is browned.

2. Meanwhile, in a bowl, combine the remaining ingredients. Spoon over the chicken. Return to the oven for 3-5 minutes or until tomato mixture is heated through. **Yield:** 4 servings.

Preparing Tomatoes

Wash and core tomatoes. To remove peel, place tomato in boiling water for 30 seconds. Immediately plunge in ice water.

Remove skin with a sharp paring knife.

Tomato Mushroom Soup

1 pound fresh mushrooms, thinly sliced
6 tablespoons butter, *divided*
2 medium onions, minced
1 garlic clove, minced
2 carrots, chopped
3 celery ribs, finely chopped
3 tablespoons all-purpose flour
8 cups beef broth
2 tomatoes, peeled, seeded and chopped
1 can (15 ounces) tomato sauce
1 teaspoon salt
1/2 teaspoon pepper
3 tablespoons minced fresh parsley
Sour cream, optional

1. In a Dutch oven, saute mushrooms in 4 tablespoons butter until tender. Remove mushrooms; set aside. In the same pan, saute the onions, garlic, carrots and celery in remaining butter until tender. Stir in flour until smooth. Add the broth, tomatoes, tomato sauce, salt, pepper and half of the mushrooms. Simmer, covered, about 30 minutes.

2. Add parsley and remaining mushrooms; simmer 5 minutes or until heated through. Garnish each serving with a dollop of sour cream if desired. **Yield:** about 12 servings (3 quarts).

This soup recipe came about while I was experimenting with the goodies from my garden...I serve it often to my family, especially in the winter.

Bonnie Hawkins
Woodstock, Illinois

Tomato Basil Linguine

1 pound Brie *or* Camembert cheese, rind removed and cut into small pieces
4 large tomatoes, coarsely chopped
1 cup chopped fresh basil
1/2 cup olive oil
3 garlic cloves, minced
1/2 teaspoon salt
1/4 teaspoon white pepper
1-1/2 pounds uncooked linguine
Shredded Parmesan cheese

In a large serving bowl, combine the first seven ingredients. Let stand at room temperature for up to 1-1/2 hours. Cook linguine according to package directions; drain. Toss with cheese mixture. Sprinkle with Parmesan cheese. Serve immediately. **Yield:** 10 servings.

Hot pasta is tossed with a fresh-tasting sauce that includes tomatoes, basil and Brie cheese in this deliciously different dish. It's very pretty, too. Even when it cools off, this pasta tastes great.

Diann Mallehan
Grand Rapids, Michigan

Tomato-Onion Phyllo Pizza

5 tablespoons butter, melted

7 sheets phyllo dough (18 inches x 14 inches)

7 tablespoons grated Parmesan cheese, *divided*

1 cup (4 ounces) shredded part-skim mozzarella cheese

1 cup thinly sliced onion

7 to 9 plum tomatoes (about 1-1/4 pounds), sliced

1-1/2 teaspoons minced fresh oregano *or* 1/2 teaspoon dried oregano

1 teaspoon minced fresh thyme *or* 1/4 teaspoon dried thyme

Salt and pepper to taste

With a delicate crust and lots of lovely tomatoes on top, this dish is a special one to serve to guests. I make it often when fresh garden tomatoes are in season. It freezes well unbaked, so I can keep one on hand to pop in the oven for a quick dinner.

Neta Cohen
Bedford, Virginia

1. Brush a 15-in. x 10-in. x 1-in. baking pan with some of the melted butter. Lay a sheet of phyllo in pan, folding edges in to fit. (Keep remaining phyllo dough covered with plastic wrap and a damp towel to prevent it from drying out.) Brush dough with butter and sprinkle with 1 tablespoon Parmesan cheese. Repeat layers five times, folding edges for each layer.

2. Top with remaining dough, folding edges to fit pan; brush with remaining butter. Sprinkle with mozzarella cheese; arrange onion and tomatoes over the cheese. Sprinkle with oregano, thyme, salt, pepper and remaining Parmesan. Bake at 375° for 20-25 minutes or until edges are golden brown. **Yield:** 28 slices.

Tomato Dill Bread

1 package (1/4 ounce) active dry yeast
2 tablespoons sugar
1/2 cup warm water (110° to 115°)
1-1/2 cups chopped peeled tomatoes
2 tablespoons vegetable oil
1 tablespoon minced fresh parsley
1 tablespoon minced fresh dill
1 tablespoon minced fresh oregano
2 teaspoons salt
3-1/2 to 4-1/2 cups all-purpose flour
3 tablespoons butter, melted

1. In a large bowl, dissolve yeast and sugar in water; set aside. In a blender or food processor, puree tomatoes with oil, parsley, dill, oregano and salt. Add to yeast mixture. Add enough flour to make a smooth dough. Turn onto a floured surface; knead until smooth and elastic, about 6-8 minutes. Place in a greased bowl, turning once to grease top. Cover and let rise in a warm place until doubled, about 1 hour.

2. Punch down and divide in half; shape into loaves. Place into two greased 8-in. x 4-in. x 2-in. loaf pans. Cover and let rise until doubled, about 1 hour.

3. Bake at 400° for 15 minutes. Reduce heat to 350°; bake for 25 minutes longer or until done. Brush with melted butter.
Yield: 2 loaves.

Delicately flavored with various herbs, this bread disappears fast at our home here in the beautiful Wallowa Mountains of Oregon. It also makes great sandwiches.

Chris Bowman
Enterprise, Oregon

Best-of-Show Tomato Quiche

3/4 cup all-purpose flour
1/2 cup cornmeal
1/2 teaspoon salt
1/8 teaspoon pepper
1/3 cup shortening
    4 to 5 tablespoons cold water

Filling:
    2 cups chopped plum tomatoes
    1 teaspoon salt
1/2 teaspoon dried basil
1/8 teaspoon pepper
1/2 cup chopped green onions
1/2 cup shredded cheddar cheese
1/2 cup shredded Swiss cheese
    2 tablespoons all-purpose flour
    1 cup evaporated milk
    2 eggs

I knew this delicious recipe was a keeper when I first tried it as a new bride—it impressed my in-laws when I made it for them! Now I sometimes substitute Mexican or Cajun seasoning for the basil. No matter how it's seasoned, it's wonderful.

Dorothy Swanson
Affton, Missouri

1. In a bowl, combine the first four ingredients. Cut in shortening until crumbly. Add water, tossing with a fork until dough forms a ball. Refrigerate for 30 minutes.

2. On a lightly floured surface, roll out dough to fit a 9-in. pie plate; transfer to plate. Trim to 1/2 in. beyond edge of plate; flute edges. Bake at 375° for 10 minutes. Cool completely.

3. Place tomatoes in the crust; sprinkle with the salt, basil, pepper, onions and cheeses. In a bowl, whisk the flour, milk and eggs until smooth. Pour over filling.

4. Bake at 375° for 40-45 minutes or until a knife inserted near the center comes out clean. Let stand for 10 minutes before cutting. **Yield:** 6-8 servings.

Dumplings with Tomatoes And Zucchini

Here's a unique and tasty side dish that has dumplings made with absolutely no flour!

Mildred Renfro
Lewiston, Michigan

1/4 cup chopped onion
2 tablespoons vegetable oil
4 large fresh tomatoes, peeled and chopped
1 tablespoon minced fresh basil *or* 1 teaspoon dried basil
1 teaspoon sugar
1 teaspoon salt
1/4 teaspoon pepper
2 medium zucchini, peeled and cubed

Parmesan Dumplings:
1 egg, lightly beaten
1 cup grated Parmesan cheese

1. In a large skillet, saute onion in oil until tender. Add tomatoes, basil, sugar, salt and pepper. Simmer, covered, for 10 minutes. Add zucchini; cook, covered, for 15 minutes or until tender.

2. For dumplings, combine egg and cheese. Drop by tablespoons onto tomato mixture. Simmer, covered, for 5 minutes or until dumplings are firm. **Yield:** 6 servings.

Tomato Crouton Casserole

8 medium tomatoes, peeled and cut into wedges
8 slices bread, crusts removed and cubed
1/2 cup plus 2 tablespoons butter, melted
1 teaspoon salt
1 teaspoon dried basil
1 teaspoon dried thyme
3/4 cup grated Parmesan cheese

Arrange tomatoes in a greased 13-in. x 9-in. x 2-in. baking dish. Top with bread cubes. Combine the butter, salt, basil and thyme; drizzle over bread and tomatoes. Sprinkle with cheese. Bake, uncovered, at 350° for 30-35 minutes or until tomatoes are tender. **Yield:** 8-10 servings.

This baked dish uses lots of delicious tomatoes and seasonings that give it an Italian twist. Every time I serve this dish, someone asks for the recipe.

Norma Nelson
Punta Gorda, Florida

Cornucopia

Peach Shortcake, p. 245

Cashew Snow Pea Salad

I like to serve this cool and refreshing dish on hot summer days. My guests enjoy the crunchy snow peas, cauliflower and cashews tossed with a light ranch dressing.

Beth Gambro
Yorkville, Illinois

3 cups fresh snow peas, halved
2 cups chopped cauliflower
1 cup chopped celery
1/4 cup chopped green onions
1/2 cup sour cream
1/2 cup ranch salad dressing
Leaf lettuce, optional
3 bacon strips, cooked and crumbled
1/3 cup chopped cashews

In a bowl, combine the peas, cauliflower, celery and onions. Combine sour cream and salad dressing; pour over vegetables and toss to coat. Serve in a lettuce-lined bowl if desired. Sprinkle with bacon and cashews. **Yield:** 5 servings.

Grilled Mushrooms

1/2 pound medium fresh mushrooms
1/4 cup butter, melted
1/2 teaspoon dill weed
1/2 teaspoon garlic salt

Thread mushrooms on metal or soaked wooden skewers. Combine the butter, dill and garlic salt; brush over mushrooms. Grill over hot heat for 10-15 minutes, basting and turning every 5 minutes. **Yield:** 4 servings.

Mushrooms cooked over hot coals always taste good, but this easy recipe makes the mushrooms taste fantastic!

Melanie Knoll
Marshalltown, Iowa

Curried Cucumbers

1/3 cup sour cream
1/2 cup mayonnaise
1/4 to 1/2 teaspoon
  lemon-pepper seasoning
1/4 to 1/2 teaspoon curry
  powder
1/4 teaspoon garlic salt
1/2 teaspoon dried parsley
  flakes
Hot pepper sauce to taste
  3 cucumbers, peeled and
    thinly sliced
1/2 medium onion, thinly
  sliced
Salt and pepper to taste
Fresh parsley *or* chopped
  chives, optional

In a bowl, combine first seven ingredients. Toss with cucumbers and onion slices. Cover and refrigerate for 2-3 hours. Stir just before serving. Season with salt and pepper to taste; garnish with parsley or chives if desired. **Yield:** 6-8 servings.

This is a variation of a cucumber salad I once enjoyed at a salad bar. I use mayonnaise to cut the tartness of the sour cream. It has a rich flavor, too!

Debra Creed-Broeker
Rocky Mount, Missouri

Summer Veggie Salad

1 cup thinly sliced carrots
1 cup fresh green beans,
    cut into 2-inch pieces
1 cup fresh sugar snap peas
1 cup thinly sliced zucchini
1 cup thinly sliced yellow
    summer squash
1/2 cup thinly sliced green
    onions
1/2 cup chopped sweet red
    pepper
1 can (2-1/4 ounces)
    sliced ripe olives, drained

Dressing:
6 tablespoons olive oil
4-1/2 teaspoons lemon juice
1 tablespoon red wine
    vinegar
1 tablespoon minced fresh
    parsley
1-1/2 teaspoons sugar
1 garlic clove, minced
1/8 teaspoon salt
Dash pepper
1/4 cup shredded Parmesan
    cheese, optional

For a deliciously different salad, try this lightly dressed version without lettuce. It's especially good when I use fresh bounty from our garden. My friends and family love vegetables, so when I serve this colorful salad, it goes fast!

Kimberly Walsh
Fishers, Indiana

1. In a large saucepan, bring 4 in. of water to a boil. Add the carrots, beans and peas; cook for 4 minutes. Drain and rinse in cold water. Place in a bowl; add zucchini, summer squash, onions, red pepper and olives.

2. In a jar with a tight-fitting lid, combine the oil, lemon juice, vinegar, parsley, sugar, garlic, salt and pepper; shake well. Pour over vegetable mixture and toss to coat. Cover and refrigerate for up to 1 hour. Just before serving, sprinkle with Parmesan cheese if desired. **Yield:** 12 servings.

Mushroom Olive Salad

1/4 pound fresh mushrooms, chopped
2 tablespoons chopped stuffed olives
2 tablespoons olive oil
1 garlic clove, minced
1/8 teaspoon dried basil
Salt and pepper to taste

In a bowl, combine all the ingredients. Cover and refrigerate for at least 1-1/2 hours before serving. **Yield:** 2 servings.

We like fresh mushrooms and have them often, so I try to be a little inventive. This salad "happened" one night when there was nothing but a carton of mushrooms in the refrigerator. The simple addition of chopped stuffed olives was such a hit that this salad has been one of our favorites ever since.

Mary Johnston
Palestine, Texas

Onion Beef Au Jus

1 boneless beef rump roast (4 pounds)
2 tablespoons vegetable oil
2 large sweet onions, cut into 1/4-inch slices
6 tablespoons butter, softened, *divided*
5 cups water
1/2 cup soy sauce
1 envelope onion soup mix
1 garlic clove, minced
1 teaspoon browning sauce, optional
1 loaf (1 pound) French bread
1 cup (4 ounces) shredded Swiss cheese

1. In a Dutch oven over medium-high heat, brown roast on all sides in oil; drain. In a large skillet, saute onions in 2 tablespoons butter until tender. Add the water, soy sauce, soup mix, garlic and browning sauce if desired. Pour over roast. Cover and bake at 325° for 2-1/2 hours or until meat is tender.

2. Let stand for 10 minutes before slicing. Return meat to pan juices. Slice bread in half lengthwise; cut into 3-in. sections. Spread remaining butter over bread.

3. Place on a baking sheet. Broil 4-6 in. from the heat for 2-3 minutes or until golden brown. Top with beef and onions; sprinkle with cheese. Broil 4-6 in. from the heat for 1-2 minutes or until cheese is melted. Serve with pan juices. **Yield:** 12 servings.

Garlic, onions, soy sauce and onion soup mix flavor the tender beef in these savory hot sandwiches served with a tasty rich broth for dipping. The seasoned beef makes delicious cold sandwiches, too.

Marilyn Brown
West Union, Iowa

Garden Bounty Beef Kabobs

1/4 cup soy sauce

2 tablespoons olive oil

1 tablespoon molasses

3 garlic cloves, minced

1 teaspoon ground ginger

1 teaspoon ground mustard

1 pound boneless beef sirloin steak, cut into 1-inch cubes

1 large sweet onion, cut into 1-inch pieces

1 large green *or* sweet red pepper, cut into 1-inch pieces

1 medium zucchini, cut into 1-inch slices

1 pint cherry tomatoes

1/2 pound large fresh mushrooms

Dipping Sauce:

1 cup (8 ounces) sour cream

1/4 cup milk

3 tablespoons dry onion soup mix

2 tablespoons Dijon mustard

1/8 teaspoon pepper

These classic kabobs are a hearty way to use up your garden harvest. At our house, everyone fixes their own skewers for an all-in-one dinner.

Christine Klessig
Amherst Junction, Wisconsin

1. In a large resealable plastic bag, combine first six ingredients; add the beef. Seal bag and turn to coat; refrigerate for 1 hour.

2. If grilling the kabobs, coat grill rack with nonstick cooking spray before starting the grill. Drain and discard marinade. On eight metal or soaked wooden skewers, alternately thread beef and vegetables. Grill, covered, over medium heat or broil 4-6 in. from the heat for 3-4 minutes on each side or until beef reaches desired doneness, turning three times.

3. In a saucepan, combine the dipping sauce ingredients; mix well. Cook over low heat until heated through. Serve with kabobs. **Yield:** 4 servings.

Preparing Mushrooms

Gently remove dirt by rubbing with a mushroom brush or wipe mushrooms with a damp paper towel. Or quickly rinse under cold water, drain and pat dry with paper towels. Do not peel mushrooms. Trim stems. For shiitake mushrooms, remove and discard stems. For enoki, trim base and separate stems. Mushrooms can be eaten raw, marinated, sauteed, stir-fried, baked, broiled or grilled.

Fresh Veggie Pizza

1 tube (8 ounces)
  reduced-fat crescent rolls
1 package (8 ounces)
  reduced-fat cream cheese
1 envelope ranch salad
  dressing mix
2 tablespoons fat-free milk
1/2 cup *each* chopped fresh
  broccoli, cauliflower,
  carrots, green pepper,
  sweet red pepper and
  mushrooms

1. Unroll crescent roll dough into one long rectangle. Press onto the bottom of a 13-in. x 9-in. x 2-in. baking pan coated with nonstick cooking spray; seal seams and perforations. Bake at 375° for 11-13 minutes or until golden brown. Cool completely.

2. In a mixing bowl, beat cream cheese, salad dressing mix and milk until smooth. Spread over crust. Sprinkle with vegetables. Cover and refrigerate for at least 1 hour before serving. Cut into 16 pieces. **Yield:** 8 servings.

This colorful pizza is topped with a rainbow of crunchy vegetables. Guests usually don't even guess this delicious pizza is low-fat.

Brooke Wiley
Halifax, Virginia

Kohlrabi with Honey Butter

1 pound kohlrabi (4 to 5
  small), peeled and cut
  into 1/4-inch strips
1 medium carrot, cut into
  1/8-inch strips
1 tablespoon minced chives
1 tablespoon lemon juice

1 tablespoon butter, melted
2 teaspoons honey
1/4 teaspoon grated lemon
  peel
1/8 teaspoon pepper
4 lemon slices

If you're not acquainted with kohlrabi, this recipe will serve as a pleasant introduction. Honey and lemon lend a sweet, citrusy taste to the turnip-like veggie.

Wanda Holoubek
Salina, Kansas

1. In a large skillet, bring 1 in. of water, kohlrabi and carrot to a boil. Reduce heat; cover and simmer for 6-10 minutes or until crisp-tender.

2. In a small bowl, combine the chives, lemon juice, butter, honey, lemon peel and pepper. Drain vegetables and transfer to a serving bowl. Add honey butter and toss to coat. Garnish with lemon slices. **Yield:** 4 servings.

Spiced Baked Beets

4 cups shredded peeled
   beets (about 4 to 5
   medium)
1 medium onion, shredded
1 medium potato, shredded
3 tablespoons brown sugar
3 tablespoons vegetable oil
2 tablespoons water
1 tablespoon cider vinegar
1/2 teaspoon salt, optional
1/4 teaspoon pepper
1/4 teaspoon celery seed
1/8 to 1/4 teaspoon ground
   cloves

Especially during the fall and winter months, this recipe is a favorite. With its red color, it looks great served at Christmastime. It's nice for taking to potlucks as well.

Margery Richmond
Lacombe, Alberta

1. In a large bowl, combine the beets, onion and potato; set aside. In a small bowl, combine brown sugar, oil, water, vinegar and seasonings. Pour over vegetables; toss to coat.

2. Pour into a greased 1-1/2-qt. baking dish. Cover and bake at 350° for 45 minutes, stirring occasionally. Uncover and bake 15-25 minutes longer or until vegetables are tender. **Yield:** 8-10 servings.

Preparing Brussels Sprouts

Remove any loose or yellowed outer leaves; trim stem end. Rinse sprouts. When cooking brussels sprouts whole, cut an X in the core end with a sharp knife.

Nutty Brussels Sprouts

1 pound fresh *or* frozen brussels sprouts, thawed and halved
1 cup water
1/2 teaspoon salt
1/4 teaspoon pepper
1/4 cup chopped pecans
3 tablespoons butter

1. In a large saucepan, bring brussels sprouts, water and salt to a boil. Reduce heat; cover and simmer for 6-8 minutes or until crisp-tender. Drain. Sprinkle with pepper; keep warm.

2. In a skillet, toast pecans in butter over medium heat for 1-2 minutes or until lightly browned. Add brussels sprouts; toss to coat. **Yield:** 4-6 servings.

Even my son will eat brussels sprouts when I make this side dish. I use pecans, but this English recipe is traditionally made with chestnuts.

Laura Hamrick
Buena Park, California

Eggplant with Mushroom Stuffing

1 small eggplant
1 tablespoon salt
1 small onion, chopped
1/4 cup butter
3/4 cup soft bread crumbs
1/2 cup chopped fresh mushrooms
1 tablespoon minced fresh parsley
Dash pepper
1/2 cup shredded Swiss cheese

1. Cut eggplant in half lengthwise; scoop out pulp, leaving a 1/4-in.-thick shell. Set shell aside. Chop pulp; place in a colander over a plate. Sprinkle with salt; let stand for 30 minutes. Blot moisture with a paper towel.

2. In a skillet, saute eggplant pulp and onion in butter until tender. Add the bread crumbs, mushrooms, parsley and pepper. Spoon into eggplant shells.

3. Place in a greased 8-in. square baking dish. Bake, uncovered, at 350° for 15 minutes. Sprinkle with cheese; bake 5 minutes longer or until cheese is melted. **Yield:** 2 servings.

We had an abundance of eggplant in our garden one year, so I was happy to find this recipe, especially since it was such a hit with my family. It's not hard to make, and the best part is it's perfect for two people.

Joyce Towles
Houston, Texas

Pea Pod Carrot Medley

1 cup sliced carrots	**2 teaspoons soy sauce**
2 cups fresh sugar snap peas	**1/2 teaspoon grated orange peel**
1 teaspoon cornstarch	**1/4 teaspoon salt**
1/3 cup orange juice	

1. Place carrots in a small saucepan; cover with water. Bring to a boil. Reduce heat; cover and simmer for 5 minutes. Add the peas. Cover and simmer 2-4 minutes longer or until vegetables are crisp-tender. Drain; set aside and keep warm.

2. In the same saucepan, whisk the cornstarch and orange juice until smooth. Bring to a boil; cook and stir for 2 minutes or until thickened. Remove from the heat. Stir in the soy sauce, orange peel and salt. Pour over vegetables; toss to coat. **Yield:** 2 servings.

Okra Pilaf

4 bacon strips, cut into 1/2-inch pieces	**2 medium tomatoes, peeled, seeded and chopped**
1 medium onion, chopped	**1/2 teaspoon salt, optional**
1/2 cup chopped green pepper	**1/4 teaspoon pepper**
1 cup sliced fresh *or* frozen okra	**3 cups cooked rice**

1. In a skillet, cook the bacon over medium heat until crisp. Using a slotted spoon, remove to paper towel to drain; reserve drippings. Saute onion and green pepper in reserved drippings for 6-8 minutes or until tender.

2. Stir in the okra, tomatoes, salt if desired and pepper; cook over medium heat for 5 minutes. Add rice; cook for 10-15 minutes or until okra is tender and liquid is absorbed. Crumble bacon; stir into rice mixture and serve immediately. **Yield:** 8 servings.

Artichoke Steak Salad

3/4 cup vegetable oil
1/4 cup cider vinegar
1/4 cup soy sauce
1/2 teaspoon dried thyme
1/2 teaspoon ground mustard
1/2 teaspoon pepper
1/4 teaspoon dried oregano
1-1/2 pounds boneless beef sirloin steak
1/2 pound fresh mushrooms, quartered
1 can (14 ounces) artichoke hearts, rinsed, drained and quartered
12 cherry tomatoes, halved
5 green onions, chopped
2 heads Bibb lettuce, separated into leaves
2 hard-cooked eggs, cut into wedges

1. In a jar with a tight-fitting lid, combine the first seven ingredients; set aside.

2. Grill or broil steak until a meat thermometer reaches at least 145° (medium-rare). Slice across the grain into thin strips.

3. In a bowl, combine the steak, mushrooms, artichokes, tomatoes and onions. Shake dressing; pour over steak mixture and toss to coat. Cover and refrigerate for at least 4 hours, stirring occasionally.

4. Line a serving platter with lettuce; top with steak mixture and dressing. Garnish with eggs. **Yield:** 6-8 servings.

I came up with my hearty main-course salad to take to picnics instead of lugging along a grill. It's perfect for potlucks, too. Feel free to substitute other meats for the steak, such as leftover roast beef, grilled pork or chicken.

Pat Briggs
Sarasota, Florida

Scalloped Turnips

3 cups diced peeled turnips
2 cups water
1 teaspoon sugar
2 tablespoons butter
3 tablespoons all-purpose flour
3/4 teaspoon salt, optional
1-1/2 cups milk
1/4 cup crushed cornflakes
2 tablespoons grated cheddar *or* Parmesan cheese, optional
Chopped fresh parsley, optional

This is the only kind of cooked turnips our five grown children and 13 grandchildren will eat. The crunchy cornflake topping adds a special touch.

Mrs. Eldon Larabee
Clearmont, Missouri

1. Place the turnips, water and sugar in a saucepan. Bring to a boil. Reduce heat; simmer, uncovered, for 5-8 minutes or until tender. Drain and set aside.

2. In another saucepan, melt butter; stir in flour and salt if desired until smooth. Gradually add milk. Bring to a boil; cook and stir for 1-2 minutes or until thickened. Stir in turnips.

3. Pour into a greased 1-qt. baking dish; sprinkle with cornflakes and cheese if desired. Bake, uncovered, at 350° for 20 minutes or until bubbly. Garnish with parsley if desired. **Yield:** 5 servings.

————Seeding a Cucumber————

Peel or score cucumber if desired. Cut lengthwise in half. Using a teaspoon, run the tip under the seeds to loosen and remove.

Greek Chicken Salad

3 cups cubed cooked chicken
2 medium cucumbers, peeled, seeded and chopped
1 cup crumbled feta cheese
2/3 cup sliced pitted ripe olives
1/4 cup minced fresh parsley
1 cup mayonnaise
3 garlic cloves, minced
1/2 cup plain yogurt
1 tablespoon dried oregano

Combine the first five ingredients. Set aside. In a small bowl, combine remaining ingredients. Toss with chicken mixture. Cover and refrigerate for several hours. **Yield:** 7 servings.

My family loves this salad—I receive nothing but raves when I serve it. Even if you or your family are not garlic lovers, I'd advise you use the full measurement of garlic and oregano for the proper flavoring.

Donna Smith
Palisade, Colorado

Amish Onion Cake

3 to 4 medium onions, chopped
2 cups cold butter, *divided*
1 tablespoon poppy seeds
1-1/2 teaspoons salt
1-1/2 teaspoons paprika
1 teaspoon coarsely ground pepper
4 cups all-purpose flour
1/2 cup cornstarch
1 tablespoon baking powder
1 tablespoon sugar
1 tablespoon brown sugar
5 eggs
3/4 cup milk
3/4 cup sour cream

1. In a large skillet, cook onions in 1/2 cup butter over low heat for 10 minutes. Stir in the poppy seeds, salt, paprika and pepper; cook until golden brown, stirring occasionally. Remove from the heat; set aside.

2. In a bowl, combine the flour, cornstarch, baking powder and sugars. Cut in 1-1/4 cups butter until mixture resembles coarse crumbs. Melt the remaining butter. In a bowl, whisk the eggs, milk, sour cream and melted butter. Make a well in dry ingredients; stir in egg mixture just until moistened. Spread into a greased 10-in. springform pan. Spoon onion mixture over the dough. Place pan on a baking sheet.

3. Bake at 350° for 35-40 minutes or until a toothpick inserted near the center comes out clean. Serve warm. **Yield:** 10-12 servings.

This rich, moist bread with an onion-poppy seed topping is a wonderful break from your everyday bread routine. You can serve it with any meat, and it's a nice accompaniment to soup or salad. I've made it many times and have often been asked to share the recipe.

Mitzi Sentiff
Alexandria, Virginia

Chicken-Stuffed Green Peppers

Both for a family meal and for entertaining, this is a dish I serve frequently. It's very appealing to the eye, and people like the wild rice and the peppers. What I learned about cooking came from an expert—my husband! He's the real chef in the family.

Shelley Armstrong
Buffalo Center, Iowa

4 large green peppers
1/3 cup chopped onion
1 garlic clove, minced
2 tablespoons butter
3 cups diced cooked chicken
2 cups chicken broth
1 package (6 ounces) long grain brown and wild rice blend
1/3 cup sliced celery
1/4 cup finely chopped carrot
1/4 teaspoon dried basil
1/4 teaspoon dried thyme
1 can (14-1/2 ounces) diced tomatoes, undrained
1 cup chopped fresh mushrooms
1/2 cup chopped zucchini
1/3 cup grated Parmesan cheese

1. Cut tops off peppers; remove seeds. In a Dutch oven, cook peppers in boiling water for 3 minutes. Drain and rinse in cold water; set aside.

2. In a large saucepan, saute onion and garlic in butter until tender. Add the chicken, broth, rice with contents of seasoning packet, celery, carrot, basil and thyme; bring to a boil. Reduce heat; cover and simmer for 25 minutes or until the rice is almost tender.

3. Remove from the heat; stir in the tomatoes, mushrooms and zucchini. Spoon rice mixture into the peppers; place in a greased shallow 2-qt. baking dish. Spoon the remaining rice mixture around peppers.

4. Cover and bake at 350° for 25-30 minutes or until the peppers are tender and filling is heated through. Uncover and sprinkle with Parmesan cheese; bake 5 minutes longer. **Yield:** 4 servings.

California Roast Lamb

1 leg of lamb (4 to 5 pounds)
2 to 3 garlic cloves, halved
1 teaspoon seasoned salt
1 teaspoon pepper
1 teaspoon dried oregano
2 cans (8 ounces *each*) tomato sauce
1 cup water
Juice of 1 lemon
3 to 5 large fresh artichokes, quartered
Fresh lemon slices

1. Cut slits in lamb; insert garlic. Rub meat with salt, pepper and oregano. Roast at 400° for 30 minutes. Reduce heat to 350°; roast 1 hour more.

2. Skim off any fat in pan; pour tomato sauce, water and lemon juice over lamb. Place artichokes around meat. Roast 1 hour longer or to desired doneness, basting occasionally with pan juices. Garnish with lemon. **Yield:** 10-12 servings.

This recipe is very easy to make and requires little attention. It goes well with any rice dish, and it's perfect for just about any occasion.

Ann Eastman
Greenville, California

Pumpkin Burgers

1-1/2 pounds ground beef
1 medium onion, chopped
1 bottle (12 ounces) chili sauce
1 can (10-3/4 ounces) condensed tomato soup, undiluted
1/2 cup cooked pumpkin
1 teaspoon salt
1/2 to 1 teaspoon pumpkin pie spice
1/4 teaspoon pepper
6 to 8 hamburger buns, split

In a large skillet, cook beef and onion over medium heat until meat is no longer pink; drain. Add the chili sauce, soup, pumpkin, salt, pumpkin pie spice and pepper. Bring to a boil. Reduce heat; cover and simmer for 1 hour. Serve on buns. **Yield:** 6-8 servings.

In our town, we have a pumpkin festival in late October and use pumpkins many different ways. This is always a popular recipe for "sandwich night" at our house.

Linda Shuttleworth
Circleville, Ohio

Cantaloupe Salsa

The sweet taste of cantaloupe tempers the spicy jalapeno pepper in this super simple salsa.

Debbie Smith
Tucson, Arizona

- 2 cups coarsely chopped cantaloupe
- 2 cups coarsely chopped cherry tomatoes
- 1/4 cup chopped green onions
- 1/4 cup minced fresh basil *or* 4 teaspoons dried basil
- 2 tablespoons diced seeded jalapeno pepper
- 2 tablespoons lime juice
- 2 tablespoons orange juice
- 1 to 2 teaspoons grated orange peel
- 1/4 teaspoon salt
- 1/8 teaspoon pepper

In a large bowl, combine all ingredients; toss to coat. Cover and refrigerate for at least 30 minutes before serving. **Yield:** 3 cups.

Editor's Note: When cutting or seeding hot peppers, use rubber or plastic gloves to protect your hands. Avoid touching your face.

Cherry Waldorf Salad

- 2 large apples (about 1 pound), chopped
- 1 tablespoon lemon juice
- 2 celery ribs, chopped
- 1 cup fresh *or* frozen pitted tart cherries, thawed
- 1/2 cup dried cranberries
- 1/2 cup slivered almonds, toasted
- 1/4 cup mayonnaise
- 1/4 cup sour cream
- 2 tablespoons honey
- 1/8 teaspoon salt

I combined apples with cherries and cranberries to give a new twist to the classic Waldorf salad.

Marie Hattrup
The Dalles, Oregon

1. In a large salad bowl, toss apples with lemon juice. Add the celery, cherries, cranberries and almonds.

2. In a small bowl, whisk the mayonnaise, sour cream, honey and salt until well blended. Pour over salad and toss to coat. Cover and refrigerate for 1 hour before serving. **Yield:** 6-8 servings.

Grilled Chicken With Peaches

1 cup 100% peach spreadable fruit
2 tablespoons olive oil
4 teaspoons soy sauce
1 tablespoon ground mustard
1 garlic clove, minced
1/2 teaspoon salt
1/4 teaspoon pepper
1/4 teaspoon cayenne pepper
8 bone-in chicken breast halves, skin removed (8 ounces *each*)
8 medium ripe peaches, halved and pitted

1. Coat grill rack with nonstick cooking spray before starting grill for indirect heat. In a small bowl, combine the first eight ingredients; set aside. Grill chicken, covered, over indirect medium heat for 10 minutes on each side. Brush chicken with glaze. Grill 10-15 minutes longer or until juices run clear, turning every 5 minutes and brushing with glaze. Transfer to a serving platter and keep warm.

2. Grill peach halves cut side down over indirect heat for 2 minutes. Turn; brush with glaze and grill for 3-4 minutes longer or until tender. Serve grilled peaches with chicken.
Yield: 8 servings.

My grandmother gave me this recipe. My children loved it when they were little, and now my grandchildren ask for it when they come over. The peaches are delicious hot off the grill.

Linda McCluskey
Cullman, Alabama

Pear-Stuffed Tenderloin

1 cup chopped peeled ripe pears
1/4 cup hazelnuts, toasted
1/4 cup soft bread crumbs
1/4 cup finely shredded carrot
2 tablespoons chopped onion
1/8 teaspoon ground ginger
1/4 teaspoon salt
1/4 teaspoon pepper
1 pork tenderloin (3/4 to 1 pound)
Vegetable oil
2 tablespoons orange marmalade

This succulent entree is a classic you'll be proud to serve your family. There's very little fuss to making this main dish, and the meat always turns out tender.

Aloma Hawkins
Bixby, Missouri

1. In a bowl, combine the first eight ingredients; set aside. Make a lengthwise cut three-quarters of the way through the tenderloin; open and flatten to 1/4-in. thickness. Spread pear mixture over tenderloin. Roll up from a long side; tuck in ends. Secure with toothpicks.

2. Place tenderloin on a rack in a shallow roasting pan. Brush lightly with oil. Bake, uncovered, at 425° for 20-25 minutes or until a meat thermometer inserted into pork reads 155°. Brush with marmalade. Bake 5-10 minutes longer or until thermometer reads 160°-170°. Let stand for 5 minutes. Discard toothpicks and slice. **Yield:** 2-3 servings.

Melon Balls with Lime Sauce

1/2 cup sugar
1/2 cup water
Juice and grated peel of 1 lime

2 cups watermelon balls
2 cups cantaloupe balls
2 cups honeydew balls

In a small saucepan, heat sugar, water, lime juice and peel; bring to a boil. Reduce heat and simmer 5 minutes. Cool. Pour sauce over fruit and toss to coat. Chill 4 hours. **Yield:** 12-16 servings.

This refreshing salad comes together in just minutes. Even though it's hard to wait, give it a few hours to chill. The delightful result is worth the wait.

Barbara Mctighe
Butler, Pennsylvania

Cantaloupe with Chicken Salad

2 cups cubed cooked
   chicken
1-1/2 to 2 cups fresh
   blueberries
1 cup sliced celery
1 cup seedless green
   grapes, halved
1/2 cup sliced almonds
3 cantaloupe, halved and
   seeded

Dressing:
   1/2 cup mayonnaise
   1/4 cup sour cream
   1 tablespoon fresh lemon
      juice
1-1/2 teaspoons grated lemon
      peel
1-1/2 teaspoons sugar
   1/2 teaspoon ground ginger
   1/4 teaspoon salt, optional

In a large bowl, combine chicken, blueberries, celery, grapes and almonds. In a small bowl, mix dressing ingredients. Pour over the chicken mixture; toss to coat. Spoon into cantaloupe halves. **Yield:** 6 servings.

This recipe is one of my favorite ways to eat blueberries. That delicious fruit is just one of the important crops grown here in the fertile Willamette Valley. We usually pick about 60 pounds each summer for pies and other dishes.

Elsie Trude
Keizer, Oregon

Pecan Pear Bread

1 cup sugar
1/2 cup vegetable oil
2 eggs
1/4 cup sour cream
1 teaspoon vanilla extract
2 cups all-purpose flour
1 teaspoon baking soda
1/2 teaspoon salt

1/4 to 1/2 teaspoon ground cardamom
1/4 to 1/2 teaspoon ground cinnamon
1-1/2 cups chopped peeled pears
2/3 cup chopped pecans
1/2 teaspoon grated lemon peel

1. In a mixing bowl, combine sugar and oil. Add eggs, one at a time, beating well after each addition. Add sour cream and vanilla; mix well. Combine dry ingredients; add to sour cream mixture and mix well. Stir in pears, pecans and lemon peel.

2. Spread into a greased 8-in. x 4-in. x 2-in. loaf pan. Bake at 350° for 65-75 minutes or until a toothpick inserted near the center comes out clean. Cool for 10 minutes; remove from pan to a wire rack to cool completely. **Yield:** 1 loaf.

Cajun Catfish with Fruit Salsa

6 catfish fillets (6 ounces *each*)
3 tablespoons butter, melted
2 tablespoons Cajun seasoning

Salsa:
2 medium navel oranges, peeled, sectioned and diced
1 cup diced cantaloupe
1/2 cup diced honeydew
2 tablespoons lime juice

1. Brush both sides of fillets with butter; sprinkle with Cajun seasoning. Place on a broiler pan; broil 6 in. from the heat for 8-10 minutes or until fish flakes easily with a fork.

2. For salsa, in a small bowl, combine remaining ingredients. Serve with fish. **Yield:** 6 servings.

Grilled Sole With Nectarines

4 sole fillets (6 ounces *each*)
**2 medium nectarines,
   peeled and sliced**
1/2 cup sliced green onions
**1-1/2 teaspoons chopped fresh
   tarragon *or* 1/2 teaspoon
   dried tarragon**
1/4 teaspoon salt
1/8 teaspoon pepper
1 teaspoon butter, melted

1. Place each fillet on a double thickness of heavy-duty foil (about 18 in. x 12 in.). Arrange nectarines around the fillets. Sprinkle with green onions, tarragon, salt, pepper and butter. Fold foil around fish and seal tightly.

2. Grill, covered, over medium heat for 7-8 minutes or until fish flakes easily with a fork. **Yield:** 4 servings.

I found this recipe years ago and adapted it to suit my family's tastes. We enjoy the delicate herb flavor.

Mary Rhoden
Waldport, Oregon

Sweet Cherry Pork Chops

**4 boneless pork chops
   (1 inch thick and 4
   ounces *each*)**
1 tablespoon vegetable oil
1 cup orange juice
**3/4 cup pitted sweet
   cherries, halved**
2 green onions, sliced
1/4 cup cherry preserves
4 teaspoons cornstarch
3 tablespoons cold water
Hot cooked rice

1. In a large skillet, brown pork chops in oil on both sides; drain. Add orange juice, cherries and onions to skillet; bring to a boil. Reduce heat; simmer, uncovered, for 15 minutes or until a meat thermometer reads 160°, turning chops twice.

2. Remove chops and keep warm. Stir preserves into pan juices. In a bowl, combine cornstarch and cold water until smooth; stir into pan juices. Bring to a boil; cook and stir for 1-2 minutes or until thickened. Serve over pork and rice. **Yield:** 4 servings.

I make pork chops often, so I like to experiment with different ideas. I dreamed up this recipe using ingredients that I had on hand. The cherry-orange sauce makes these chops special enough for guests.

Shannon Mink
Columbus, Ohio

Polynesian Sausage Kabobs

1/2 cup lemon juice
1/2 cup soy sauce
1/3 cup water
1/3 cup honey
1/4 teaspoon salt
1-1/2 pounds fully cooked
kielbasa *or* Polish
sausage, cut into
1-1/2-inch slices

1 small pineapple, cut into
1-inch cubes
1 small cantaloupe, cut
into 1-inch cubes
2 medium green peppers,
cut into 1-inch pieces

Here's a meal on a skewer with a unique twist. The pineapple, cantaloupe and peppers complement the sausage perfectly. I frequently fire up the grill for these simple kabobs in summer.

Patricia Eggemeyer
Ellis Grove, Illinois

1. In a large bowl, combine first five ingredients; mix well. Set aside half of the marinade for basting; cover and refrigerate. Pour remaining marinade into a large resealable plastic bag; add sausage. Seal bag and turn to coat. Refrigerate for 3 hours.

2. Drain and discard the marinade from sausage. On metal or soaked wooded skewers, alternate the sausage, pineapple, cantaloupe and green peppers. Grill, uncovered, over medium heat for 10 minutes or until sausage is browned, turning and basting frequently with reserved marinade. **Yield:** 5 servings.

This tantalizing recipe is easy enough for weeknight meals, but don't hesitate to serve it for special occasions. If you don't have plums on hand, feel free to substitute nectarines.

Taste of Home Test Kitchen
Greendale, Wisconsin

Fillets with Plum Sauce

4 beef tenderloin fillets
(4 ounces *each*)
2 tablespoons butter
1/4 teaspoon salt
1/8 teaspoon pepper

2 medium plums, sliced
3 green onions, sliced
1/4 cup orange marmalade
2 tablespoons balsamic
vinegar

1. In a large skillet over medium-high heat, cook fillets in butter until meat reaches desired doneness (for medium-rare, a meat thermometer should read 145°; medium, 160°; well-done, 170°). Season with salt and pepper. Remove and keep warm.

2. In the same skillet, cook plums and onions for 2-3 minutes or until plums are tender. Add marmalade and vinegar; cook and stir until heated through. Serve over fillets. **Yield:** 4 servings.

Watermelon Sherbet

8 cups seeded chopped watermelon
1-1/2 cups sugar
1/2 cup lemon juice
2 envelopes unflavored gelatin
1/2 cup cold water
2 cups milk

1. In a large bowl, combine watermelon, sugar and lemon juice. Chill for 30 minutes; place half in a blender. Blend until smooth; pour into a large bowl. Repeat with the other half; set aside.

2. In a saucepan, cook and stir gelatin and water over low heat until gelatin dissolves. Add to watermelon mixture; mix well. Stir in the milk until well blended.

3. Freeze in an ice cream freezer according to the manufacturer's directions. Serve immediately or freeze and allow to thaw about 20 minutes before serving. **Yield:** 1/2 gallon.

This recipe is a great way to use up an abundance of watermelon. Come fall, a taste of this sweet treat is like a little bit of leftover summer.

Lisa McAdoo
Rush Springs, Oklahoma

Plum Kuchen

2 eggs
1/3 cup milk
3 tablespoons butter, melted
1 cup all-purpose flour
1/2 cup plus 2 tablespoons sugar, *divided*
1 teaspoon baking powder
1-1/4 teaspoons ground cinnamon, *divided*
1/4 teaspoon salt
1/4 teaspoon ground nutmeg
6 medium plums, pitted and halved
Whipped cream and additional ground nutmeg, optional

1. In a mixing bowl, beat the eggs, milk and butter. Combine the flour, 1/2 cup sugar, baking powder, 3/4 teaspoon cinnamon, salt and nutmeg; add to the egg mixture and beat just until combined. Pour into a greased 9-in. round baking pan. Place plums cut side up over batter. Combine remaining sugar and cinnamon; sprinkle over the top.

2. Bake at 375° for 20-25 minutes or until a toothpick inserted near the center comes out clean. Cool for 10 minutes before removing from pan to a wire rack to cool completely. Serve with whipped cream and sprinkle with nutmeg if desired. **Yield:** 6 servings.

I remember my mother making plum kuchen. She never followed a recipe, but this recipe tastes like hers.

Gretchen Berendt
Carroll Valley, Pennsylvania

Golden Peach Pie

Pastry for double-crust pie (9 inches)
1 cup sugar
1/4 cup cornstarch
1/4 teaspoon ground nutmeg
1/8 teaspoon salt
2 teaspoons lemon juice
1/2 teaspoon grated orange peel
1/8 teaspoon almond extract
5 cups sliced peeled fresh peaches (about 5 medium)
2 tablespoons butter
Milk

1. Line a 9-in. pie plate with bottom pastry; trim even with edge of plate. Set aside. In a large bowl, combine the sugar, cornstarch, nutmeg and salt; stir in lemon juice, orange peel and extract. Add peaches; toss gently. Pour into crust; dot with butter.

2. Roll out remaining pastry to fit top of pie; make decorative cutouts in pastry. Set cutouts aside. Place top crust over filling. Trim, seal and flute edges. Brush pastry and cutouts with milk; place cutouts on top of pie. Cover the edges loosely with foil.

3. Bake at 400° for 40 minutes. Remove foil; bake 10-15 minutes longer or until crust is golden brown and filling is bubbly. Cool on a wire rack. Store in the refrigerator. **Yield:** 8 servings.

Peeling Peaches

1. Place peaches in a large pot of boiling water for 10-20 seconds or until the skin splits.

2. Remove with a slotted spoon. Immediately place in an ice water bath to cool the peaches and stop the cooking process.

3. Use a paring knife to peel the skin, which should easily peel off. If stubborn areas of skin won't peel off, just return fruit to the boiling water for a few more seconds.

Peach Shortcake

2 cups all-purpose flour

2 tablespoons brown sugar

1 tablespoon baking powder

1/2 teaspoon salt

1/2 teaspoon ground ginger

1/2 cup cold butter

2/3 cup milk

Filling:

1-1/2 pound ripe fresh peaches *or* nectarines, peeled and thinly sliced

6 tablespoons brown sugar, *divided*

1/4 teaspoon ground ginger

1 cup heavy whipping cream

1/4 cup chopped pecans, toasted

1. Combine first five ingredients in a bowl; cut in butter until mixture resembles coarse crumbs. Add milk, stirring only until moistened. Turn onto a lightly floured surface; knead 10 times.

2. Pat evenly into a greased 8-in. round baking pan. Bake at 425° for 20-25 minutes or until golden brown. Remove from pan to cool on a wire rack.

3. Just before serving, combine peaches, 4 tablespoons brown sugar and ginger. Whip cream with remaining brown sugar until stiff.

4. Split shortcake into two layers; place bottom layer on a serving platter. Spoon half of the peach mixture over cake; top with half of cream. Cover with second cake layer and remaining peach mixture. Garnish with remaining cream; sprinkle with pecans. **Yield:** 8-10 servings.

Brown sugar and ginger give this shortcake its mellow, sweet-spicy flavor.

Karen Owen
Rising Sun, Indiana

Cherry Cheese Blintzes

1-1/2 cups milk
   3 eggs
   2 tablespoons butter, melted
2/3 cup all-purpose flour
1/2 teaspoon salt

Filling:
   1 cup (8 ounces) small-curd cottage cheese
   1 package (3 ounces) cream cheese, softened

1/4 cup sugar
1/2 teaspoon vanilla extract

Cherry Sauce:
   1 pound fresh *or* frozen pitted sweet cherries
2/3 cup plus 1 tablespoon water, *divided*
1/4 cup sugar
   1 tablespoon cornstarch

These elegant blintzes can be served as an attractive dessert or a brunch entree. The bright cherry sauce gives them a delightful flavor. You can try other fruits, such as raspberries, blueberries or peaches.

Jessica Vantrease
Anderson, Alaska

1. In a small mixing bowl, combine the milk, eggs and butter. Combine the flour and salt; add to milk mixture and mix well. Cover and refrigerate for 2 hours.

2. Heat a lightly greased 8-in. nonstick skillet; pour 2 tablespoons batter into the center of skillet. Lift and tilt pan to evenly coat bottom. Cook until top appears dry; turn and cook 15-20 seconds longer. Remove to a wire rack. Repeat with remaining batter. When cool, stack crepes with waxed paper or paper towels in between. Wrap in foil; refrigerate.

3. In a blender, process cottage cheese until smooth. Transfer to a small mixing bowl; add cream cheese. Beat until smooth. Add sugar and vanilla; mix well. Spread about 1 rounded tablespoonful onto each crepe. Fold opposite sides of crepe over filling, forming a little bundle.

4. Place seam side down in a greased 15-in. x 10-in. x 1-in. baking pan. Bake, uncovered, at 350° for 10 minutes or until heated through.

5. Meanwhile, in a saucepan, bring the cherries, 2/3 cup water and sugar to a boil over medium heat. Reduce heat; cover and simmer for 5 minutes or until cherries are heated through. Combine cornstarch and remaining water until smooth; stir into cherry mixture. Bring to a boil; cook and stir for 2 minutes or until thickened. Serve over crepes. **Yield:** 9 servings.

Plum Upside-Down Cake

1/3 cup butter, cubed
1/2 cup packed brown sugar
2 pounds fresh plums, pitted and halved
2 eggs
2/3 cup sugar
1 cup all-purpose flour
1 teaspoon baking powder
1/4 teaspoon salt
1/3 cup hot water
1/2 teaspoon lemon extract
Whipped cream, optional

1. Melt butter in a 10-in. cast-iron skillet. Sprinkle brown sugar over butter. Arrange plums cut side down over sugar; set aside.

2. In a mixing bowl, beat eggs until thick and lemon-colored; gradually beat in sugar. Combine flour, baking powder and salt; add to egg mixture and mix well. Blend water and lemon extract; beat into batter. Pour over plums.

3. Bake at 350° for 40-45 minutes or until a toothpick inserted near the center comes out clean. Immediately invert onto a serving plate. Serve warm. **Yield:** 8-10 servings.

A scoop of this warm from the oven and served with a dollop of whipped cream is simply heaven!

Marie Hattrup
The Dalles, Oregon

Caramel Pear Pie

6 cups sliced peeled ripe pears (about 6 medium)
1 tablespoon lemon juice
1/2 cup plus 3 tablespoons sugar, *divided*
2 tablespoons quick-cooking tapioca
3/4 teaspoon ground cinnamon
1/4 teaspoon salt
1/4 teaspoon ground nutmeg
1 unbaked pastry shell (9 inches)
3/4 cup old-fashioned oats
1 tablespoon all-purpose flour
1/4 cup cold butter
18 caramels
5 tablespoons milk
1/4 cup chopped pecans

1. In a large bowl, combine pears and lemon juice. In another bowl, combine 1/2 cup sugar, tapioca, cinnamon, salt and nutmeg. Add to pears; stir gently. Let stand for 15 minutes.

2. Pour into pastry shell. In a bowl, combine the oats, flour and remaining sugar. Cut in butter until crumbly. Sprinkle over pears. Bake at 400° for 45 minutes.

3. Meanwhile, in a saucepan over low heat, melt caramels with milk. Stir until smooth; add pecans. Drizzle over pie. Bake 8-10 minutes longer or until crust is golden brown and filling is bubbly. Cool on a wire rack. **Yield:** 6-8 servings.

A dear friend shared the recipe for this attractive pie. The caramel drizzle and streusel topping make it almost too pretty to eat. Knowing this dessert is waiting, is great motivation for our children to eat all their vegetables.

Mary Kaehler
Lodi, California

General Recipe Index

Alphabetical Index